NIZAMI GANJAVI: Abû Muhammad Ilyâs ibn Yûsuf ibn Zakî Mu'ayyad, known by his pen-name of Nizâmî, was born around 1141 in Ganja, the capital of Arran in Transcaucasian Azerbaijan, where he remained until his death in about 1209. His father, who had migrated to Ganja from Qom in north central Iran, may have been a civil servant; his mother was the daughter of a Kurdish chieftain; having lost both parents early in his life, Nizâmî was brought up by an uncle. He was married three times, and in his poems laments the death of each of his wives, as well as proffering advice to his son Muhammad. He lived in an age of both political instability and intense intellectual activity, which his poems reflect; but little is known about his life, his relations with his patrons, or the precise dates of his works, as the accounts of later biographers are coloured by the many legends built up around the poet. Although he left a small corpus of lyric poetry, Nizâmî is best known for his five long narrative poems, of which the *Haft Paykar*, completed in 1197, is his acknowledged masterpiece. Often referred to by the honorific Hakîm, 'the sage', Nizâmî is both a learned poet and master of a lyrical and sensuous style, qualities seen to advantage in the *Haft Paykar*.

JULIE SCOTT MEISAMI, a native of California, studied Arabic, Persian, and Comparative Literature at the University of California at Berkeley. From 1971 to 1980 she lived and taught in Tehran, Iran, where she pursued her study of Persian literature; since 1985 she has been Lecturer in Persian at the University of Oxford. Her books include *Medieval Persian Court Poetry* (Princeton, NJ, 1987) and *The Sea of Precious Virtues (Bahr al-Fava'id): A Medieval Islamic Mirror for Princes* (Salt Lake City, 1991), translated from the Persian. She is co-editor of *Edebiyât: The Journal of Middle Eastern Literatures*.

THE WORLD'S CLASSICS

━━

NIZAMI GANJAVI

# *The* Haft Paykar
## *A Medieval Persian Romance*

━━

Translated with an Introduction and Notes by
JULIE SCOTT MEISAMI

Oxford   New York
OXFORD UNIVERSITY PRESS
1995

Oxford University Press, Walton Street. Oxford OX2 6DP

Oxford New York
Athens Auckland Bangkok Bombay
Calcutta Cape Town Dar es Salaam Delhi
Florence Hong Kong Istanbul Karachi
Kuala Lumpur Madras Madrid Melbourne
Mexico City Nairobi Paris Singapore
Taipei Tokyo Toronto
and associated companies in
Berlin Ibadan

Oxford is a trade mark of Oxford University Press

First published as a World's Classics paperback 1995

British Library Cataloguing in Publication Data
Data available

Library of Congress Cataloging in Publication Data
Niẓāmī Ganjavī, 1140 or 41–1202 or 3.
[Haft paykar. English]
The haft paykar: a medieval Persian romance / translated with an introduction and
notes, Julie Scott Meisami.
p.  cm. – (World's classics)
Includes bibliographical references.
I. Meisami, Julie Scott, 1937–  .  II. Title.  III. Series.
PK6501. H4A26  1955  891'.5511 – dc20  94-33161
ISBN 0–19–283184–4

1 3 5 7 9 10 8 6 4 2

Typeset by Best-set Typesetter Ltd., Hong Kong
Printed in Great Britain
by BPC Paperbacks Ltd
Aylesbury, Bucks

# CONTENTS

# ACKNOWLEDGEMENTS

I would like to thank the National Endowment for the Humanities for providing a two-year Translation Grant during which the bulk of the translation was completed. Excerpts from the translation previously published in my *Medieval Persian Court Poetry* (© Princeton University Press 1987) have been used with the kind permission of the publishers. Of the many individuals who encouraged me in this translation, the first and foremost was the late Peter Whigham, an inspired interpreter of Martial and Catullus, whose guidance through the labyrinths and pitfalls of verse translation made of him a veritable Sîmurgh. My thanks also to the students with whom I have read and discussed the poem; to friends who have (somewhat unexpectedly) enthused about it; and to Mona and Ayda, who (so they tell me) have enjoyed it.

# INTRODUCTION

## Nizâmî the Poet

The region of Azerbaijan, where Nizâmî lived and wrote, had in his time only recently become the scene of significant literary activity in Persian. Persian poetry first appeared in the east, where in the tenth and eleventh centuries it flourished at the courts of the Samanids in Bukhara and their successors the Ghaznavids, centred in eastern Iran and Afghanistan. When the Ghaznavids were defeated in 1040 by the Seljuk Turks and the latter extended their power westwards into Iraq, which was predominantly Arabophone, Persian literary activity similarly spread westwards to the Seljuk courts.[1] In Azerbaijan, where numerous languages and dialects were spoken, the original language was a local dialect, Âzarî; but with increasing westward migrations of Turks in the eleventh century Turkish became widespread. When in the twelfth century the Seljuks extended their control into the region, their provincial governors, virtually autonomous local princes, encouraged Persian letters. By the mid-twelfth century many important poets enjoyed their patronage, and there developed a distinctive 'Azerbaijani' style of poetry which contrasted with the 'Khurasani' or 'Eastern' style in its rhetorical sophistication, its innovative use of metaphor, and its use of technical terminology and Christian imagery.

Ganja, the capital of Arran (Transcaucasian Azerbaijan), described by the geographers as one of the most beautiful cities in Western Asia, was an important and well-fortified border town and a flourishing centre of silk manufacture and trade; from the 1150s onwards it was ruled by the Eldigüzids (see below, 'Nizâmî and his Times'), under whom it became a major centre of literary and scholarly activity. Among the many poets Ganja produced, Nizâmî stands out as a towering figure.

[1] On the Samanids and Ghaznavids, see the relevant chapters in *The Cambridge History of Iran*, iv. *From the Arab Invasion to the Saljuqs*, ed. R. N. Frye (London, 1975); on the Seljuks, see v.5: *The Saljuq and Mongol Periods*, ed. A. J. Boyle (Cambridge, 1968).

Although the chief source of support for poets was court patronage, which would both provide a poet's livelihood and ensure his work's copying and diffusion, and although Nizâmî's poems are dedicated to various local princes and contain appeals to his patrons' generosity, the poet seems to have avoided court life. It is often held that he did so in order to preserve his artistic independence and integrity; yet his frequent complaints of 'imprisonment' in Ganja and of the envy of rivals and detractors suggest that his isolation may not have been by choice. Despite attempts to reconstruct Nizâmî's biography from statements in his poems, the details of his life seem destined to remain obscure. As with all medieval poets, complaints of poverty and old age, pleas for generosity and favour, and inveighing against envious rivals are well-established poetic topoi. Nor can the poet's precise relations with his patrons, or the exact dates of composition of his poems, be accurately determined; the extant manuscripts are all considerably later than his own time, and undoubtedly contain many errors, alterations, and interpolations.

About Nizâmî's prodigious learning there is no doubt. Poets were expected to be well versed in many subjects; but Nizâmî seems to have been exceptionally so. His poems show that not only was he fully acquainted with Arabic and Persian literature and with oral and written popular and local traditions, but was also familiar with such diverse fields as mathematics, geometry, astronomy and astrology, alchemy, medicine, Koranic exegesis, Islamic theology and law, history, ethics, philosophy and esoteric thought, music, and the visual arts. The *Haft Paykar* is virtually a summmum of medieval knowledge adapted to poetic ends, and contains many allusions to contemporary events and issues.

Nizâmî held a high view of the poetic art. If speech is the divine gift to humanity, that which distinguishes humans from beasts, poetry is the highest form of speech. In his *Makhzan al-Asrâr* Nizâmî calls poets 'Heaven's nightingales', second in rank only to the prophets, and poetry 'a shadow of the Prophetic veil'. He boasts that his own poetry, inspired by religion and the sacred Law, will 'seat thee on the Tree of Paradise [and] make thee ruler of the empire of the spirit'. When in the *Haft Paykar* he compares himself to a jeweller working with precious gems to create a poetic treasure (§4: 21–3), he calls attention both to the value of his work and to his own creative skill in selecting, weighing, and shaping his materials, in arranging and ornamenting his poem; and when he asserts that speech is man's sole memorial and teaches him the nature of his own design (§7: 6, 9–10), he asserts his belief in the imaginative role of poetry in leading to self-knowledge. While these, too, are well-known poetic topoi, their recurrence and continued emphasis suggest that they were meant quite seriously.

Of Nizâmî's lyric output (estimated by the notoriously unreliable fifteenth-century biographer Dawlatshâh of Samarqand at 20,000 verses) only a few poems survive. One long poem deals with poetry; others blend ethical and religious topics with panegyric, a blend seen also in many of his short *ghazal*s or love poems. Nizâmî's true fame, however, lies in his five long poems in *masnavî* form (written in rhyming couplets, *aa bb cc* etc., rather than the monorhyme of lyric, and used for narrative and didactic purposes) and in particular his four romances, in which he brings this genre to its peak of sophistication. His five *masnavî*s, collected under the title *Khamsa*, 'Quintet' (also known as the *Panj Ganj*, 'Five Treasures'), were widely imitated by later poets.

The first, the ethico–philosophical *Makhzan al-Asrâr*,[2] was composed perhaps as early as 1163–4 (some put it at 1176 or even later) and dedicated to Fakhr al-Dîn Bahrâmshâh (r. *c.*1160–1220), the most notable ruler of a minor Turkmen dynasty centred in Erzinjan in eastern Anatolia, who is said to have rewarded the poet lavishly for its composition. In his prologue Nizâmî refers to an earlier poem dedicated to another Bahrâmshâh (the Ghaznavid ruler, r. 1117–57?), the *Hadîqat al-Haqîqa* ('Garden of Truth') of Majd al-Dîn Sanâ'î (d. 1131); but it is doubtful if it in fact provided his model, as Nizâmî's poem is significantly different from his predecessor's in its lyricism and economy of style. It contains twenty discourses, each illustrated with an exemplary story, on religious and ethical topics—enjoining kingly justice, inveighing against hypocrisy, warning of the

---

[2] English translation by G. H. Darab, *The Treasury of Mysteries* (London, 1945).

vanity of this world and the need to prepare for the next—in a
manner which joins spiritual with practical concerns.

*Khusraw and Shîrîn*[3] is the first of Nizâmî's romances. Its
precise date (probably *c*.1180) is uncertain; in it the poet
addresses the Seljuk sultan Toghrïl II, Toghrïl's Atabak
Muhammad ibn Eldigüz Jahân Pahlavân the ruler of Ganja, and
Jahân Pahlavân's brother Qïzïl Arslân and son Nusrat al-Din
Abû Bakr, and tells of being summoned to converse with Jahân
Pahlavân and Qïzïl Arslân and of the latter's rewarding him with
a village for the poem's composition. Based on the story of the
love of the Sassanian ruler Khusraw II Parvîz (r. 590–628) for
the beautiful Shîrîn, the chief source for which is Firdawsî's
(d. 1020) great epico-historical poem the *Shâhnâma* ('Book of
Kings'), it celebrates love as a cosmic force for harmony and
justice. The love-story also provides a vehicle for treating
broader issues of kingship and justice; and in the person of
Shîrîn (perhaps inspired by his first wife, the Kipchak slave
Âfâq, whose death he laments at the end of the poem) Nizâmî
provides one of the most beautiful portrayals of woman in
Islamic literature.

Nizâmî's second romance, *Laylî and Majnûn*,[4] was completed around 1188 or 1192 and dedicated to the Sharvânshâh
Akhsatân I (r. *c*.1162–99 or later), who ruled the small
Transcaucasian principality of Sharvan from his capital at Baku.
The poem is based on a popular Arab legend of ill-starred lovers:
the poet Qays falls in love with his cousin Laylî, is prevented
from marrying her, goes mad (hence his sobriquet Majnûn,
Arabic for 'mad, possessed'), and abandons human society to live
in the desert among the animals and compose poems lamenting
his love for Laylî, who has been married to another. Never
united in life, when the lovers die they are buried in a single
grave.

The *Haft Paykar*, Nizâmî's masterpiece, was completed in
1197 and dedicated to the ruler of Maragha, 'Alâ' al-Din Körp

---

[3] French translation by Henri Massé, *Le Roman de Chosroës et Chîrîn* (Paris,
1970); German translation by J.-C. Bürgel, *Chosrou und Schirin* (Zurich, 1980).
[4] Partial English translation by James Atkinson, *Laila and Majnun* (London,
1836; repr. 1968); partial German translation by R. Gelpke, *Lejla und Medschnun*
(Zurich, 1963); English version, *The Story of Layla and Majnun* (Oxford, 1966).

Arslân (on whom see below, 'Nizâmî and his Times'). Little is known of this ruler or why he commissioned the poem, which, the poet boasts, is a precious gift of advice to the prince (§53: 23–9); no mere versified mirror for princes, however, the poem is a complex allegory of spiritual and moral growth. (See further below, 'The *Haft Paykar*'.)

Nizâmî's last work was the *Iskandarnâma* ('Book of Alexander'), in two parts, the *Sharafnâma* ('Book of Honour') and *Iqbâlnâma* ('Book of Fortune');[5] its precise date (around 1200–2?) and the names of its dedicatees are uncertain. The *Sharafnâma* deals with Alexander as king and world-conqueror; the *Iqbâlnâma* shows him as philosopher and prophet. Nizâmî's major source was, again, Firdawsî's *Shâhnâma* (whose metre he employs), as well as materials from the Alexander Romance; but his treatment of Alexander is far different from Firdawsî's, and the poem broaches many important philosophical and ethical questions.

All five poems deal with the theme of human perfectibility, on the level of both the individual and the ruler, expressed directly or by means of stories of love which show that personal virtue and wisdom are necessary prerequisites for just rule. Nizâmî evokes the concept of the Perfect Man, mediator between God and His creation who unites spiritual and temporal, universal and particular, embodied in religious terms in the Prophet Muhammad, in temporal society in the king. The image of Muhammad as Perfect Man expounded by ʿAbd al-Qâdir al-Jîlânî (d. 1166), founder of the Qâdiriyya Sufi order, was developed extensively by later mystics; the related concept of man as microcosm was treated by many philosophers, from the Ikhwân al-Safâʾ (tenth century) to Nasîr al-Dîn Tûsî (d. 1275), who observed:

When Man reaches this degree he becomes a world unto himself, comparable to this macrocosm, and merits to be called a 'microcosm'. Thus he becomes Almighty God's vice-gerent among His creatures, entering among His particular Saints, and standing as a Complete and Absolute

---

[5] English translation of the first book by H. Wilberforce Clarke, *Sikandar Nama, e Bará or The Book of Alexander the Great* (London, 1881); complete German translation by J.-C. Bürgel, *Das Alexanderbuch* (Zurich, 1991).

Man. . . . At length, between him and his Master no veil intervenes, but he receives the ennoblement of proximity to the Divine Presence.[6]

## Nizâmî and his Times

Nizâmî lived in an age in which the gap between the ideal of kingship and the actualities of politics was a wide one, rule was based on power, and political instability was endemic. The Abbasid caliphate, whose empire had once stretched from India to North Africa but whose power had long since waned, was controlled by the powerful Seljuk sultans, staunch supporters of Sunni Islam and implacable opponents of all forms of heterodoxy. By Nizâmî's time the Seljuks themselves were in disarray, their unity riven by succession disputes, fragmented by the growing power of local princes, and threatened both by internal conflicts and by rival dynasties in Syria and Egypt.

Arran and Azerbaijan, over which the Seljuks had only nominal control, were the scene of clashes between local princes and between Muslim princes and their Christian neighbours. Nizâmî numbered among his patrons some of the most important of these princes, including members of the powerful Eldigüzid family of atabegs. (Atabegs were officials appointed as tutors to the young Seljuk princes, who through their positions often achieved enormous power.) Shams al-Dîn Eldigüz (d. 1175–6), the governor of Arran, by 1146 controlled most of Azerbaijan; in 1161 he secured the succession to the sultanate for his stepson Arslân ibn Toghrïl and, with Arslân firmly under his control, was undisputed master of the Seljuk territories in Iraq and Azerbaijan. His son Muhammad Jahân Pahlavân (r. 1175–87) extended his control to the cities of the Jibal (western Iran), Rayy, Hamadan, and Isfahan, and established his brother Qïzïl Arslân as ruler in Tabriz; he is said to have poisoned Sultan Arslân, who had attempted to rebel against his tutelage, and set up Arslân's, son Toghrïl II as his successor in 1176.

On Jahân Pahlavân's death Qïzïl Arslân (r. 1187–91) succeeded him as atabeg. In 1190 he imprisoned Toghrïl II, who had sought to oppose his power, near Tabriz, with the approval of the caliph al-Nâsir li-Dîn Allâh, who also supported his claim

---

[6] *The Nasirean Ethics*, trans. G. M. Wickens (London, 1964), 52.

to the sultanate of Iraq and Azerbaijan. When Qïzïl Arslân was murdered in 1191 his nephews Qutlugh Ïnanch (r. 1191–5) and Nusrat al-Dîn Abû Bakr (r. 1195–210) engaged in a lengthy power struggle; the latter managed to maintain his hold on Azerbaijan, defeating the Ahmadili ʿAlâʾ al-Dîn Körp Arslân's attempt to overthrow him in 1205–6, and taking over most of his territories three years later.

The ultimate outcome of this power struggle was the fall of the Seljuk dynasty. Qutlugh Ïnanch, supported by the caliph al-Nâsir, sought the help of the Khwârazmshah Takesh against Toghrïl and Abû Bakr. When in 1194 Takesh defeated and killed Toghrïl in battle, he occupied the former Seljuk territories and claimed them for his own. Iran and Iraq were devastated by successive waves of Khwârazmian invaders, and were briefly absorbed into the Khwârazmshah's empire, which stretched from Transoxiana to the Caspian and which itself fell to the Mongols shortly after.

ʿAlâʾ al-Dîn Körp Arslân (also called Qara Sonqor), who commissioned the *Haft Paykar*, succeeded his brother Arslân Abâ ibn Âq Sonqor as the Ahmadili ruler of Maragha in south-western Azerbaijan somewhere around 1169–70. His father, the slave commander Âq Sonqor, had assumed the rule of Maragha after the assassination of the eponymous Ahmadîl ibn Ibrâhîm al-Rawwâdî in 1116; he himself was murdered in 1133. The Ahmadilis had a chequered career, owing to their involvement in Seljuk succession struggles and their enmity with the Eldigüzids, but managed to defend their territories against the latter until early in the twelfth century.

The Seljuk sultans and their atabegs were noted for their religious zealotry and support of Sunni traditionalism and their relentless persecution of anything remotely associated in their minds with heterodoxy. Both philosophy and esoteric thought were in disrepute, linked with Ismaili 'heresies' (the Ismailis were heterodox Shiites who supported the claim of the Prophet's son-in-law ʿAlî ibn Abî Tâlib and his successors to the caliphate).[7] Nizâmî's city of Ganja was described by the geographer Qazwînî (d. 1283) as being notorious for its intolerance

---

[7] On the Ismailis, see Farhad Daftary, *The Ismāʿilīs: Their History and Doctrines* (Cambridge, 1990).

of heterodoxy. However, in the poet's time a balance between orthodoxy and heterodoxy was coming about which is reflected in the policies of the Abbasid caliph al-Nâsir.

In the two decades preceding the investiture of al-Nâsir li-Dîn Allâh (r. 1180–225) at the age of 22, successive caliphs had managed to wrest an increasing degree of independence from the Seljuk sultans. Al-Nâsir had ambitions to restore the authority of the Abbasid caliphate and free it from Seljuk control. He was by no means universally admired: his army had suffered an ignominious defeat by Toghrïl II in 1188; he was, exceptionally, tolerant of Shiites and of other heterodox movements; and his efficient spy system sought out critics and dissidents who were given short shrift.

Al-Nâsir was notable both for his tolerance of heterodoxy and for his patronage of the *futuwwa*, brotherhoods of young men from all levels of society who embraced ideals of chivalry and true religion. In 1182 he officialized one branch of this movement, placed himself at its head, and invited other Muslim rulers, both Sunni and moderate Shiite, to join the brotherhood under his leadership. In 1207 he declared illegal all brotherhoods except that which he headed and announced that he, as caliph, divinely entrusted with maintaining the sacred Law, was the model for others to follow.[8] The caliph's activities represent the political manifestation of the trend towards a synthesis of various esoteric and heterodox doctrines under Sunni Islam; and one of his advisers, the famous Sufi *shaykh* ʿUmar ibn Muhammad Suhrawardî (1145–1234), conceived a theory which would unify the Caliphate, the *futuwwa*, and Sufism.

The esoteric teachings of the *futuwwa* and of Sufism have much in common, and moreover share many features with the teachings of the Ismailis, whose synthesis of scientific and religious knowledge, and esoteric interpretation of both, led to a complex symbolism expressive of the correspondences between the created and the transcendental worlds, between macrocosm and microcosm. In this period all three movements were moving towards a coalescence: mysticism and mystical literature, ortho-

---

[8] On al-Nâsir and the *futuwwa*, see H. Mason, *Two Statesmen of Medieval Islam: Vizir Ibn Hubayra ... and Caliph an-Nâṣir li Dîn Allâh* (The Hague, 1972).

dox and heterodox theology, and gnosticism (reflected in the interest in astrology, alchemy, and magic) were all heavily coloured by Ismaili esotericism with its Pythagorean, Neoplatonic, and Islamic elements. As Alessandro Bausani observes: 'It is no exaggeration to say that after this period all of eastern Islam felt, to a lesser or greater degree according to spiritual areas and particular cases, the influence of Ismaili esotericism, diffused through channels often subtle and difficult to single out into both art and poetry.'[9]

In the *Haft Paykar* Nizâmî draws on this esoteric symbolism in a manner which speaks to different movements and is susceptible of different interpretations. Nizâmî is thought to have been associated with a *futuwwa* brotherhood known as the Akhis, who drew their members from the artisan classes, and to have received his education at the hands of one of their masters; and the *Haft Paykar* reflects their ideal of human perfectibility as well as the respect they accorded to the artisan. But these notions were widely shared, notably by the Ismailis and Sufis, and were expounded in detail in the compendium of sciences known as the *Rasâ'il* ('Epistles') of the tenth-century Arabic writers the Ikhwân al-Safâ' (Brethren of Purity), with which Nizâmî was clearly well acquainted. But Nizâmî was first and foremost a poet; and the *Haft Paykar*, rather than reflecting any specific system of thought, is a poetic synthesis which draws upon many different sources.

## The *Haft Paykar*

The *Haft Paykar* recounts the history of the Sassanian ruler Bahrâm V Gûr; its biographical narrative, framed by a prologue and an epilogue, is divided into two unequal parts by a central interlude consisting of seven tales. The poem begins with praise of God and of the Prophet Muhammad (§§1, 2) and a description of the Prophet's Mi'râj, his celestial ascent (§3). There follow an account of the poem's composition (§4), praise of its patron (§§5, 6) and of discourse (§7), and a lengthy section of advice to the poet's son (§8); then the story begins.

[9] A. Pagliaro and A. Bausani, *Storia della letteratura persiana* (Milan, 1960), 173.

A son, Bahrâm, is born to the ageing and childless king
Yazdigird. When his horoscope predicts that he will become
ruler of the world, Yazdigird sends Bahrâm to the court of the
Arab king Nuʿmân and his son Munzir, where he is educated in
all the arts and skills befitting a prince (§9). Nuʿmân builds for
him the marvelous palace of Khavarnaq; when its architect,
Simnâr, suggests he could have built an even finer one, Nuʿmân
has him thrown from the battlements to his death. Repenting, he
himself disappears into the desert (§§10, 11).

Bahrâm's skill in hunting his favourite prey, the onager (*gûr*),
earns him the sobriquet 'Bahrâm Gûr', and his exploits are
painted on the walls of Khavarnaq (§§12, 13). The pun on the
two meanings of *gûr*, 'onager' and 'grave', provides a recurrent
motif throughout the poem: that of the prince who hunts the
wild ass as the grave hunts him. In the first of four linked
episodes (§14) Bahrâm pursues a female onager of great beauty
who leads him to a cave before which lies a dragon. Bahrâm slays
the dragon and cuts open its belly, from which the onager's foal
emerges; the onager leads him into the cave where he finds a
fabulous treasure.

One day, returning from the hunt, Bahrâm disocovers a mysterious room in the palace (§15); obtaining the key, he enters and
sees the portraits of the Princesses of the Seven Climes—India,
Chîn ('China', Turkestan), Khwârazm, Siqlab (Slavonia), the
Maghreb (North Africa), Rûm (Byzantium), and Persia—
ranged in a circle, with his own portrait at the centre (§15: 17–
24). After this discovery he often returns to the room to muse in
solitude over the portraits of these beauties.

Yazdigird dies, having ruled with such injustice that he has
become known as 'the Sinner'; the Iranians, fearing that the son
will be like the father, place an outsider on the throne. Bahrâm
marches on Iran to assert his claim and proposes a test: should he
succeed in seizing the crown from between two lions, it will be
his without dispute (§§16–20). He performs this feat, is proclaimed king, and swears to rule justly (§§21–3). Entrusting the
administration of his realm to the wise vizier Narsî and his sons,
he himself devotes most of his time to pleasure (§23). During a
period of famine he proves to be a compassionate ruler, and
thereafter his kingdom prospers (§24).

Bahrâm goes hunting with his harpist Fitna, in the second of the four linked episodes (§25). When Fitna withholds praise of his skill, he orders her killed; she persuades the officer who has been given this task to conceal her in his palace, where for six years she practises carrying a new-born ox calf to the palace roof until it is fully grown. On her advice the officer invites Bahrâm to the palace after the hunt. Fitna, veiled, carries the ox to the top of the tower where Bahrâm has been feasting; when she reveals her identity to the suitably amazed king, the two are reunited and married (§26).

Bahrâm's kingdom is invaded by the ruler of Chîn, who thinks the king's devotion to pleasure signals negligence (§27). Bahrâm repels the invasion, rebukes his generals, then sends his messengers to seek the Princesses of the Seven Climes as his brides (§28–9). At a feast in his winter chambers the architect Shîda, the apprentice of Simnâr, proposes to build a palace containing seven domes or pavilions for his brides, each dedicated to one day of the week, governed by that day's planet and bearing its emblematic colour (§§30–1). Bahrâm spends a lengthy period visiting each dome in turn, where he feasts, drinks, enjoys the favours of his brides, and listens to a tale told by each.

These seven tales, which form the central interlude, tell of love and its frustration or fulfilment. In the first (§32: the Black Dome/Saturn/Saturday) a king, his curiosity aroused by word of a mysterious city where all dress in black, travels there in disguise and persuades a citizen to reveal the city's secret. Taken to a remote ruin where stands a tall column with a basket at its foot, he climbs into the basket, is raised to the top, and is carried off by a gigantic bird. When the bird descends, he falls into a magical garden, where he meets the beautiful Turktâz, who comes there each night to feast with her companions. Though he is allowed the favours of any of the maidens, his true desire is for their queen; but when he seeks to embrace her before the designated time, lady and garden disappear, and he is left in perpetual mourning. Donning black robes, he is known thenceforth as the King of Black.

The king of the second tale (§33: the Yellow Dome/Sun/Sunday), whose horoscope has predicted danger in marriage, becomes disillusioned by his concubines, who are corrupted by an old crone and seek only their own advantage; he takes a new girl to his bed each night and discards her in the morning. The devoted service of one companion causes him to fall in love with her; when she rejects his advances, he tells her a tale which exemplifies the importance of honesty and truthfulness, and she reveals that the women of her race are doomed to die in child-birth. Through a ruse devised by the old woman, the king achieves his desire and finds his love returned; vowing eternal honesty, the lovers are united in marriage.

In the third tale (§34: the Green Dome/Moon/Monday) Bishr falls in love with a passing woman whose veil is lifted by the wind. He goes on pilgrimage to Jerusalem to purify himself of temptation; on his return journey he is accompanied by a godless know-it-all named Malîkhâ, who meets a suitably grue-some end when he drowns in a well which he mistakes for a jar of water buried in the desert. When Bishr returns Malîkhâ's belongings to his wife, he finds that she is the same woman by whom he was tempted; impressed by his honesty, she persuades him to marry her.

The heroine of the fourth tale (§35: the Red Dome/Mars/Tuesday) is a Russian princess skilled in all the arts who can find no man worthy of her. She shuts herself up in a fortress sur-rounded by talismans and with a secret entrance, and declares that only he who can find his way to her will win her. As the heads of failed contenders multiply above the city gate, a prince arrives, falls in love with her portrait, and determines to succeed. Through the guidance of a wise hermit, he defeats the talismans and discovers the entrance; after he has successfully answered a set of riddles set by the princess, they are wed.

In the fifth tale (§36: the Turquoise Dome/Mercury/Wednesday) the beautiful Egyptian youth Mâhân is led into the desert by a demon disguised as his partner. Lost and terrified, Mâhân comes upon an old man and woman who promise to guide him to safety; but at daybreak they disappear, having led him even further astray. He then encounters a rider who also promises to lead him aright, but who takes him to a dreadful waste filled with frolicking demons who invite Mâhân to join them; he is tormented until he falls senseless to the ground. When day comes, he manages to escape the desert, and discovers a garden presided over by an old man who offers to adopt Mâhân and make him his heir if he will wait in a giant sandalwood tree till summoned, and pay no heed to anyone. But Mâhân is enticed from his tree by a lovely lady who comes to the garden with her attendants; joining their feast, he embraces her, but she turns into a dreadful afreet who torments him till he faints. Awakening to find the ladies vanished and the garden a waste land filled with corruption, he appeals to God, and is rewarded by the apparition of the prophet Khizr, who leads him safely home. There he finds his friends in mourning for him, and dons blue robes of mourning in renunciation of the world.

In the sixth tale (§37: the Sandal Dome/Jupiter/Thursday) Good, travelling in the desert, is blinded and robbed by his companion, Bad, and left for dead. He is found by the daughter of a Kurdish chief, who cures his sight and restores him to health. Good marries the Kurdish maid; then, using the Kurd's remedies, he cures a king's daughter of epilepsy and his vizier's daughter of blindness, marries both, and finally becomes king himself. Encountering Bad one day by chance, he pardons him, but Bad is summarily dispatched by the less forgiving Kurd.

In the seventh and final tale (§38: the White Dome/Venus/Friday) a young man visits his garden and hears sounds of music and song from within. Entering through a breach in the wall, he finds a group of maidens feasting and sporting and falls in love with one of them, the beautiful Bakht ('Fortune'). His passion is returned, but the lovers' attempts at union are thwarted by a variety of ludicrous incidents. The young master, realizing that the cause is the illicit nature of his desire, makes Bakht his legal wife; the tale ends with a hymn to the colour white, symbol of purity, worship, and illumination.

Bahrâm emerges from his sojourn in the Seven Domes to hold court in the spring and celebrate the New Year (§39). His kingdom is in disarray: the evil vizier Râst-Rawshan has abused his power in Bahrâm's absence, and his subjects are too frightened to tell him the truth. Again threatened by war with Chîn, he finds his soldiers unequipped and his treasury empty. In the third of the linked episodes (§41) Bahrâm goes hunting to allay his cares; on his return he seeks water from an old shepherd, outside whose hut he sees a heap of dead sheep and a dog hung from a gibbet. He asks the shepherd the story of the dog, and is told. The dog was guardian of the flock; but one day the shepherd noticed that sheep were missing. So many disappeared that he was impoverished and reduced from owner of the flock to humble shepherd. One day, watching his dog in secret, he saw a female wolf approach; the dog mounted her, then gave her a fat sheep in return for her favours. The shepherd punished the dog by hanging him.

Returning home, Bahrâm ponders this lesson, and realizes its import: he is the shepherd of his flock and must bring its wicked guardian to justice. He investigates the vizier's crimes, removes him from his post, and brings him to trial, hearing the testimony of seven witnesses whom the vizier had unjustly imprisoned (§§43–9). Bahrâm executes the vizier; the Chinese king sends his apologies and evidence of the vizier's treachery (§§50–1). Bahrâm renounces his seven brides and turns their domes into fire-temples, wedding himself solely to Justice (§§51–2).

At the end of a prosperous reign, in the final linked episode (§52) Bahrâm turns once more to the hunt; this time, however, it is not wild beasts he seeks to slay, but his own faults. Again he is led to a remote and mysterious cave by a beautiful female onager; he plunges on horseback into a deep chasm within the cave, and disappears forever. His soldiers can find no trace of him; his mother appears and has the ground dug up all around, but to no avail. She laments bitterly until a heavenly voice consoles her; she then delivers the kingdom to Bahrâm's heir. Nizâmî concludes this section with a discourse on the vanity of this world and an exhortation to seek wisdom; in the epilogue (§53) he again addresses the ruler to whom he has offered his poem— in which 'Each story is a treasure-house, | and no mere fable' (§53: 29)—requests his generosity, and ends with a prayer for his well-being.

Nizâmî took the basic elements of his romance from both history and legend. The historical Bahrâm V Gûr (more properly, Gōr), son and successor of Yazdigird I (r. 399–420), ruled the Sassanian empire from 421 to 439. His upbringing at the court of the Lakhmid kings of Hira, who supported his claim against the prince Khusraw, placed on the throne of Iran by the powerful nobles and priests after the death of Yazdigird (murdered, the historians suggest, by those same nobles); his trial by ordeal, his appointment of the minister Mihr Narseh (the Narsî of §23), and his defeat of the Hephtalites or White Huns (the 'Chinese' of §§27 and 40) are matters of historical record. Because of his just rule and attractive personal traits, he was an extremely popular ruler; known for his love of pleasure and his hunting skills, he promoted musicians to high rank and imported thousands of Indian minstrels to entertain the populace at festivals (cf. §23). (He is also celebrated, probably apocryphally, as the first person to compose poetry in Persian.)

The historical figure of Bahrâm pales, however, before the legendary personality built up by both literary and popular tradition. While the early historians stress his military achievements and good government, other accounts both embroider these and add a wide range of heroic and romantic adventures. As W. L. Hanaway observes:

[These] accounts contain many of the characteristics of popular romance: a childless king . . . who eventually fathers a son, the boy's auspicious horoscope, his precocious physical and intellectual development, his education in the three areas of letters, manly arts, and kingship, and a life devoted to military and amorous adventures and the chase.[10]

While Nizâmî draws upon both historical accounts and popular legends, he uses these in a manner uniquely his own; and many of the *Haft Paykar*'s crucial episodes—such as Bahrâm's killing of the dragon (§14) and disappearance into the cave (§52), his discovery of the portraits of the Seven Princesses (§15), the building of the Seven Domes (§30-1) and the seven tales—are his own invention.

Other literary treatments of Bahrâm Gûr include Firdawsî's *Shâhnâma* (see below, 'Nizâmî and his Sources'), and later popular romances. The pun on his sobriquet *gûr* has given rise to many poetic verses, from ʿUmar Khayyâm (in Fitzgerald's version)—

> They say the Lion and the Lizard keep
> The Court where Jamshyd gloried and drank deep;

[10] W. L. Hanaway, art. 'Bahrām V Gōr in Persian Literature and Legend', *Encyclopaedia Iranica*.

> And Bahrám, that great Hunter—the Wild Ass
> Stamps o'er his Head, and he lies fast asleep—

to Hâfiz (d. 1394)—

> Cast aside Bahrâm's hunting noose and take up Jamshîd's cup;
> for I've traversed that desert: neither Bahrâm nor his *gûr* are there.

Bahrâm Gûr's adventures were a popular subject in the fine and applied arts, not only in the miniatures which adorn their historical and literary treatments, but in ceramics, metalwork, and carpets as well. Bahrâm also appears as an exemplary figure (not always in a positive sense) in histories and mirrors for princes.

It is difficult to estimate the effect of the *Haft Paykar* on its contemporary audience; no records survive which testify to the poem's impact, and the political and social disruptions produced by the instability of the last half-century of Seljuk rule, the depredations of the Khwârazmians and, after them, the Mongols, left in their wake a society radically changed in every way, including matters of literary taste. The *Haft Paykar* (and the *Khamsa* as a whole) did, however, find many later imitators; over a hundred poets in Persian, Turkish, Urdu, and other languages modelled poems upon it, including the Indo-Persian poet Amîr Khusraw of Delhi (d. 1325) in his *Hasht Bihisht* ('Eight Paradises'); Maktabî of Shiraz (fifteenth century), said to have written a parallel poem (now lost); and the sixteenth-century Azerbaijani Turkish poet Fuzûlî.

## Nizâmî and his Sources

The *Haft Paykar* blends historical and legendary materials concerning the pre-Islamic Iranian past with Islamic beliefs and esoteric symbolism. Over a century earlier, Firdawsî had in his *Shâhnâma* ('Book of Kings'; *c.*1010) chronicled the history of Iranian monarchy from its mythical beginnings to the defeat of the Sassanians by the Muslim Arabs in 637, incorporating materials drawn from popular legend and saga as well as panegyrics in which he presented the poem's dedicatee, Mahmûd of Ghazna (r. 997–1030), as embodying both Iranian and Islamic kingship. But Mahmûd received the work coolly; and both historians and panegyrists of this and the early Seljuk period speak slightingly of the 'false' and fabulous history represented by the *Shâhnâma*. Nizâmî both recuperates and reworks Firdawsî's treatment of the Iranian past to create a different sort of poem, one that reflects the concerns of his own age.

A detailed survey of Nizâmî's sources cannot be undertaken here; Mechtild Pantke's study indicates that these sources include not only historical and geographical works and mirrors for princes but a wide variety of writings on astrology, astronomy, and magic.[11] Many others undoubtedly remain to be discovered. In the prologue to the *Haft Paykar* Nizâmî describes his search for sources and gives pride of place to one: the *Shâhnâma* (§4: 19–20, 24–5). Since Nizâmî's treatment of his known literary models sheds light on both his method and his intent, we may briefly consider two important instances, beginning with the story of Bahrâm and his harp-girl (§§25–6), the first part of which (§25: 1–72) is calqued on Firdawsî's story of Bahrâm and Azâda in the *Shâhnâma*.

Firdawsî, following the historical sources closely, presents this as an episode in the prince's youth; its brevity (thirty-four couplets) indicates its relatively minor importance. Bahrâm goes hunting with his favourite, the harp-girl Âzâda. Spying two pair of gazelles, he asks which of them she wishes him to shoot; she challenges him to change the female to a male, the male to a female, and to transfix another through head, ear, and hoof. When he does so, Âzâda bursts into tears and accuses him of having a demonic nature; Bahrâm, enraged, tramples her beneath his riding camel and never takes women hunting again.

Nizâmî's version of this story is marked by increased length, the addition of a continuation (§26), and changes in significant details. The hunt takes place after Bahrâm has become king; the quarry is onager, not gazelle; the details of the challenge are simplified and its occasion altered. While in Firdawsî's version Bahrâm hunted alone, in Nizâmî's he is accompanied by his soldiers, and the account of his hunt (§25: 1–11) is balanced by an extended description of the slave-girl (§25: 12–19), here named not Âzâda ('noble') but Fitna, a name which suggests both temptation and testing. The description of Fitna's talents elevates her

[11] Mechtild Pantke, *Das arabische Bahrām-Roman: Untersuchungen zur Quellen- und Stoffgeschichte* (Berlin, 1974).

from the status of one of the king's chattels to one complementary to his own. If we take the end of the first part, that calqued
on Firdawsî's version, as the report of Fitna's death, Nizâmî's
version is almost exactly twice as long (seventy-two lines); this
near-doubling in length recalls his claim in the prologue to tell in
full what Firdawsî had left 'half-said' (§4: 24) and directs us to
his reworking of the model, the most important feature of which
is his development of the figure of Fitna, whose association with
music evokes notions of cosmic harmony, and that with the
moon her role of guidance, as she sets Bahrâm on the path to
spiritual and moral growth.

   This growth is achieved in the episode in which the old shepherd teaches Bahrâm his kingly role (§41), followed by the account of the trial and execution of the evil vizier (§§42–9) and the
apology of the Chinese ruler (§50). The model for this account is
found in the *Siyâsatnâma* ('Book of Government') of Nizâm al-
Mulk (d. 1092), vizier to the Seljuk sultan Malikshâh (r. 1032–
92) and founder (in 1067) of the famous Nizamiyya *madrasa*
(college) in Baghdad, whom Nizâmî mentions in his prologue
(§6: 39); it illustrates the principle that kings must closely observe the conduct of viziers and officials. Nizâmî alters the name
of the vizier, Râst-Ravishn, 'Right-Conduct', to 'Râst-Rawshan',
'Right and Bright', on which he makes a series of puns; otherwise
his account amounts to a near-verbatim versification of Nizâm
al-Mulk's. Only in the trial of the vizier does Nizâmî make
several significant changes: for Nizâm al-Mulk's fifth victim (a
chieftain whose father was robbed and killed and he himself
imprisoned) he substitutes (as his fourth) the minstrel whose
beloved was stolen by the vizier (§46); and to Nizâm al-Mulk's
six witnesses he adds a seventh, the ascetic whose prayers the
vizier feared and who, instead of accepting compensation as do
the other victims, renounces the world and disappears (§49).
Thus Nizâmî signals the spiritual dimension of his tale.

## Structure, Symbolism, and Themes

The *Haft Paykar* is an allegorical romance of profound dimensions, constructed according to a plan which echoes the design of
the cosmos itself, filled with a universal and syncretic symbol-

ism, and evoking a wide network of intertextual allusion. Rich in fantasy, evoking the worlds of faerie, of magic, and of dream, it is charged with a powerful eroticism expressed in vivid sensuous imagery. All these elements are bound together in a whole of unparalleled richness and diversity.

Self-knowledge is the principle theme of the *Haft Paykar*, the goal both of Bahrâm's journey through life and of the protagonists of the seven tales. It is knowledge of the self that leads to knowledge of the world and its Creator; as the Prophet Muhammad said, 'He who knows himself knows his Lord.' It is only through knowledge that the soul can return to its origin in God; the purpose of its sojourn in this world is to perfect itself in preparation for that return.

Discourse—specifically, structured discourse—is the medium through which both Bahrâm and the reader learn the nature of the human design. In his prologue Nizâmî calls attention to the importance of his poem's design (§4: 33–40); and design is a recurrent motif throughout the poem, reiterated in the references to building (of the palace of Khavarnaq and of the Seven Domes, ultimately transformed into fire-temples (§51: 17–§52: 10), exemplifying building for this world and building for the next) and to astrology and astronomy, and expressed in terms of number and geometry. Design and number are, indeed, the principles upon which the poem is based.

The *Haft Paykar* is ordered by three complementary structural patterns. The *linear* movement of Bahrâm's life, from birth to kingship to death, paralleled in the seven tales by the progress from dark to light, ignorance to wisdom, is complemented by one of *alternance*. In the narrative, kingship segments, usually set in palace or court or on the battlefield and involving public issues (matters of state, the conduct of war, and so on), alternate with adventure episodes, which are introduced by Bahrâm's departure for the hunt, occur in natural settings, and deal with acts or encounters of a private nature. The seven tales alternate between those in which the action is motivated by the faculty of concupiscence (I, III, V, VII), represented by temptation and/or desire for gain, and those in which it is motivated by the faculty of irascibility (II, IV, VI), represented by the desire to ward off harm and/or to pursue a worthy goal. Tales II, IV, and VI also

emphasize wit and intelligence, Tales I, III, V, and VII faith, as
the guide to felicity.

The third pattern, that of the *circle*, is the overall unifying
pattern of the poem and that which links the four analogical
adventure episodes, two preceding and two following the central
interlude of the tales (§§14, 25; §§41, 52). These episodes involve
Bahrâm and a second figure who functions as guide; a conflict
which may be external or internal; the resolution of the conflict,
linked with the motifs of rebirth and of discovery; and the gain
achieved: the treasure, material or spiritual, acquired by Bahrâm.

These structural patterns evoke spatial and numerical sym-
bologies echoed throughout the poem. The spatial pattern of the
circle, symbol of perfection and of divine Unicity, and that of the
line, symbol of earthly motion through time and space, appear
first in the description of the Prophet as 'The primal Circle's
centre, and | the Seal upon Creation's line' (§2: 1). When Bahrâm
has slain the dragon and is rejoined by his guards, they form a
circle round him (§14: 58); the portraits of the seven princesses
are ranged round his own at the centre (§15: 17–19); in the hunt
with Fitna his soldiers, again forming a ring, beat game towards
him as he stands at the centre of this circle (§25: 4–5). Nizâmî's
reference to 'lines and points' (§4: 36) asserts the principle
that 'intellectual geometry' provides the means of passing from
material to spiritual understanding, and echoes his predecessor Sanâ'î, who likened 'the ability to behold the divine
manifestation . . . to the intellectual way of perception of a
geometrician: "You only see with your imagination and your
senses, | when you have not learned about lines, planes and
points." '[12] Like astronomy, the purpose of whose study is to
purify the soul and instil in it the desire for celestial ascent,
geometry leads to an understanding both of human justice and
of divine wisdom; it is no coincidence that these two sciences
are those to which Bahrâm devoted himself during his early
education.

Like the created universe itself, the *Haft Paykar* is a work of
art through which knowledge of the Creator may be achieved
through the truth of number. If circle and line represent one and

---

[12] J. T. P. de Bruijn, *Of Piety and Poetry: The Interaction of Religion and
Literature in the Life and Works of Ḥakīm Sanā'ī of Ghazna* (Leiden, 1983), 216.

two, their sum, *three*, embodied in the poem's tripartite division
narrative–tales–narrative, is the number of the soul (signifying
its vegetative, animal, and rational aspects); of the 'three kingdoms' of creation (mineral, plant, and animal; cf. §7: 7); of the
three astral agents of the Universal Soul (the signs of the Zodiac,
the spheres, and the planets); of the trivium (grammar, rhetoric,
and poetry); and of the division of the universe into material
world, astral world, and world of universals. *Four*, embodied in
the four linked adventure episodes, is the number of matter; of
the categories of nature (the elements, the humours, the seasons); of the virtues and vices; of the quadrivium (arithmetic,
geometry, astronomy, and music). The four elements and humours (the bases of creation), when maintained in equilibrium,
are symbolized by the image of a square within a circle, the
symbol which lies at the heart of the *Haft Paykar*'s design; the
circle of the four adventure episodes transforms the line of
Bahrâm's physical journey (now a square, symbolizing its material aspect) into a circle of perfection representing a journey
which is not merely from ignorance to wisdom but from his
origin in God to his return.

*Seven*, the sum of three and four and the number of the
cosmos, is embodied in the seven tales (4 + 3). *Five*, the number
of the senses, is seen in the alternating kingship segments/linked
adventure episodes in each half of the narrative (K + A + K +
A + K × 2), recalling the distinction between the external or
physical senses (taste, smell, sight, touch, and hearing) and the
internal or spiritual senses (common sense, imagination, reflection, estimation, and recollection). Five is also a fundamental
number of Islam, with its 'five pillars': affirmation of God's
Unicity, ritual prayer (five times daily), the pilgrimage to Mecca,
fasting in the month of Ramadan, and giving alms (of which
there are five types). Finally, the sum of the 'seven lines and ten
designs' of which the poet speaks (§4: 36–7) is *seventeen*, viewed
by esoteric philosophers as the key to the understanding of
nature, sum of the first complete (7) and first perfect (10) numbers and of the harmonic proportion 9:8 which is the sign of
felicity, and a number of particular significance to Shiites.[13]

---

[13] See I. Mélikoff, 'Nombres symboliques dans la littérature épico-religieuse
des Turcs d'Anatolie', *Journal asiatique*, 250 (1962), 435–45.

If the section numbering is authentic (and we cannot be sure, since rubrification varies from manuscript to manuscript), certain important sections occur at numerologically significant points: Praise of Discourse (§7); the building of Khavarnaq (§10); Bahrâm and the dragon (§14); Bahrâm's march on Iran (§17; 17 is also the number of conquest) and his seizure of the crown (§21); Bahrâm's wedding to Justice (§51 = 3 × 17) and his disappearance into the cave (§52, the number of Unicity (51 + 1); the testimony of the ascetic (§49 = 7 × 7); Fitna's lesson (§26 = ¹/₂ of 52). In the tales significant numbers are also found, for example, in that of the Russian princess (§35 = 5 × 5, the 'magic square' of Mars, product of the five internal senses), where the numerical riddles also figure, and in that of Mâhân (§36 = 6 × 6, product of the inauspicious number six; Wednesday is, moreover, considered an unlucky day). While this may be conjecture, the presence of similar procedures in both Classical and medieval European works also influenced by number symbolism suggests that they inform the *Haft Paykar* as well.[14]

The poem's tripartite structure recalls the division by the Ikhwân al-Safâ' of the stages of self-knowledge into three: (1) knowledge of the body (the first part of the poem, dominated by physical action); (2) knowledge of the soul (the tales, reflection on which enables Bahrâm to progress towards wisdom); and (3) knowledge of the two together (the third part, in which Bahrâm is able to excercise his knowledge of both body and soul). In the tales, the interaction between three and four (exemplified by the alternation of the motivation of the tales' action between the faculties of irascibility and of concupiscence) further figures this movement towards spiritual balance: these faculties can motivate for good or evil; what is important is that equilibrium be established between them, a necessity reflected by their alternation, as the balance swings from one to the other. The tales exemplify divergences from equilibrium; through contemplating them, Bahrâm is enabled to perfect his speculative faculty so that he can interpret the lesson of the shepherd and bring about moral equilibrium in his person and justice in his kingdom.

---

[14] See e.g. Caroline D. Eckhardt (ed.), *Essays in the Numerical Criticism of Medieval Literature* (Lewisburg, Ky., 1980).

The ............................................. stage in Bahrâm's
progres ......................................... degrees of human
perfec ..................................... craftsmen, religious
and le ................................. ...gs and sultans, and
proph ............................... ...ch of these degrees:
crafts ........................... ...olitical chief, as he
achie ....................... ...bining temporal and
spiritu.. ................... ...e Law; and sage or
prophet, as he disappears ............ ...here he is rejoined with
his Creator.

Bahrâm's biographical journey through time is thus also a
spiritual journey from ignorance to wisdom; its prototype is the
Prophet's Mi'râj, his celestial Ascent to the Divinity. The theme
of the celestial ascent is an ancient one; and Muhammad's Mi'râj
has been a constant inspiration to Muslim writers. Accounts of
the Mi'râj (based on Koran 17: 2, 53: 9–19 and 81: 23–4 and on
various Prophetic Traditions) were later elaborated and vary
greatly. Nizâmî combines elements of various stories and adds
others of his own; with him the Mi'râj becomes a standard
element of prologues to *masnavî* poems.[15] In the *Haft Paykar* the
Prophet passes by the seven planets—the moon, Mercury,
Venus, the sun, Mars, Jupiter, and Saturn—in their normal
cosmological order, and bestows upon them their emblematic
colours—turquoise (or green) for the moon, blue for Mercury,
white for Venus, yellow for the sun, red for Mars, sandal (red-
brown) for Jupiter, black for Saturn—which are repeated in the
Seven Domes, though in a different order. As Peter Chelkowski
notes:

[The] colors are also expressed geometrically. Black, white, and sandalwood form a triangle: earthly sandalwood is the base, black the ascend-
ing side and white the descending side. This triangle symbolizes body,
spirit, and soul. The remaining four colors—red, yellow, green, and

---

[15] On the theme of the celestial ascent, see e.g. Geo Windengren, *Muhammad,
the Apostle of God, and His Ascension* (Uppsala and Wiesbaden, 1955); *Encyclopaedia of Islam* (new edn.), art. 'Mi'radj'; A. Schimmel, *And Muhammad is His
Messenger* (Chapel Hill, NY, 1985), 158–75. On Nizâmî's use of the Mi'râj
account, see C.-H. de Fouchécour, 'Les Récits d'ascension (Me'râj) dans l'œuvre
de Nezâmî', in C.-H. de Fouchécour and Ph. Gignoux (eds.), *Études irano-
aryennes offertes à Gilbert Lazard* (Paris, 1989), 99–108.

blue—constitute a square and represent the active qualities of nature. . . . [16]

Bahrâm's journey through the Seven Domes follows the temporal order of the days of the week; but, though this would appear to relate it to human time and space, it is a symbolic progress in which Bahrâm experiences vicariously the lessons learned by the protagonists of the tales. George Krotkoff estimates the duration of Bahrâm's sojourn in the Domes as seven years, which is borne out by the testimonies of the vizier's seven victims. [17] The Seven Domes are linked with other ancient or legendary buildings, such as the seven walls of Babylon, the seven temples of the Sabians, the seven buildings of Kaykâvûs's castle, and others; [18] and, as M. Pantke shows, Bahrâm's progress through the Seven Climes, as represented by the Seven Domes, forms the spatial pattern of a six-pointed star, the magical symbol of Solomon's Seal. [19]

The Prophet's Ascent provides the background for the colour symbolism which informs the tales told in the Seven Domes. Nizâmî's scheme of the relationship between colours and planets (like his division of the world into seven regions), while it has antecedents in various sources, is his own, geared to the purpose of his poem; nevertheless, it reflects a tendency, particularly marked in Nizâmî's time and seen in the work of a number of his contemporaries, to express imagistically the correspondences between the material and spiritual worlds. The mystical writer Najm al-Dîn Kubrâ (1145–221) posited a scheme relating the seven levels of the universe with the seven major colours: the worlds of Intelligence (white), Spirit (yellow), Soul (green), Nature (red), Matter (ashen), Image (dark green), and the Material Body (black); in yet another scheme he associated white with Islam, yellow with faith, dark blue with beneficence, green with tranquillity, light blue with certitude, red with gnosis, and

---

[16] *Mirror of the Invisible World* (New York, 1975), 113.

[17] 'Colour and Number in the *Haft Paykar*', in R. M. Savory and D. A. Agius (eds.), *Logos Islamikos: Studia Islamica in honorem Georgii Michaelis Wickens* (Toronto, 1984), 102.

[18] See Pantke, *Das arabische Bahrām-Roman*, 176 ff.

[19] 'Colour and Number', 172.

black with 'passionate love and ecstatic bewilderment'.[20] The Illuminationist (Ishrâqî) philosopher Shihâb al-Dîn Suhrawardî (executed in 1191) in one of his allegorical treatises depicted the soul's progress from black through red to white, a progress paralleled in the seven tales of the *Haft Paykar*.

Astrology plays a prominent role throughout the poem, not only in Bahrâm's natal (§9: 14–18) and regnal (§22: 2–7) horoscopes but in numerous astrological allusions. For Nizâmî, as for his philosophical sources such as the writings of the Ikhwân al-Safâ', the stars do not determine events (cf. §1: 35–7) but are agents of the divine Will which, when read aright, provide guidance into the mysteries of existence. Geometry provides the means for ascertaining the configurations of the stars and the relationships between them; magic (seen in the talismans of §35) is one outcome of understanding these relationships. When Bahrâm achieves perfect wisdom, he is able to dispense with the guidance of the stars (see §52: 2–10)—not false guidance, as H. Ritter suggested,[21] but one divinely appointed, with respect to which (taking issue with Ritter) Rudolf Gelpke expressed his conviction that 'in astrology Nizâmî perceived a suitable bridge not only between Divinity and humanity but also between individual religions—a bridge, to be sure, for which, once one has reached the other side, he has is no further need'.[22]

The human means to Bahrâm's progress is love, the desire for union which arises from the correspondence or harmony between 'lover' and 'beloved' and which is above all a spiritual force, the source not only of human felicity but of justice and cosmic harmony. Fitna's love for Bahrâm enables her to guide him; his for the seven princesses leads to the tales, love-stories in which the protagonists seek union with their loves. The culmination of this search is the perfect union figured by marriage—not, as is sometimes suggested, because Nizâmî, as a Muslim,

---

[20] A. Schimmel, *Mystical Dimensions of Islam*, p. 256; see also Henry Corbin, 'The Realism and Symbolism of Colours', in *Temple and Contemplation*, trans. Philip Sherrard (London, 1986), 25.

[21] *Über die bildersprache Nizamis* (Berlin, 1927), 50.

[22] 'Das astrologische Weltbild in Nizamis Heft Peiker', *Symbolon*, 2 (1961), 69

was constrained to subject the erotic to the laws of Islam, but because perfect union can only be achieved through perfect virtue. 'The supreme goal of love is to awaken the soul from the sleep of negligence and ignorance by raising it from the sensible and corporeal to the psychic and rational.'[23] Nizâmî's eroticism is neither unduly spiritualized nor tainted with either prudery or licence; it colours the poem, and in particular the tales, with an atmosphere of sensuous delight in which the cosmic and the carnal aspects of love combine to form the driving force which impels (or should impel) their protagonists to virtue.

The tales highlight the importance of story-telling as a means of conveying both wisdom and delight. The validity of story-telling was often challenged in the Islamic tradition: philosophers, historians, and religious conservatives alike condemned 'fanciful' tales as misleading falsehoods with no moral value. There is, however, a long-standing connection between women and story-telling, as between story-telling and the entertainment and instruction of princes; we have only to recall that paradigmatic example, the *Thousand and One Nights*, in which, through story-telling, Scheherazade leads the king to justice and understanding. Story-telling is a night-time activity, performed largely by women, to divert and relax the ruler and encourage sleep, a motif central to the *Nights* and which recurs in Nizâmî's *Khusraw and Shîrîn* as well as in the *Haft Paykar*, whose seven tales bear many affinities to those of the *Nights*; indeed, the second tale, in which the king does not slay his concubines-for-a-night but merely sells them back the next morning, parodies the *Nights*' frame-story.

Recurrent imagery is a prominent feature of the *Haft Paykar*. Much of this imagery is based on the fundamental contrast between darkness and light, ignorance and illuminated wisdom. The Prophet, in his Ascent, is described as the sphere's moon (§3: 7); moonlike beauties—Fitna, Turktâz, Bakht—provide guidance to their respective lovers. Black, coiling dragons, likened to tar or smoke, guard shining treasures and threaten these moons, as the 'Sky-Dragon' causes Fitna's 'eclipse' (§25: 71, §26: 90). Bahrâm's arrows strike fire in the hunt (§25: 7–9), kindling

---

[23] Y. Marquet, *La Philosophie des Iḫwān al-Ṣafāʾ* (Algiers, 1973), 357.

a flame by which he himself is burned (§26: 80). Water, the greatest need of the thirsting man, is linked with the legendary Water of Life, for which Alexander fruitlessly searched the Realms of Darkness but which was found only by his companion, the prophet Khizr, who thereby gained not only immortality but spiritual wisdom.

A pervasive image is that of the cave, entrance into which both inaugurates and concludes Bahrâm's journey (§§14, 52). For the *futuwwa*, the cave was a symbol both of initiation and of closeness to the divine; their initiation ritual included the recitation of Koranic passages, among them one from *Sûrat al-Kahf*, the 'Sura of the Cave' (18: 10): 'When the young men fled for refuge to the cave and said: Our Lord! Give us mercy from thy presence and shape for us right conduct in our plight.' The Koranic story of the Seven Sleepers in the Cave (Ahl al-Kahf) came to symbolize perfect piety and divine protection, and provided an important allegory for esoteric writers; it is linked to the Prophet's flight (Hijra) from Mecca to Medina in 622, during which he and his companion Abû Bakr hid in a cave to evade their pursuers. Bahrâm's initial discovery of the treasure in the dragon's cave recalls such prophetic figures as Zoroaster, Mânî, and Muhammad, who emerged from retreat into a cave with the treasure of divine revelation; his final disappearance links him with such eschatological figures as the ancient Iranian saviour-king Saoshyant (whose coming would be preceded by the reign of the king Varhrân (= Bahrâm)), the Sunnite 'rightly guided leader' (*imâm mahdî*), and the Shiite 'occulted imam' (*imâm ghâʾib*), and with the Kayânid prince Kaykhusraw who renounced the world to vanish into a cave (the story is told in the *Shâhnâma*; Nizâmî alludes to it in §52: 27: 'He spurred his horse within, and gave | his kingly treasure [*ganj-i kaykhusravî*] to the cave'). The reference to the cave which follows (§52: 109: 'Existence's length and breadth are great; | but all *we* know of is this cave') seems directly reminiscent of Plato's cave. The cave is also evoked in the imagery of penetration linked to various protagonists in the tales: the basket and column of the King of Black (§32: 130–52), Malîkhâ's drowning in the supposed jar (§34: 131–4), Mâhân's penetration into the garden from the pit into which he falls (§36: 170–83), the young master's breach in the wall of his garden (§38: 48–9), his spy-hole in the brick chamber (§38: 91–4, 124–5), the lovers' retreat into a cave overgrown by jasmine (§38: 260–3).

The garden is perhaps the most powerful of these recurrent images. The seven tales are framed by gardens: Bahrâm's winter chamber mimics the four seasons (§30: 18–45); he emerges from the Seven Domes into the royal garden in spring (§39). The chief locus of the action of Tales I, V, and VII is the garden (in V, contrasted with the ghoul-inhabited waste), each introduced by the controlling metaphor of Iram: the first identified with it (§32: 194), the second surpassing it (§36: 185), the third merely like it (§38: 27). The association of the garden with Paradise is self-evident; but in Tale V Nizâmî seems to allude directly to the 'garden of the Sharî'at' described by the Ismaili poet Nâsir-i Khusraw (d. after 1074) as 'God's garden', full of grain and seed, with abundant trees of every kind, 'planted both by the All-Merciful and by Satan'; he who desires the garden's blessings and fruits may not enter without permission of its gardener, 'a great man, famed and virtuous'.

> If you must have fruit, go towards its apples and quinces;
> pay no attention to its fruitless, thorny plants.

The 'thorny plants' are the camel-thorn ((khâr-i) mughîlân, a word derived from the same root as 'ghoul' (cf. §36: 107–9)). The garden is perhaps the greatest of God's signs , the World-Book which reflects His Paradise—

> In the meadow, every petal is the book of a different state;
> what a pity should you remain ignorant of all of them,

wrote Hâfiz—but, like any book, it must be read aright.

With its creative use of religious, esoteric, literary, and popular traditions, mingling epic motifs with romantic and magical adventures, the whole informed by a cosmic symbolism based on number and colour and ordered by a complex and overarching structure, the *Haft Paykar* is far more than a 'mirror for princes'; it is a mirror of the world itself, in its material and spiritual aspects, both reflecting and figuring forth the correspondences between the two, a speculum by means of which man may come to know both himself and his Lord.

## The *Haft Paykar* in the West

Despite its position as one of the great masterpieces of Persian poetry, and perhaps because of the complexity that makes it so, the *Haft Paykar* has received less attention in the West than it deserves. Nizâmî received a brief mention in D'Herbelot's *Bibliothèque orientale*; in the early nineteenth century scholars in Hungary (Wilhelm Bacher) and Russia (Franz von Erdmann) addressed themselves to the poet and his works, and interest increased (primarily in Russia and Germany) throughout the nineteenth and early twentieth centuries. Some scholars have sought to reconstruct both Nizâmî's biography and his beliefs from statements in his poems, but with little success; others have been concerned with the sources of the *Haft Paykar*, its relationship to 'Oriental tales' and to the spread of such tales to the West.[24] Nizâmî's imagery was the subject of a study by Hellmut Ritter,[25] who compared the Persian poet's style to that of Goethe, contrasting the vividness and immediacy of the latter to Nizâmî's supposed 'metaphorical transformation' of physical phenomena which permits the invention of new relationships which have no basis in 'reality'.

Other scholars have addressed problems of the *Haft Paykar*'s structure and symbolism. George Krotkoff divides the seven tales into a sequence of four plus three: the first four represent matter and correspond to the four humours (black bile, yellow bile (= choler), green (phlegm), red blood) reflected in the characters of their protagonists, and constitute the early stages of a ritual of initiation; the last three (blue, sandal, white) represent spirit. He relates the poem's numerical symbolism to the concept of the three trines (feminine + masculine + spiritual), the sum of which constitutes the Grand Trine of the cosmos, noting the apparent absence of the eighth and ninth spheres (identified with Sophia and Logos) and associating these implicitly with the wisdom and justice gained by Bahrâm.[26] The present writer has discussed the poem's structure and symbolism, its ethical

---

[24] For a relatively complete bibliography of studies on the poet, see Peter Chelkowski, art. 'Niẓāmī Gandjawī', *Encyclopaedia of Islam* (new edn.).

[25] *Über die bildersprache Nizamis.*     [26] 'Colour and Number', 106–11.

intent, and its status as a literary microcosm (see further the Bibliography).

The *Haft Paykar* has sometimes been viewed as mere 'entertainment'. M. V. McDonald deemed it 'the most inconsequential of [Nizâmî's] works,' which 'points no moral and seeks only to amuse' and offers 'little scope for philosophy'.[27] Earlier scholars were often unappreciative of Nizâmî's style (as of that of Persian poetry generally); but more recent scholars have begun to call attention to its many excellences. Peter Chelkowski has called the poet 'a master dramatist', commenting on the use of plot and character to enhance the 'psychological complexities' of the romances.[28] While we should beware of reading 'plot' or 'character' in modern, 'novelistic' terms, the vividness of Nizâmî's description of crucial moments in his protagonists' lives is no less striking for their linkage to the broader themes of his poems, and his mastery of dialogue may be seen, for example, in Fitna's confrontation with Bahrâm (§26), or in the rantings of the insufferable Malîkhâ (§34).

Negative moral judgements on the poet have not been lacking. Even the sympathetic Jan Rypka criticized the ending of the sixth tale (§37), in which Good marries three brides—the Kurdish maid who restored his sight, and the daughters of the king and the vizier whom he cured of epilepsy and blindness respectively: 'We are irritated all the more because [the Kurdish maid] does not remain the only wife—whereas this would be a matter of course in Western tales—but on the contrary must give precedence to two wives of higher birth.'[29] Happily, such anachronistic attitudes are becoming rare.

The earliest translation of the *Haft Paykar* into English, C. E. Wilson's *The Haft Paikar* (*The Seven Beauties*) (London, 1924), was largely motivated by the pervasive interest in 'Eastern spirituality' of the late nineteenth and early twentieth centuries. Wilson rendered the poem into unrhymed iambic decameter, and supplemented his translation with a volume of not always reliable notes and commentary (Wilson, for example, confused the 'Dragon'—the twenty-eighth lunar station—with the con-

[27] 'The Religious and Social Views [of] Nizami of Ganjeh', *Iran*, 1 (1963), 100.

[28] 'Nizāmī Gandjawī', *Encyclopaedia of Islam* (new edn.).

[29] 'Les Sept Princesses de Nizhami', in *L'Âme de l'Iran* (Paris, 1951), 112.

stellation Draco, known in Western astrology for its malefic
influence; Eastern astrology is, however, less interested in con-
stellations than in planetary movements through the Zodiac).
His reading of the poem is heavily tinged with mystical
interpretation, seen, for example, in his attempt to correlate the
seven tales with the seven stages of the mystical Path, or his
mystical readings of various episodes (for example, Malîkhâ's
drowning in the 'jar' of water (§34: 134–7), 'taking [the real
meaning] of the jar and water as Universal Spirit' (2: 156 nn.
1513–14)). Wilson also had reservations about the poet's style.

[Nizâmî's] defects are those common to all Persian poets, who have little
skill in delineating character, or in inspiring a sense of the spirit of
nature. Each different character is cast in its own conventional mould,
and has no individuality, whilst the depicting of nature is also conventional and artificial. Emotional, especially pathetic situations . . . are
often drawn with great artistic power, but the expression to which they
lead in those affected is not convincing. . . . The depicting of nature
reveals, it is true, the most close and accurate observation, but the
images offered are fantastic: they are neither poetic nor scientific, and
convey nothing of the spirit of nature such as we see it in Shelley and
Wordsworth. (i, p. xvii)

There have been a number of other translations into various
languages, largely confined to prose, and some only partial. F.
Gabrieli rendered the story of the Russian princess (§35), the
description of spring (§39), and Bahrâm's disappearance (§52)
into Italian prose;[30] A. Bausani later produced an Italian prose
translation of the entire poem (slightly abridged), accompanied
by a valuable introduction and glossary, which is the most reliable of prior translations (see the Bibliography). R. Gelpke
published a German prose paraphrase of the seven tales, with an
extensive 'Afterword' on their symbolism (unfortunately not
reproduced in full in the English version);[31] J.-C. Bürgel translated the story of Bahrâm and Fitna into German verse.[32] There

---

[30] 'Versioni da Niẓāmī', *Annali dell'Istituto superiore orientale di Napoli*, 10:
1–2 (Dec. 1937–Mar. 1938), 31–72.

[31] *Die sieben Geschichten der sieben Prinzessinnen* (Zurich, 1959); *The Story of
the Seven Princesses*, English version by Elsie and George Hill (London, 1976).

[32] 'Die Geschichte von König Bahram Gor und seinem Sklavenmädchen',
*Bustan*, 8/2 (1967), 26–35.

are, to my knowledge, no French translations, but there exist a number of Russian ones. Peter Chelkowski presented an English prose summary of the poem in his *Mirror of the Invisible World* (see the Bibliography), with a commentary and an introduction on the poet's life, accompanied by reproductions of miniatures from the Metropolitan Museum manuscript dated 1524–5.

The present translation seeks to present Nizâmî's poem, as befits its importance in the Persian romance tradition, as a work of poetry first and foremost, and in a style approximating that of European romances. While explanatory notes have been provided, the poem has been regarded not as a philological document but as a work of the imagination; nor has it been reduced to the status of mere entertaining tales, to be read for the 'story' alone. All the elements of the *Haft Paykar* must be seen as working together, combined into a whole which balances entertainment with didacticism, romantic adventure with symbolic meaning, as indeed is true of all medieval romances. Above all, the poem should be seen as a testimony both to the ennobling power of love and to the inspiring force of story, the twin means by which its protagonist, and its reader, learn the nature of their own design.

# NOTE ON THE TRANSLATION

The *Haft Paykar* presents particular problems for the translator, especially for one who attempts to render it into verse (prose renderings, however competent, tend to move the poem into the 'storybook' genre) and to retain as much as possible of the flavour of the original. It consists of approximately 5,000 rhyming couplets of *masnavî* verse, written in the *Khafîf* metre; the 'apocopated' form used here (-⏑--/⏑-⏑-/⏑⏑- × 2) is generally considered a 'light' or 'festive' metre. I have chosen to render the poem in octosyllabic couplets, a roughly parallel prosodic form widely used in medieval narrative poetry in the West which is close in rhythm to the original and sufficiently flexible to prevent monotony, and to retain the characteristic rhyme *aa bb cc* etc. (a far more difficult task in English, with its limited rhymes, than in Persian, and with which I have necessarily had to take some liberties). Another characteristic of Persian verse is the relative infrequency (though not, as is often supposed, total absence) of enjambment: end-stopped lines (in *masnavî* each half-line) tend to be complete statements, grammatically and syntactically (though not conceptually) independent of what precedes and follows, reflecting the fundamentally oral nature of Persian poetry which, if composed in writing, was still intended to be read aloud. I have increased the proportion of overlapped lines, partly to provide variety, partly to facilitate translation.

The second problem relates to the traditional nature and complex allusivity of the poem's imagery. Persian poetry is noted for its abundant use of rhetorical figures and its elaborate (often termed 'artificial' or 'decorative') imagery, and the *Haft Paykar* is no exception. Many translators find the flowery, hyperbolic style of Persian poetry not congenial to Western tastes, and deliberately modify the style of their originals to make it more 'palatable'. Many complex figures prove difficult or impossible to translate literally, particularly when they involve language-specific figures such as paronomasia (e.g. the pun on the meanings of *gûr*; some such figures are explained in the Notes). A key to translating such features lies in a proper understanding of their function; and a certain amount of consistency must be observed in order to bring out the recurrent images which characterize the poem—for example, 'moon', in the sense of 'a beautiful face/person', must be rendered literally, as it is tied in with the poem's astrological symbolism.

The allusions, commonplaces, and types found in Persian poetry will often be unfamiliar to Western readers. Some are self-explanatory; others require glossing or annotation, which I have provided. In general I have attempted to stay close to the conceits of the original; on some occasions, however, I have substituted an equivalent expression where a literal translation would be meaningless (e.g. §7: 125, 'shoes/sealing-wax' for the Persian *âsmân va-rîsmân*, 'sky/rope', where the sense is based not on meaning but on rhyme). I have not hesitated to call a handsome man or lovely girl a cypress, a beautiful maiden a perî or hourî, an eye a narcissus, dark curls surrounding a bright face 'Ethiops attacking Greeks', and so on, when Nizâmî does. Nor have I attempted to 'clean up' Nizâmî's rather colourful, and certainly unobjectionable, sexual imagery, which Wilson routinely and relentlessly Latinized. Neither have I suppressed Nizâmî's many allusions to, for example, the heroes of the *Shâhnâma*; these and other proper names, along with such untranslated and untranslateable terms as *qibla* (the Muslim direction of prayer) or *farr* (the aura of royal glory and divine support which surrounds legitimate Iranian rulers) will be found in the Glossary. More complicated allusions to cosmology, astrology and astronomy, alchemy and magic, even orthography, have been explained when necessary. Finally, I have retained the title in its original Persian: *haft paykar* can be translated as seven 'images', 'portraits', 'beauties', or 'planets' (the poem is also known as the *Haft Gunbad*, 'Seven Domes'); to prefer any one of these would be to destroy the polysemy implicit in the original.

A further difficulty lies in the text itself. The establishment of a 'definitive' text of the *Haft Paykar* may never be achieved, owing both to the proliferation of manuscripts and to flexible medieval notions of literary property and textual transmission. I have based my translation on the edition of H. Ritter and J. Rypka (Prague, 1934), who compared fourteen manuscripts and provided a complete apparatus criticus; I have also consulted the

edition by Vahîd Dastgirdî (2nd edn., Tehran, 1955–6) and the
Moscow edition (1987), as well as the translations by Wilson and
Bausani. (The edition of the poem by H. Pizhmân Bakhtiyârî
(Tehran, 1965) used the editions of Ritter and Rypka and
Dastgirdî, as well as several additional manuscripts; it contains
neither variants nor annotations, is even less critical than that of
Dastgirdî, and thus has not been consulted.) Line numbering,
section numbering, and rubrification follow Ritter and Rypka; I
have not omitted any of the lines in their edition (though some
are problematic), but have sometimes included others which
they omit or consider interpolations, and have numbered these *a*,
*b*, etc. (e.g. §51: 19*a–e*, included on the basis of Nizâmî's fidelity
to his model in the *Siyâsatnâma*). In compiling the Notes I have
had recourse to a wide range of sources, both primary and sec-
ondary, some of which are indicated when they might be of
further interest to the reader; most, however, are not. Translit-
eration of names and terms has been simplified, with only long
vowels (â, î, û) and (Arabic) *hamza* (’) and *ʿayn* (ʿ) (pronounced
identically as glottal stops in Persian) indicated. Arabic words
and phrases in the text have been italicized.

# SELECT BIBLIOGRAPHY

With a few important exceptions, I have restricted the
Bibliography to works in English; for works in other languages,
both the Notes to the Introduction and the Translation and
the article on Nizâmî in the *Encyclopaedia of Islam* may be
consulted.

## General Background

Nizâm al-Mulk, *The Book of Government or Rules for Kings*,
trans. H. Darke (London, 1960; repr., 1978).

Nasîr al-Dîn Tûsî, *The Nasirean Ethics*, trans. G. M. Wickens
(London, 1964).

Seyyed Hossein Nasr, *An Introduction to Islamic Cosmological
Doctrines* (Cambridge, Mass., 1964; repr. Boulder, Colo.,
1978).

J. S. Meisami, 'Kings and Lovers: Ethical Dimensions of Medi-
aeval Persian Romance', *Edebiyât*, NS 1 (1987), 1–27.

J.-C. Bürgel, 'The Romance', in Ehsan Yarshater (ed.), *Persian
Literature* (New York, 1988), 161–78.

## On Nizâmî

M. V. McDonald, 'The Religious and Social Views [of] Niẓami
of Ganjeh', *Iran*, 1 (1963), 97–101.

Priscilla P. Soucek, 'Niẓāmī on Painters and Painting', in
Richard Ettinghausen (ed.), *Islamic Art in the Metropolitan
Museum of Art* (New York, 1972), 9–21.

Peter J. Chelkowski, *Mirror of the Invisible World: Tales from the
Khamseh of Nizami* (New York, 1975).

J. S. Meisami, 'Allegorical Gardens in the Persian Poetic Tradition: Neẓāmī, Rūmī, Ḥāfeẓ', *IJMES* 17 (1985), 229–60.

——— *Medieval Persian Court Poetry* (Princeton, NJ, 1987), chs.
3–5, 7.

Peter J. Chelkowski, 'Neẓāmī: Master Dramatist', in Ehsan
Yarshater (ed.), *Persian Literature* (New York, 1988), 179–89.

## The *Haft Paykar*

### Editions

*Heft Peyker, ein romantisches Epos*, ed. H. Ritter and J. Rypka (Prague, 1934).

*Haft Paykar*, ed. Vahîd Dastgirdî (2nd edn., Tehran, 1956).

*Haft Paykar*, ed. T. A. Muharramov (Moscow, 1987).

### Translations

*The Haft Paikar (The Seven Beauties)*, trans. C. E. Wilson (2 vols., London, 1924).

*Le sette principesse*, trans. Alessandro Bausani (Bari, 1967).

*The Story of the Seven Princesses*, trans. R. Gelpke; English version by Elsie and George Hill (London, 1976).

### Interpretation

George Krotkoff, 'Colour and Number in the *Haft Paykar*', in R. M. Savory and D. A. Agius (eds.), *Logos Islamikos: Studia Islamica in honorem Georgii Michaelis Wickens* (Toronto, 1984), 97–118.

J. S. Meisami, 'Fitnah or Azadah? Nizami's Ethical Poetic', *Edebiyât*, NS 1/2 (1988), 41–75.

—— 'The Theme of the Journey in Niẓāmī's *Haft Paykar*', *Edebiyât*, NS 4/2 (1993), 5–22.

# A CHRONOLOGY OF NIZAMI

| | |
|---|---|
| 1141 | ? Birth of Nizâmî in Ganja. |
| 1146 | Shams al-Dîn Eldigüz (d. 1175–6), governor of Arran, controls most of Azerbaijan. |
| 1150s+ | Ganja ruled by Eldigüzids. |
| 1155–84 | Reign of Giorgi III, king of Georgia; increased military activities against Muslim territories. |
| 1157 | Death of Sanjar, Seljuk sultan of Iran; loss of the Seljuks' Iranian territories. |
| 1161 | Accession of sultan Arslân ibn Toghrïl, stepson of Shams al-Dîn Eldigüz. |
| 1162 | Invasion of Georgia by Muslim coalition (including Sultan Arslân, Âq Sonqor II, and Shams al-Dîn Eldigüz); defeat of King Giorgi. |
| 1163–4 | ? *Makhzan al-Asrâr*, dedicated to Fakhr al-Dîn Bahrâmshâh (r. *c.*1160–1220), Menjukid ruler of Erzinjan. |
| 1166 | Georgian raids into Arran as far as Ganja. |
| 1169–70 | ? ʿAlâʾ al-Dîn Körp Arslân (or Qara Sonqor) succeeds his brother Âq Sonqor II as Ahmadili ruler of Maragha. |
| 1175–87 | Atabegate of Muhammad Jahân Pahlavân; his brother Qïzïl Arslân ruler in Tabriz. |
| 1176 | Accession of Toghrïl II ibn Arslân. |
| 1180 | ? *Khusraw and Shîrîn*; praises Toghrïl II, Muhammad ibn Eldigüz Jahân Pahlavân the ruler of Ganja, Qïzïl Arslân, and Nusrat al-Dîn Abû Bakr. |
| 1180–1225 | Caliphate of al-Nâsir li-Dîn Allâh. |
| 1182–3 | al-Nasir officializes the Rahhâsiyya order of the *futuwwa*. |
| 1184–1212 | Reign of Queen Tamara of Georgia. |
| 1187–91 | Atabegate of Qïzïl Arslân. |
| 1188 | Toghrïl defeats caliphal forces at Hamadan. |
| 1188–92 | ? *Laylî and Majnûn*, dedicated to the Sharvânshâh Akhsatân I (r. *c.*1162–99 or later). |
| 1188 | Saladin retakes Jerusalem from the Franks. |
| 1190 | Qïzïl Arslân imprisons Toghrïl II near Tabriz and claims the sultanate of Iraq and Azerbaijan, with the support of the caliph al-Nâsir. |
| 1191 | Qïzïl Arslân murdered; power struggle between his nephews Qutlugh İnanch and Nusrat al-Dîn Abû Bakr. |
| 1191–5 | Atabegate of Qutlugh İnanch. |

1193    ? Defeat of Nusrat al-Dîn Abû Bakr by Georgians outside
        Ganja. Death of Saladin.

1194    Toghrïl II defeated and killed in battle by the Khwarazmshah
        Takesh; Takesh occupies Saljuq territories; Iran and Iraq
        devasted by Khwarazmian troops.

1195–1210 Atabegate of Nusrat al-Dîn Abû Bakr.

1197    *Haft Paykar*, dedicated to ʿAlâʾ al-Dîn Körp Arslân, ruler of
        Maragha.

1120    Death of Takesh; massacre of Khwarazmians in Western Iran.

1200–2  ? *Iskandarnâma* ('Book of Alexander'), in two parts, the
        *Sharafnâma* ('Book of Honour') and *Iqbâlnâma*.

1205–6  Nusrat al-Dîn Abû Bakr repels Bakr attack by ʿAlâʾ al-Dîn
        Körp Arslân; takes over most of the Ahmadili territories three
        years later.

1209    ? Death of Nizâmî.

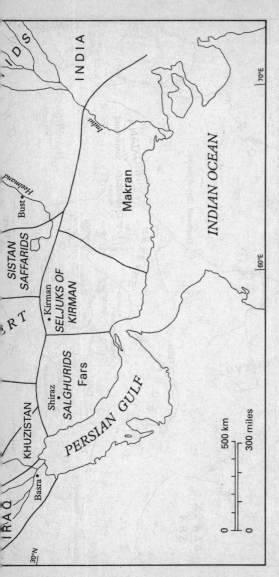

AZERBAIJAN AND SURROUNDING AREAS

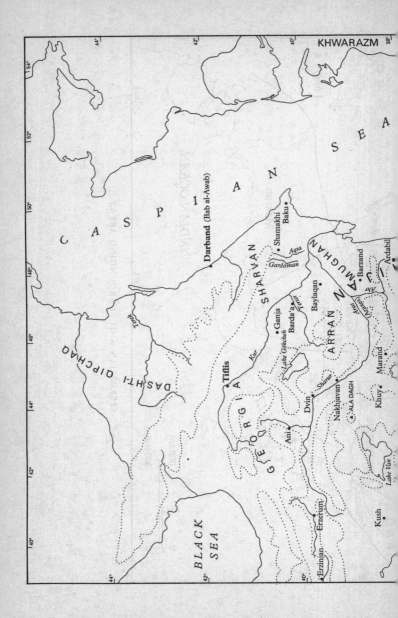

THE IRANIAN WORLD *c.* 1180

Damghan •   36°

MT DAMAVAND

Firuzkuh

Amul •   Rayy •

MAZANDARAN

GILAN (DAYLAM)

Miyana •

MT SAHAND

Maragha •

*Jaghatu*

Lake Urmiyeh

Zanjan •   Sultaniya •

Abhar •   Kharraqan

Qazvin •

JIBAL

Sava •

Qum •

Kashan •

Isfahan •

Hamadan •

Nihavand •

Bisitun •

Shushtar •

K U R D I S T A N

Mosul •

Baghdad •

Najaf •

*Tigris*

I R A Q

*Euphrates*

32°   34°   36°

42°   44°   46°   48°   50°   52°

# THE *HAFT PAYKAR*
## A Medieval Persian Romance

# CONTENTS

# Contents

# 1

## Invocation

*In the name of God, the Merciful, the Compassionate*

O You from Whom the world began,　　　　1
before Whom nought had ever been;
The Source from Whom all things have come,　　2
the End* to Whom all will return:
O You Who raised the lofty sphere,　　　　3
kindled the stars in order fair,
Created Bounty's endless store,　　　　4
and fashioned Being through Your power:
All men's affairs You order well　　　　5
Who are All, and created all.
You *are*, and have no like nor peer;*　　　6
to all wise men You thus appear,
Enlightening men of insight—though　　　7
without form—through the forms You show.
All beings live by vital force;　　　　8
but Your sole Being is their source.
O You who formed the world from nought;　　9
Who cherished it, and plenty brought:
Your Name is first among all names;　　　10
You first Beginning, final End;
You *were*, before all reckonings,　　　11
and still will *be*, when all else ends.
Each creature's being You have formed;　　12
to You alone will each return.
Thought cannot reach Your high estate,　　13
nor death's dust sully Your high gate.
You were not born, all others were;　　　14
You are the Lord, all others air.
You show the way with one swift thought;　　15
one word untangles every knot;
And he who would not bow to man*　　　16

is prisoned fast with lock and band.

17 To night You give the radiant dawn,
to day the birds, to birds their grain.

18 You have bestowed on sun and moon
two tents with white and black adorned.

19 Both day and night traverse Your way,
true servants of Your royal sway;

20 By Your command both good and ill
they do, but nought by their own will.

21 You kindled in man's mind the light
of reason, than a lamp more bright;

22 And yet with all its quickness, it
cannot perceive You, as is fit.

23 If reason on Your path goes lame,
how should man's fancy there incline?

24 The soul—that substance in our selves—
none knows the place wherein it dwells;

25 You, Who're no substance, know no place,
how should bewildered fancy trace?

26 You're guided not, but are the Guide;
present in all, nowhere reside.

27 We, of the seven spheres a part,
stand far outside Your noble court.

28 The Universal Intellect,*
though by You guided, from respect

29 Regards You not. O You whose aid
in bright day and black night we need;

30 Who are the Changer of all states,
He Who alone such changes makes:

31 No good or bad, but by Your wish,
no being, of itself, exists.

32 You give to stone the ruby's flame;
bring forth from it the fiery gem.*

33 Both earth and earth-revolving sky
cry out before your door, 'Make way!'

34 All, on Your fine-wove tapestry,
are figures; You their forms array.

35 How should the stars cause good or ill,
which are by good and ill enthralled?

Great Kayqubâd—were such the case—                    36
would stem from the stargazers' race;
But what stargazer, through his vain                    37
predictions, ever treasure gained?
To him alone You treasure give                    38
who knows not seven stars from five.
The subtle secrets of the stars                    39
I've studied; pondered occult lore,
And puzzled what each page might mean:                    40
when I found You, I washed them clean:
I saw that all things turn to God,                    41
and knew You as their mighty Lord.
O You Who give to all their lives;                    42
Whose ovens their daily bread provides:
Before Your gate exalt me then,                    43
that I may have no need for men.
Without another's aid, bestow                    44
my bread, Who nourish all below.
Since from my youth I never turned                    45
away from You, my bread to earn
At others' doors, Your grace has sent,                    46
without my asking, all to mine.
Now, an old man, I stand before                    47
Your court; protect me from all fear.
What words are these? an error plain:                    48
with Your support, the world is mine.
O Lord, the world bewilders me.                    49
Yours is the power to set me free.
To whom should I complain? to You                    50
Who welcome all; receive me, too.
Though many secrets lie concealed,                    51
before You all things are revealed.
My poem's goal, not hid from You                    52
Who know it well, You can make true;
But should You will it that I fail,                    53
I'll bend my purpose to Your will.
'Tis best to seek from You alone                    54
my purpose, and with You commune.
To tell the mystery to mankind                    55

degrades me; if to You, I'll find
56  You'll raise me high. You, Nizâmî's
sole refuge, turn him not away
57  To others' doors, but honour him;
bestow contentment's diadem,
58  That, when all deeds to You are shown,
though poor, he'll boast a kingly crown.

## 2

### In Praise of the Chief among Prophets
*Benedictions and peace be upon him!*

1  The primal Circle's centre, and
the Seal upon Creation's line;*
2  The ancient sphere's first fruits; the crown
of lofty discourse; reason's gem:
3  Who, but the lord of confirmed faith,
God's Prophet, Messenger most praised.*
4  By sword and crown the prophets' lord:
the Ascent his crown, the Law his sword.*
5  Unlettered, source of all that's made,
the Carpet's light, the High Throne's shade,*
6  Who sounds the Law's five turns; arrays
his fourfold rule* o'er earthly clay.
7  He foremost goal, we all in need:
Muhammad he, his mission praised.*
8  Of that first clay that Adam pressed,*
he essence pure, all others dregs;
9  And when Heaven turns its final round,
his word shall seal its final sound.
10  On right are based his yeas and nays,
enjoining good, and banning base.
11  His boast, of poverty;* no pain
to him, who such a treasure gained!
12  He put day's brightness in the shade:
what talk of shade,* with sun displayed!
13  Of worldly rule the godly stay,

he worldly rulers mates and slays,
Abasing all who would rebel, 14
grasping the hand of those who fell.

With righteous men he dealt aright, 15
but anger showed towards evil might.

His vengeful sword struck evil down; 16
for good his kindness mixed sweet balm,
Elixir to sore hearts; his blade 17
to hearts of stone his wrath displayed.

Those foes who barred the road of faith, 18
and girded up their loins with hate,
Now beat their thongs upon his drum, 19
and, after years, all follow him.

Though God chose him from every age; 20
created this world for his sake;
'*Turned not aside*'* his eyes hath sealed, 21
a garden beyond this revealed.

From seven hundred thousand years, 22
seven thousand* servitude declare.

The servants of the blue-robed sphere* 23
his service's ring wear in their ear.

His four true friends,* both root and branch, 24
are walls for the Law's treasure, staunch.

From the divine Creator came 25
his eyes' bright light—blessings on him!

His soul life's every breath maintains; 26
his body* both earth and Heaven spans.

This soul that body's life does bring; 27
all others throne, he Solomon.

His breath like musk the air perfumes, 28
and shakes moist dates from dry date-palms.

His miracle: dates from dry thorns, 29
that for his foes to sharp barbs turn!

His nail did split the moon in twain, 30
a two-halved apple in his hand.

Despite its fear, he rent away 31
the cataract that blinds the sky.*

He was most blessed by the Creator, 32

the chosen one of that Elector;
33 And may on both our praises fall,
longer than the blue sphere shall roll.

# 3

## On the Prophet's Ascent to Heaven

1 Since this world compassed not his crown,
his Ladder* bore him to God's Throne.

2 To raise him high from low degree
came Gabriel with Burâq,* his steed.

3 'Place now on air your foot of clay,
that your earth be made heavenly.

4 The Holy Presence you will guard
tonight; be purity's staunch ward.

5 Yours now is Burâq's lightning speed;
mount, to perform your watchman's deed.

6 Since I've conveyed your guardian's lot,
Burâq, your mount, I've also brought.

7 Traverse the sphere, for you're its moon;
speed o'er the stars, for you're their king;

8 From their seven roots, uproot the six
directions; the nine spheres unfix

9 From their four nails; pass by the Fish,*
and bend the heavens to your wish.

10 The stars blend night's dark musk for you;
the green-robed angels wait for you.

11 The Egyptian beauties of this sphere
adore you, like a Joseph fair.

12 Rise, that your face they all may see,
and wound themselves in ecstasy.*

13 Beneath you, form new vaulted whorls
for Heaven, from your shadow's curls.

14 Lamp-like,* give the stars blooms of light;
fresh-faced as garden flowers, shine bright.

15 This night is yours;* this hour, of prayer;
you'll gain whatever you desire.

16 Make new the angels' carpet; raise

your tent at the Divine Throne's base;
Brighten the Throne's eyes with your light;    16a
fold up the carpet* in your flight;
Then grasp the crown, for you are king;    17
exalted, rule created things.
Raise high your head in grandeur; make    18
both worlds* your own, through your attack.
Then cleanse your path of dust; speed on    19
to the court of the Eternal One,
So that—your meed for coming nigh—    20
your flag may over both worlds fly.'
When he, in secret converse, heard    21
from Gabriel these soul-moving words,
His intellect perfect thereby,    22
the Prophet hastened to obey.
One God's trustee in revelation,    23
the other in wise deliberation:
Both guardians of a wealthy trust:    24
no demon this, no sinner that.
One brought the message as decreed;    25
the other did its secrets heed.
In dark night, that light-giving lamp    26
was sealed by his high wish's stamp.
He shook not off that lasso's bond;    27
no yoke of gold but this is known.
Like lightning on Burâq he leapt;    28
his steed beneath, he grasped his whip.
He mounted; that celestial steed    29
traversed the sky with eagle's speed.
Like peacocks' wings his striking hoofs;    30
the moon like Kâvûs' throne above;
And in its flight—so quick it climbed—    31
the four eagles* shed their wings behind.
It quickly passed o'er all it found;    32
the night was spurned, the moon reined in.
Have you seen how swift a fancy speeds?    33
how lightning quick unsheathes its blade?
Both world-traversing Reason's speed    34
and the soul's leap towards generous deed:

35  All, by its flight, were left as lame;
    all by its lengthy stride constrained.

36  Its speed outstripped the Poles' swift course:
    one moment south, the other north.

37  The Fish in that swift rushing stream
    showed now as Lancer, now unarmed.*

38  When he with Burâq's dancing feet
    inscribed that volume, sheet by sheet,

39  He left behind the worldly road,
    and far above the heavens soared;

40  Cut through the stations of the sky,
    with angel's wings, a broad highway.

41  From his own verdant nature, he
    gave to the moon new verdancy.

42  His silver-work to Mercury gave
    the bluish shade of leaden glaze.

43  O'er Venus, from the moon's bright light,
    he drew a veil of silvery white.

44  His dust, as he attacked the heavens,
    set on the sun a golden crown.

45  Green-robed like Caliph of the West,*
    red garments bright to Mars he left;

46  And, finding Jupiter consumed
    by pain, rubbed sandalwood* thereon.

47  When Saturn's crown* his feet had kissed,
    he placed its flag in ambergris.

48  As he rushed on like morning's wind,
    astride a mount like raging lion,

49  His comrade left off his attack,
    and in his course Burâq grew slack.

50  For he had reached a stage so far
    that Gabriel dared not come near.

51  From Michael's couch he rose, until
    he reached the tower of Isrâfîl.

52  He left that throne behind, and soared
    beyond both Rafraf and the Lote.*

53  Companions left behind, he pressed
    on to the Sea of Selflessness;

54  Passed o'er that ocean, drop by drop;

traversed all Being, step by step.
When he came to the Throne's support,    55
he made a ladder from prayer's rope.
He went beyond the radiant Throne,    56
to the mystery of 'Praise be Mine'.*
When, lost in his bewilderment,    57
God's Mercy came and seized his reins,
His distance of '*two bowlengths*' went    58
from '*he came near*' to '*nearer yet*'.*
Rending the veil of thousand lights,*    59
that unveiled Brilliance reached his sight.
Beyond his being's bounds* he trod,    60
till he achieved the sight of God.
He saw outright the Worshipped One,    61
and cleansed his eyes of all but Him;
Nor did in one place rest his sight,    62
as greetings came from left and right.
All one—front, back, left, right, high, low;    63
the six directions were no more.
When Non-direction's flame burns high,    64
world and direction swiftly flee.
God, without form, knows no direction;    65
and so he turned towards Non-direction.
When sight is veiled by direction,    66
the heart's not free from false perception;
But when direction's hid from sight,    67
He who has none is seen aright.
Nought but the Prophet's breath remained;    68
for God alone then dwelled in him.
How can direction compass Him,    69
the All and All-encompassing?
When the Prophet saw God thus,    70
he heard words spoken without voice.
He drank a special draught; attained    71
great honour; from his closeness gained
The way to Truth; Fortune his cup,    72
Wisdom his sâqî: nought else left.
With myriad prayers in tribute rendered,    73
from that high summit he descended;

74    Spent all he brought* upon his friends;
      placed it in trust for sinful men.

75    How long, Nizâmî, love this world?
      How long be base? Raise high your head!

76    The eternal realm strive to attain,
      which through Muhammad's faith you'll gain.

77    If reason guard your faith aright,
      you'll cleave to Truth through the Law's light.


## 4

## On the Cause of the Work's Composition

1     When, from the court of Solomon,*
      a hidden sign to me was borne,

2     Fleet as a bird on wings wide spread,
      straight to the royal gate I sped.

3     'Twas told me: 'Make a new moon rise;*
      begin your pen's festivities:

4     So slim a moon, that not an eye
      shall it through darkness' veil descry.

5     Make sorcerers, with your fancy's play,
      to your enchanted words* fall prey;

6     Some pepper grains on fire pour,*
      and let its hot flames crack and roar:

7     And in that heat make cold wax flow
      and weep, till soft of heart it grow.

8     Bring forth from out this narrow road
      your couch; how long a lame mule* goad?

9     Bid your pen sprinkle musky dew;
      let the dawn breeze grow musky too;

10    And bid the wind o'er amber dance:
      the grass, like silk, with musk enhance.

11    Toil, for your time of toil begins,
      and count each page the wealth of kings.

12    Your toil the way to riches winds,
      for he who toils a treasure finds.

13    Until the vine weeps bitter tears,
      its smiling harvest ne'er appears.

For marrow one must crack the bone,    14
and flies round honey swarm and drone.

Will your cloud ne'er its sweet rain shed?    15
Your oven's hot: now bake the bread.

Raise the curtain;* show your skill;    16
the virgins' faces now unveil.'

When to this end the envoy spoke,    17
my grief subsided; joy awoke.

I searched through books both fine and rare    18
for what would free sore hearts from care.

All chronicles of kings of yore    19
were gathered in one book of lore;

Already one of keenest mind    20
had ordered it in verse refined.

From that, some ruby dust remained,    21
shards* from which others something feigned.

I, from those fragments, jeweller-wise,    22
this precious treasure cut to size,

So that the experts who assay    23
all efforts, *this* most worthy weigh.

That which was left by him half-said    24
*I* say; the half-pierced pearl *I* thread;

While that which I found right and true,    25
just as before I've left to view.

I strove that this fair jointure, too,    26
should be adorned in foreign hue.

Again I sought, from books concealed    27
and scattered through the world's broad field;

From Persia's speech, and Araby's;    28
Bukhârî's pen, and Tabarî's;*

From other texts, all scattered wide:    29
each pearl, in hiding, cast aside.

The pages coming to my hand    30
I wrapped in leather, tied with band.

When all was chosen, ordered well,    31
when 'neath my pen's black ink all fell,

A poem I wrote that would win praise,    32
and not the scholars' laughter raise.

This written temple I've adorned,    33

with seven brides, like Magian Zand,

34  So that, should the sky-brides* decide
to turn their gaze upon *my* brides,

35  Through like affairs and ornaments
each of them aid to mine might lend.

36  For when the seven lines converge,
one point at centre shall emerge.

37  The painter, ten designs in hand,
of one main thread yet grasps the end;

38  If that thread from the line should stray,
the others would be set awry.

39  Though one trace not this thread aright,
rightness remains, nor quits our sight.

40  I follow this thread, painter-wise;
on that main thread I've fixed my gaze.*

41  This single thread's with peril fraught
since such abundant pearls I've brought.

42  One must wash in a thousand streams
to find one fit to drink, and clean;

43  From but a droplet man is made;*
yet how much water's thrown away.

44  If, shell-like, I from raindrops make
a pearl,* I'm surely worth my keep.

45  Sweeter than honeyed morsels are
my words; how should not bounty hear?

46  But why wind on about such things?
I'm nought; the luck-star fortune brings.

47  Firdawsî's bounty, Mahmûd's greed
the Bow and Scorpion decreed.*

48  Bû Dulaf kept in fruitful ease
Asadî,* since their signs agreed.

49  What do I say? what idle words;
my prince's rain forms precious pearls.

50  If the cloud nourishes the shell,
it sees in turn its due fulfilled.

51  When rain it scatters from the skies
the shell with royal pearls replies.

52  By Gabriel taught, my reed-pen's muse

my marks on paper thus construes:
'Go, deck this muse-taught magic fine
in garments new for New Year's time;*
From demons' eyes keep it concealed,
to none but Solomon* revealed.
*Here* lies my pith; seek me therein:
the rest's a mouldering bit of skin.
I'm pure wax, by no seal impressed,
with neither bees nor honey blessed,
Till Solomon, with his own seal,
impress upon me what he will.
Whether I'm honoured or disgraced,
the prince's scribe will seal my fate.
In weighing words I give the full
of worth, debasing not their gold.
If none will buy my musk so fine,
it still perfumes this silk of mine.
Those poets rare who sang their songs
grew old, departed, now sleep long.
I, their executor, to their
sage legacy the noble heir:
None more than I has made anew
those ancient modes that men once knew.
Although of words I may fall short,
of meanings I give full report;
Like dreams, I found an empty rind,
in answer left the pith behind.
And yet, with all my rare new lays,
I turn not from those ancient ways.
My fine-strung pearls bring me no gain,
but measuring the wind in vain.
What have I, jeweller-wise, not weighed
of precious gems and wealth arrayed?—
So many private treasures breached,
but found no key to bring release.
And now, with all this plenteous hoard,
I seek forgiveness from my Lord.
—Nizâmî! Jesus' breath your speech,

53
54
55
56
57
58
59
60
61
62
63
64
65
66
67
68
69
70
71

and Mary's tree\* your wisdom rich:
72      Now you have scattered wide its dates,
        rest well! good fortune is your fate.

## 5

## In Praise of the August Ruler
*May God illumine him!*

1       Oh heart, how long these fancies weave?
        How long illusions vain conceive?

2       I'll quit these false imaginings
        and turn my thoughts to better things.

3       The goal I've chosen in this sphere,
        fourfold, is better than spring's cheer.

4       The first part is the praise of God
        Whose grace maintains this mortal world.

5       The next the Prophet's praise has been,
        he who renewed this world's old coin.

6       And then, praise of the sovereign king,
        which from my lips rare pearls shall bring.

7       The final chapter\* counsel gives
        to him—may he victorious live:

8       That king whose rule the Seven Climes,
        unto his fortune bound, proclaim.

9       The kingdom's proof, in word and might;
        his rule a wonder in time's sight.

10      Crown-giver and king-maker he,
        showering on all his treasury.

11      'Alâ al-Dîn,\* the kingdom's base,
        protector, guard of time and place.

12      Körp Arslân the world-conquerer, he
        whose state excels Alp Arslân's sway.

13      Upholder of Âq Sonqor's line,
        through whom his sires perfection find.

14      Sun of this world, a saviour sage,\*
        whose rule will seal this final age.

15      A Rustam whose steed strides the sky;
        both great, and giving greatness, he.

The heavens' mate, the rain-cloud's palm,     16
a lion in form as well as name.*

When Being's lock had found its key,     17
one Essence caused this world to be.

*He* is that world, from whose hand rain,     18
each moment, pearls without end.*

His wisdom makes Heaven's book leaf out;     19
his bounty makes the shamed sea sweat.

Both land and sea his rule commands,     20
his praise sung by their denizens.

His noble nature soars to heights     21
unreachable by flagging thoughts.

In greatness like an angel he,     22
the sphere's twin* in nobility.

Shroud-stitcher for his foes, his blade,     23
like lightning, sets their mail ablaze.

Before him conquest bows its head;     24
sedition drowns in his sword's waves.

His bright blade sets the sky aflame;     25
his noble earth the air perfumes.*

In war, where lions grow faint from dread,     26
his foes' swift steeds crash down in death.

When grapes' blood in his cup is poured,     27
that frozen crystal fire brings forth;

And when he hones his blade for war,     28
for Armageddon* all prepare.

But when he opens bounty's mine,     29
he gives great wealth, forgives great crime.

Sea-like, not grudging, ever true,     30
the whip and sword his ebb and flow.

That which by force of sword he's gained     31
he gives as if the whip ordained.

Like Jupiter he strides the sphere;     32
his steed's hoofs black Saturn inter.

If you've not seen a lion ride     33
a dragon; a sun draw a sword,

Behold the king, in fray and hunt,     34
a dragon-burner on a lion.

Beneath his dragon flag, his lance     35

cleaves the fell dragon like a snake.

36  With two–barbed shaft, his narrow aim
prepares wide graves for raging lions.

37  Fierce bears are vanquished by his sword,
and lions tamed like dancing bears.

38  His lion-taking no drunken riot:*
he tames the lion with dragon's might.

39  Near Mount Sahand,* his two–barbed shaft
struck hand and foot a ravening wolf;

40  That feat would make the fiercest lion
tremble with fear in all its limbs.

41  His bolts, which strike down pards and wolves,
make the plain strait for asses' hoofs.

42  His hunting-ground's a sea of blood,
now striped like wolves, now spotted pard.

43  When 'gainst the boar he draws his blade,
the boar flees from its blow. The hide

44  Of stags, when he his bowstring bends,
becomes a grave enfolding them.

45  And when he treads the battlefield
he makes the very stones to bleed.

46  His deadly blade makes fierce sparks fly,
and raises smoke from earth to sky.

47  Famed both in battle and in feast,
his cup gives life, his sword life takes.

48  The earth is darkened by his light;
the eye is brightened by his sight.

49  His nature, like an artist's reed,
scatters black musk and rubies red.

50  His musk and rubies everywhere
string necklaces, perfume the air.

51  His crowned head, his robes of might,
make heaven and earth abased and slight.

52  His conqueror's bow, for its least dart,
takes the ninth heaven as its mark.

53  His thought such greatness does display,
the elements proclaim his sway.

54  Upon his gates his enemies
are nailed fast, like uprooted trees.

Moon-like beneath his sun of might,     55
his foes' are black, our faces bright.

What wonder? for that gold-shod sun     56
gave mountains rock, gems to the mine.

The mine's bright gems their secrets gave     57
to him; the mine itself's his slave.

His life-giving largesse confers     58
the mountain's rubies, the sea's pearls.

He guards two rules in two abodes:*     59
the rule of man, and that of God,

Receiving power from God's grace,     60
conveying it unto His slaves.

May all his days most favoured be,     61
who's brought the world brave victory.

On all his days may Fortune shine,     62
and may his kingship ne'er decline.

And may his sons, by Fortune favoured,     63
be ordered, pearl on pearl, forever.

Sun-like, may he be ever bright     64
from those two bright-faced dawns' pure light.

Two princes they, of high estate;     65
one learning seeks, one conquests makes.

One wise and sage as Farîdûn,     66
one Kaykhusraw in conquering.

One's image crown and throne both show:     67
Nusrat al-Dîn Muhammad Shâh.

The other's on Heaven's vault engraved,     68
for 'He who follows me is praised.'*

Two forms, their noble source the same,     69
one Ahmad, one Muhammad named.

See how both these auspicious names     70
within one circle are contained:

Two sides formed by a single line—     71
how can one any difference find?

One is of victory the key;     72
one conquers Heaven, plain to see.

One's strategy the earth commands,     73
the other's piety gains Heaven.

One has through victory raised a throne;     74

to one the sphere has fortune given.

75 May the king's eyes, beneath the sky,
be e'er made bright by theirs; and may,

76 In north and south, his course of rule
be ordered by these noble poles.

77 May Fortune be his fatted prey,
his life most happy night and day.

78 And may that veil* which hides his night
be of Muhammad's lineage bright.

79 He, generous as the planets; she
the seal of being's nature. May

80 Eternal Khizr be his name,
and she the Stream of Life in fame.

81 In the dark Solomonic night
may Bilqîs' throne be given light.

82 May the king's shade, light's fountain, e'er
to rose and rose garden be near.

83 Forever has he given succour;
may his kingship endure forever.

# 6

## Address of Homage

1 Oh you whose mitre fortune serves,
whose crown and throne the world preserve:

2 The night, your Hindu watchman swart
the moon's bright bells has round him girt;

3 Dawn, a lone rider, girt with Sun,
breathes at your stirrup sweet perfume.

4 Your loyal slave, Daylam-crowned dusk,
owes to your court's fair plants his musk.

5 Greek day would be a black like night
should you dismiss him from your sight.

6 The heavens' great feast, with stately spread,
can muster but two disks of bread;*

7 But he you pay the least can sup
the seven planets in one cup.

8 The signet of God's victory*

in you seals perfect sovereignty.

The sky, of which the sun's a trace,　　9
is the least girdle round your waist.

From the sphere's gold the moon has formed　　10
its own pale copy of your throne.

The water of the spring, so pure,　　11
is brackish when compared to you.

Your sword makes rubies show as clay;　　12
your patience melts the hills away.

Those kings who reign the world around,　　13
each to his hand a cloud has bound,

But save for yours—a cloud of spring—　　14
theirs are all clouds that winter bring.

They lay no feast without bloodshed,　　15
and take a life ere they give bread;

But he on whom your shadow's thrown　　16
you summon late, but cherish soon.

He knows of virtuous men the worth　　17
who's studied many books of art.

Who knows not art from fault: what man　　18
of virtue could wish gain from him?

Kingship gains honour from your being;　　19
men everywhere your praises sing.

As guardian of bounty's realm,　　20
your fortune does this world maintain;

Such light to state and faith you've given　　21
as from spring clouds no garden's seen.

The Kayânids, by Fortune blessed,　　22
seven feats, twelve champions possessed;

Those feats, those champions, that you boast　　23
are Heaven with its mighty towers.*

The world's a body, Iran its heart　　24
(no shame to him who says such words!);

Iran, the world's most precious heart,　　25
excels the body, there's no doubt.

Among the realms that kings possess,　　26
the best domain goes to the best:

You are the heart; and in like way,　　27
the kingdom's heart you hold in sway.

28    Like Khizr and Alexander famed,
      your knowledge, justice, all the realm
29    Illume. If Alexander made
      a mirror of iron;* if Khizr sped
30    To the Water of Life, *your* breast so pure
      is mirror; Life's stream within *you* flows.
31    May God protect from evil's bane
      the realm which boasts of such a king.
32    From your renowned good fortune, all
      do you 'The Seven Climes' fortune' call.
33    The Fifth Clime's* by your rule enriched;
      in you rejoice the other six.
34    All regions, seeing your benign
      beneficence, long for your reign.
35    Four kings, four royal jewels have owned,*
      and you the fifth—your life be long!
36    Much wisdom Alexander bore
      from Aristotle's precious store.
37    Nûshîrvân's feast with heaven vied
      since Buzurgmihr his earth did stride.
38    Parvîz a Bârbad had, whose airs
      a hundred—nay, a thousand—were.
39    That great king, Malikshâh by name,
      had his Nizâm, of pious fame.
40    But you, whose crown far greater be,
      have such a poet as Nizâmî.
41    Oh you who give Nizâmî fame,
      whose work is ordered by your name:
42    All other princes boast in vain
      of their largesse: an idle claim!
43    Their seeds upon salt ground they shower
      and in blind eyes collyrium pour.
44    The seed that's on the salt earth cast
      will bear no fruit but sore regret.
45    Trees must be planted in such earth
      as Paradisal fruits brings forth.
46    When wine is poured upon the ground
      how should the farmer's name be known?
47    Save you, whom right and learning guard,

who's generous to himself? Indeed,
I've seen that you protect all men 48
of learning; that you honour them;
Buy not the alchemist's false ruse, 49
nor yet the tricks of coarse buffoons.
This everlasting poem's design 50
I've bound to your felicitous name.
Happy that man whose seed, well cast, 51
returns such harvest to his house,
That, long as it endures, his name 52
opens its pages, spreads his fame;
Not such that, when time passes by, 53
the sphere will cross it out for aye.
Since, in this cycle of time,* I've brought 54
a dish with seven pictures wrought,
To sup will make your soul rejoice; 55
enjoy it; 'tis your sustenance.
I've given it garnish of my soul. 56
and offered it to you withal.
O you whose kinship elevates 57
the sphere; sphere-born and sphere-related:*
How should I, earth-born, soar the sphere, 58
or reach the angels, a human mere?
I sought, with help of sugared pen, 59
to make the earth grow green again;
Provision my way with sugar sweet, 60
to pour it out at the king's feast.*
If not so privileged, I am yet 61
the king's night-watchman, vigilant.
The king's a world-illuming sun 62
whose brilliance makes my tears to run.
Though sun on water casts its light, 63
water can't reach the sun so bright.
But though my eyes can't bear the sun, 64
I can conceive it through the mind.
The sovereign's treasure lacks for naught, 65
save this new-minted coin I've brought.
Now by your generosity, 66
accept it, that it be raised high.

67   Watered by clouds, the mountain fields
     disdain the water of the well.

68   The water of that hand I've sought,
     and closed my mouth to other draughts.

69   To price my pearl would spoil its worth;
     before the king I offer it:

70   Should my new Venus-like song please,
     as to the moon you'll point to me;*

71   But if you find my picture small,
     the wind will such poor dust dispel.

72   Live long, who faith and justice own;
     you've those; may God your life prolong.

73   May all good things Fortune bestows
     keep lasting faith with you; and those

74   Your lofty favour not esteem
     be far from you and your domain.

75   As long as Heaven's sun shall shine,
     health to your friends; your foes struck blind,

76   And, with their straitened hearts, cast down
     stones on their heads, their heads on stones.

77   May your perception ever grow
     greater in wisdom; may you long

78   Endure; may ruin's hand dwell far
     from your domains, for ever more.


# 7

## In Praise of Discourse, and a Few Words of Wisdom

1    That which at once is new and old
     is discourse; let its tale be told.

2    The mother '*Be!*'* hath never born,
     than discourse, any better son;

2a   Say not the eloquent are dead;
     'neath waves of speech they've disappeared.

2b   But should you mention one by name,
     fish-like, he'll raise his head again.

3    Discourse—like to a flawless soul—
     the keys to unseen treasure holds.

It knows the story yet unheard,     4
and reads the yet unwritten word.

Look round: of all that God has made,     5
what else, save discourse, does not fade?

The sole memorial of mankind     6
is discourse; all the rest is wind.

Strive, from the worlds of mineral,     7
plant, animal, and rational,*

To learn what in creation lives     8
that to eternity survives?

He who his own self truly knows,     9
triumphant over this life goes.

Who knows not his design must die;     10
but who can read it, lives for aye.

When once you know yourself aright,     11
though gone, you shall not pass from sight.

Those who life's mysteries ignore     12
come in through this, go out that door.

Doors cleaned of smoke, windows of grime:     13
yet none can see—what use the sun?*

Each with himself is well content;     14
no one will his own garden tend.

All offer clever pretexts; nor     15
will any say, 'My milk is sour.'

Wise men, who have great knowledge gained,     16
don't bend their minds to empty sums;

The man of substance plans ahead;     17
when substance lacks, 'tis as I've said.

But such a man, though sharp, no doubt,     18
requires a guard; there's thieves about!

The Chinese merchant, loading musk,     19
guards it with gum* against the thief.

The hoopoe, 'neath the eagle's wing,     20
in flight leaves other birds behind.

The famed are not immune to sin;     21
only the base are free from stain.

In search of grain, the clever bird     22
falls in the trap with both feet snared.

He who's a glutton like the earth,     23

takes from it but a stomach's worth;

24  Though all its stores be well devoured
and plundered, not a grain falls short;

25  For all you gather, grain by grain,
you one by one give back again.

26  If, candle-like, you'd seek a crown
of gold, tears will your laughter drown.

27  That draught of pearls and rubies made*
brings little joy, but tears unstayed.

28  Each person has a hidden friend,
a confidant, that help will lend:

29  'Tis wisdom, from which succour comes;
he has all things who wisdom owns.

30  Who gives not wisdom its just due,
though man in form, his nature true

31  Is demon-like; angelic men
are those with wisdom—wondrous thing!

32  All was decreed when Time began;*
men strive today, but reap no gain.

33  Strive to improve your nature; sloth
leads but to Hell; to Heaven, work.

34  He who's imprisoned by his deeds,
if he's not good, he will be bad.

35  To think the worst of others; that's
the habit of the bad man; but

36  Who thinks the best of others, wins:
goodness is from good conduct born.

37  Live such that, if a thorn appears,
you will not reap your foes' sharp jeers;

38  Lest this one say, 'His faults have shown,'
or that, 'His just reward has come.'

39  If no one takes your hand, at least
at your death he won't stamp his feet

40  In joy. Who treats you well is best;
not he who's by your sorrow pleased.

41  Don't eat in front of those who fast,
or else, make sure they join your feast.

42  Don't weigh your gold before the poor,
lest they twist, snake-like,* with desire.

Though New Year's breeze may gently waft, 43
best not light lamps before its draft.

Man does not live to eat his fill, 44
but that he may seek sense and skill.

A dog is nobler than the man 45
whose eyes, ass-like, for fodder scan.

Then strive to serve mankind; 'tis so 46
your nature will adorn the world.

One who's good-tempered, like the rose, 47
smells sweetly everywhere he goes.

Have you not heard the wise man tell, 48
'He dreameth best who sleepeth well'?

He who's bad-tempered at his birth 49
will be that way until his death;

But he who's with good temper born 50
will meet a good and happy end.

Don't take things hard; for many a one 51
like you, the coarse earth's fed and slain.

What use to deck out earth, when ye 52
who bear earth's form, half ashes be.

If someone says, 'Pure reason must 53
arise from man, and man's from dust,'

Say, 'From the thorny rose there comes 54
rose-water; life from the snake-stone.'*

Strive with the world; its wiles abhor; 55
don't pitch your tent in dragon's maw.

Seek not the dragon's friendship; for 56
the dragon does all men devour.

A dog may wear a patched cloak;* but 57
its currish nature's not forgot.

When friends fall out and quarrel, see 58
how speedily their foes agree.

Like flies o'er black and white they flock, 59
make black seem white and white look black.

'Tis better to avoid such thieves, 60
and cut this fourfold purse* away.

In times when pious men are base, 61
the Josephs wolves,* the ascetics dazed

With drink, one only 'scapes from peril 62

by doing, or approving, evil.

63  May God forbid His servants place
     such bonds as these upon their legs.

64  They kindle fires for Hell's sake,
     seek naphtha, and pour talc away.*

65  Rise; let us stamp out all sedition;
     observe obedience's condition.

66  How long seek gold to answer dearth?
     How long be bound by sky and earth?

67  The harsh wind rends the tulip's robes
     in search of bits of bloody dross;

68  Since wormwood* bears no golden coin,
     the wind does not assail its form.

69  Don't, like the cloud, bear treasure on
     your head; rise o'er it, like the sun,

70  That, when earth's moistened by the cloud,
     your sun-like kiss turn it to gold.

71  Scatter your gold upon the sun;
     break sun-like rubies with a stone.

72  'Tis wrong gold makes your eyes shine bright,
     for wisdom's the world's true delight.

73  'Gold' is two letters, unconnected;*
     how should you boast of something scattered?

74  Don't fill your heart with gold, like earth,
     lest, like 'gold', you be scattered forth.

75  Those beauties that have golden forms
     are by blue mourning robes* adorned.

76  Each scale which deals with gold is stoned
     before a thousand doors.* Assume

77  That, with great effort, you've obtained
     of wealth, lawful or not, some grains:

78  Some reckless rogue steals them away
     and lives, while their collector dies.

79  To spend gold brings rejoicing; but
     'tis pain and fear to lay it up.

80  'Tis loving gold, not its expense,
     that kills the self with pain immense.

81  See how the fool who seeks a stone
     sets friends at war, one against one.

'Tis best to quit this earthly ruin,                    82
which brings you nought but fear and pain.

How long be porter for the world,                      83
hiding gold's burden in the earth?

Though you may own three porters' loads,               84
you'll gain but the four porters' abode.*

'Tis earth and air that are your foes:                 85
unfriendly earth, air full of woes.

The thorn torn from the date-palm's crown              86
will serve the cooking fire to turn.

Thick noodle soup will better fill                     87
the stomach, than rose-petals will.

Pull out your teeth; don't eat your fill;              88
then you'll be worthy as the pearl.

See, with its thousand teeth, the comb                 89
can dress the beard of anyone.

Before you taste time's remedy,                        90
a thousand poisoned draughts you'll see.

From this world's butcher-shop you'll gain             91
no portion without causing pain.

A hundred hearts are rent in twain                     92
before a fat haunch is obtained.

A thousand necks are cast aside                        93
in favour of a fattened thigh.

One sets his foot upon a treasure,                     94
another toils for trifling measure.

Since none achieves his goal, 'tis best                95
to have none, than for many quest.

The man who late his goal achieves                     96
finds joy in his long-travelled life.

Long life is best, for one will find                   97
his goal perfected through long time.

The slow-born ruby long endures;                       98
the swift-come tulip swiftly goes.

How long, like candles, brightly glow?                 99
Consume yourself, your self to show.

Cast off these hoofs of beast-like greed;             100
from this clay vat pull out your head.

Cut off this seven-rooted branch;                     101

these four-nailed horseshoes,* too, renounce.

102   Don't pass o'er this straw-covered pit
      like stones and straw that cover it.

103   Like lightning, die while flashing bright;
      rude health's eclipsed by virtuous life.

104   Do as your masters teach, if you
      are a disciple; follow true

105   The path that leads to wisdom; put,
      with perfect faith, your trust in God.

106   I, who untie a hundred knots,
      possess a village, dwell without.

107   If from the road a guest should come,
      who then will lay the feast for him?

108   Reason knows well of what I speak;
      by this allusion, what I seek.

109   I don't despair, despite my want;
      I blame but those who earn complaint.

110   The Ethiop scorns my Turkish wares,*
      rejects the fine foods I prepare.

111   When I was raw as unripe grapes
      in this, old nature's cooking-place,

112   Time pressed me like a grape unripe,
      to make collyrium for the sight.*

113   Since I grew ripe, I've suffered from
      the stings of bees, just as the wine

114   That's poured upon the earth is lost.
      Is not the grape's worth more than that?

115   I tread the path on which I'm driven,
      the name of 'frozen water' given;

116   They say that water, frozen cold,
      is not water, but a spring of gold;

117   They err: still water silver forms,
      as silvery ice of this informs.

118   Whene'er did silver like gold seem?
      they're different as the moon and sun.

119   *Sîm* without *yâ* is *miss* (that's brass),
      especially when they're reversed.*

120   Observe my iron, inlaid with gold,
      its silvery work in speech unfold.

Ironmongers would wear golden robes 121
who iron at silver's prices sold.

Woe to the goldsmith when, assayed, 122
his gold is less than silver weighed.

The world's harsh treason chafes me: luck's 123
the source of fortune, wisdom's not.

That keen assessor who knows coin 124
owns not a half-grain, while the man

Who can't tell cotton plants from flax, 125
nor ships and shoes from sealing-wax,

With finest stuffs fills up his hoard: 126
with loads of silks, and chests of gold.

If this is gold and silver's case, 127
why should one then fear idleness?

How long should we this ruin grieve, 128
and draw up water in a sieve?

All from the antechamber call; 129
one day our turn will come withal.

Others, like me, this tale have told, 130
and, at the end, have found repose.

It was my task to grasp it firm, 131
lest sleep should seize me in my turn.

The traveller must have supplies, 132
and flee the perilous places. I

Walk on; my donkey does not follow; 133
I can't believe that on some morrow

I too will leave; I'll only know 134
when I have passed beyond that door.

How long, in ignorance, shall I 135
go on; string pearls with closed eyes?

Forget your eyes, and silence keep; 136
be confidant of secrets deep.

All that you know—know this, and heed— 137
you take in error, or misread.

The flood has swept the road away; 138
discard your spade; see how the sky

Digs pits for men within the earth; 139
the earth recks not such spades as yours.

Consider: when you first were born, 140

what did you have of what you own?

141   From day and night you'll bear away
what you brought with you that first day.

142   Your neck weighed down with borrowed gems
from earth and sea: how can you then

143   Dance with the sphere? repay your loan;
let but you and an empty mount

144   Remain. Without a grain of this
world's burden, go where'er you wish.

145   Before your crown's pulled from the throne,
you must cast off what wealth you own.

146   One day a hundred blossoms must
fall to the ground 'neath envy's dust.

147   I, like the rose, of weapons shorn,
have also fled from envy's thorn;

148   Donned a patched cloak,* in hope this might
scatter pure talc on flames of spite;

149   For even so is the road travelled
that passes through this place of peril.

150   When I've bid this old inn farewell,
say to the sphere, 'Do what you will.'

151   How long, Nizâmî, dwell in bonds?
Arise! send forth your voice in song;

152   Devote your soul to Unity,
and gain, fore'er, Felicity.

# 8

## The Poet's Advice to his Son

1   Those students in the school of 'Kun!'*
when they discourse's lesson learned,

2   Made knowledge treasurer of deeds,
and solved creation's mysteries.

3   All travelled to their place of rest,
and, when the time for sleep came, slept.

4   My son, give heed to what I say:
when I have slept, be you awake.

5   Since you from the eternal garden bear

a rose; by happy fortune wear
—Auspicious seal!—the Prophet's name,*          6
sound then the drum of praise and fame.

With your good name's die stamp your coin;          7
let honour raise you up to Heaven,

So that, in my confinement, I,          8
by your greatness, will be raised high.

Seek those of good repute for friends,          9
that they may bring you a good end.

Better a friend with breath that's foul,          10
than one whose words are nonsense all.

'Tis fault enough that one bad friend          11
gives to a hundred a bad name.

One simple prey that falls to him          12
a hundred more puts in his gin.

A needy man, who swallows gold,*          13
brings brigands to the pilgrims' road.

Don't sleep, like old men, on that way;          14
beware those that on weak men prey,

That in this transient, upturned dome,          15
woman-like, you're not duped; you, a man.

Heed not your mount's dance, as he goes;          16
beware the perils of the road.

Like a white falcon,* if you fly          17
along this road, fix well your eye,

Sun-like, upon this hunter's road;          18
the sky is armed with shaft and bow.*

Although your iron may be pure,          19
the road's a stone, a lodestone sure.

Load your mount lightly, that it not          20
remain upon this sharp ascent,

For many knots have hidden keys;          21
in many hardships there is ease.

How many dreams the heart distress          22
which, read aright, mean happiness.

Though sorrow's arrow pierce the heart,          23
the mail of patience turns its dart.

Make firm your pact with God, and prise          24
your heart away from other ties.

25    If to this pact you cleave, you will
      escape (I swear) from every ill.

26    Don't cast the precious pearl away,
      but from the evil-natured flee.

27    The evil-natured's true to none;
      nor will he miss a chance to sin.

28    How should he bow? have you not heard
      the saying, '*Nature does not err*'?

29    The scorpion, since its nature's ill,
      'tis harm to leave, and art to kill.

30    Learn wisdom, for when it's acquired,
      you'll close and open every door.

31    He who is not ashamed to learn
      draws pearls from water, rubies from stone;

32    He to whom wisdom's not ordained
      at studying feels scorn and shame.

33    Many quick wits whose ears are dull
      sell but base clay, not wisdom's pearls.

34    Many blind hearts, being taught, became
      chief judges of the Seven Climes.

35    The hunting dog's half-eaten prey
      is lawful food through teaching; say,

36    If teaching guides the dog aright,*
      a man might reach the angels' height.

37    Like blessed Khizr, know yourself,
      that you may taste the Spring of Life.

38    No mortal source, that spring, but soul
      with reason, reason with a soul.

39    Reason with soul's a godly gift;
      a soul with reason, eternal life.

40    These two have only one result;
      that you have both, there is no doubt.

41    Till from two you've not reached that One,*
      tell no one that he is no one.

42    When you find One, forget the two,
      and both worlds you will surely rule.

43    Ignore three, for it bears no weight;
      abandon two,* that dualist;

44    Grasp tight the single thread, like men;

abandon two; turn three to One.
Till you leave not the third of three,    45
you'll never win Unicity.

Two left behind, don't speak in jest;    46
when you've found One, seek no pretext.

When you to this high station climb,    47
mere passion all you leave behind.

While you are young and sound of frame,    48
all your desires you'll soon obtain.

When the tall cypress falls to ground,    49
how can a remedy be found?

Now that you wear the world's fresh green,    50
follow that road, since you are keen:

Gird up your loins, like the red rose,    51
on faith's path; a tall cypress grow.

I, willow-like, in green no more,    52
my violets white, my tulips sere,

Through weakness have been left behind    53
from wearing royal belt and crown.

Much manly service I've performed,    54
but now no longer am that man.

Life's seized and bound me in its toils;    55
such is the custom of this world.

My wings were broken ere I fell;    56
now that I've fallen, who can tell

My state? How shall a handsome man    57
appear when smallpox visits him?

Though shadow threaten me, my shade,    58
protecting, is of virtue made.

All in this world a shadow find:    58*a*
sheep run before, the wolves behind.

On none can I my trust bestow;    58*b*
all men are wolves, though sheep they show.

Crude are those few who seem my friends;    58*c*
in whom shall I seek safety then?

Though youth has left me, still it seems    58*d*
that, willy nilly, greed remains.

The older aged bodies grow,    59
their greed demands yet more and more.

60    Is this coin but my own alone,
      or do all suffer from this pain?

61    O You, my heart's physician, keep
      my clay from bowing at others' feet.

62    How long the darkness? Give me light,
      and heal my broken body's plight.

63    Oh, ease those cares which bring me woe;
      this is an easy task for You.

64    My neck's escaped the rope; do not
      weary it under base men's loads.

65    I am content, like the pearl-shell,
      with but a grain, and lord as well

66    Of my own house; a better aid
      is lordship, than base servitude.

67    The lion finds greatness when he frees
      his neck from service's yoke; 'tis best

68    To give your bread to others, than
      to eat sweetmeats from baser men.

69    —Now dawn's sharp dagger rends the skies;
      how long asleep? Nizâmî, rise,

70    Mine deeply; fret not at your toil;
      open for all the treasure's door.

## 9

## The Story Begins: Bahrâm is Born

1     The jeweller of the secret store
      thus opens wide his treasure's door:

2     Heaven a two-panned balance owns:
      one pan holds pearls, the other stones.

3     From it upon the piebald world
      now stones, now pearls, are fiercely hurled.

4     Even so are offspring born to kings:
      the child or sin or honour brings.

5     Sometimes a pearl brings forth a stone;
      sometimes will amber rubies form.

6     Like stone to pearl, in worth and fame,
      was Yazdigird to prince Bahrâm.

One struck, one cherished—wondrous fate!  7
But stones bear rubies, date-thorns dates.

Whoso was ruined by the lord,  8
the prince's gentleness restored.

On the first day that Bahrâm's dawn  9
bore from dark night the evil name,

Those wise in Heaven's alchemy,  10
of moon and sun knowing the ways,

Thought, in the scales which Heaven weighed,*  11
to find but silver half-alloyed.

They found instead the purest gold;  12
from dull stone gems, from salt sea pearls.

They saw, auguring victory,  13
and world-brightening nobility,

Pisces ascendant, Jupiter therein,  14
and Venus, pearl to ruby joined;

The moon in Taurus; Mercury  15
in Gemini; Mars' apogee

In Leo clear; Aquarius  16
helped Saturn strong outstrip his foes;

The Dragon's Tail towards Saturn turned,  17
the sun in Aries.* Thus in turn

Each star to his felicity,  18
like Jupiter, did testify.

With such portents as I have shown,  19
when fortunate Bahrâm was born,

His royal father, crude of thought,  20
did reason ripely; saw his fate:

That all his ripest thoughts were raw;  21
he reaps bad ends who evil sows.

Some twenty years before that time  22
some sons he'd had, but none lived on.

The astrologers advised him then  23
to send away his handsome son

From Persia to the Arabs' land,  24
his nurture-time with them to spend,

That he might there his fortune find  25
—each man finds honour in some clime—

And bring his luck to fruit; although  26

         'tis said, *'Fortune's on lands bestowed.'**

27    His father drew apart, both out
       of love, and to preserve his life;

28    Like Canopus, outside his realm,
       in Yemen's land* he raised his throne.

29    He sent for Nu'mân; gave that fair
       red blossom to that garden's care,

30    That his anemone might bloom*
       when flowers were scattered by Nu'mân;

31    Who'd teach to him all princely traits,
       and rules of royal government.

32    Nu'mân then bore him from the king,
       his breast a litter for that moon.

33    That spring, more famous than the sea,
       he held more precious than his eyes.

34    When four years o'er the youth had passed,
       he grew an onager in craft,

35    A lion in boldness. King Nu'mân
       said to his son, 'My mind's in pain.

36    Our air is dry, our land is hot;
       this princeling is of tender stock;

37    He needs a lofty nurturing place
       whose head from earth to sky is raised,

38    That he may soar upon its heights,
       be nourished by the north wind's breeze;

39    Dwell among pleasant airs; have sleep
       and rest that will his life increase;

40    His nature's gem remain untouched
       by earth's damp vapour and dry dust.'

41    Munzir then with his father went;
       their thoughts to such a search they bent,

42    Seeking a high and spacious place,
       from noxious heat and all harm safe.

# 10

## Of Simnâr and the Building of Khavarnaq

1    That region boasted no such fort,
       and useless were all other sorts.

They summoned expert builders; smoothed    2
the way for such a task. All who
Proposed to do that task, could not    3
devise a plan that came out right;
Until Nu'mân heard news that such    4
a master was within his reach.
'A famed man dwells in Grecian lands;    5
clever? stone's wax within his hands;
Learned and skilled, of matchless art;    6
of Sâm's race,* and his name Simnâr.
The whole world has observed his skill;    7
all praise him; he has built withal,
In Syria and Egypt, some    8
fine buildings, perfect every one.
The Greeks bow to his skill; in Chîn*    9
from his pick artists chips do glean.
Although a builder, clearly he    10
a myriad artists holds in sway.
And, of sound judgement, he can tell    11
the secrets of the stars as well.
His gaze draws o'er the sphere a web,    12
like the spider of the astrolabe.*
Like Apollonius* wise, he can    13
devise and loose all talismans.
He knows the veiled ones of the sky,    14
the moon's raids, the sun's hostile eye;
He'll solve this problem; only he    15
can such a precious fabric weave.
He'll raise a vault from earth so high    16
that it will plunder from the sky
The stars' bright lamps.' Nu'mân, hot bent    17
in quest of Simnâr's fire, then sent
A messenger to far-off Rûm,    18
to woo, with wiles, Simnâr to him.
So Simnâr came; and so Nu'mân's    19
hope for that task grew sevenfold strong.
He sought from him what he desired,    20
and then prepared what he required.
All that that building might demand,    21
materials, tools, were readied. Then

22  The master's hands all measured well.
    Five years he laboured on, until

23  He with his golden hands had made
    a silvery palace of stone and clay,

24  Its tower rising to the moon,
    the cynosure of everyone.

25  A palace richly decked with gold,
    flame-hued, as only he could build;

26  A palace with a heavenly dome
    round which the heavens' nine spheres turned;

27  A pole formed like those south and north,
    whose fancies seemed like Teukros' work.*

28  Its sight was rest to weary hearts,
    its image water to the parched.

29  When the sun on it cast its rays,
    the hourîs hid their dazzled gaze.

30  Within, a paradise of ease;
    without, embellished like the skies.

31  Its roof, polished with milk and glaze,
    reflected like a mirror's face.

32  Both day and night, both swift and slow,*
    like brides it would three colours show,

33  Of three opposing, varied hues:
    now white, now yellow, and now blue.

34  From the sky's azure robes, at dawn,
    like air, a blue-hued robe it donned;

35  Its face, when rose the journeying sun,
    grew yellow as the sun; and when

36  The sun was veiled by clouds, it grew,
    subtly, as white as clouds in hue.

37  Clad in the colours of the air,
    it now grew black, and now showed fair.

38  When Simnâr had achieved his task—
    accomplished more than he was asked—

39  Its splendour overwhelmed the sky;
    its brilliance gave the sun its light.

40  Nu'mân gave him the news of such
    a great reward, the half of which

41  He had not hoped for: purest gold,

rare gems and musk, by camel-load,
Beyond all reckoning, that he 42
might once again of service be.

If with dry wood the fire's not stoked, 43
the meat thereon remains uncooked.

The generous hand, silver dirhams' hurt, 44
is guardian of bounty's court.

The architect, at this largesse, 45
hoped for more bounteous promises.

'If I had known before', said he, 46
'of all the king has promised me,

I would have made, in my design, 47
the best that all the world could find.

I would have taken greater pains, 48
and even greater treasure gained;

A palace built whose brilliance would 49
daily increase, long as it stood.'

Asked Nu'mân, 'Were you given more, 50
could you build better than before?'

'If you'd so wished,' he said, 'forewarned, 51
I'd built one to put this to scorn.

This has three hues; that would have owned 52
a hundred; it ruby, this but stone.

This shows but one sphere; that would seven 53
high domes display, like seven heavens.'

Nu'mân's face kindled at these words, 54
his store of human kindness burnt.

The king's a fire; who sees its light 55
from far off will escape its heat;

A fiery rose-bush raining gems, 56
close by a rose, in its breast thorns.

The king's a vine,* which does not twist 57
round plants that flourish far from it;

But that round which he closely twines 58
has branch uprooted, fruit brought down.

'If I spare him (he thought), with gold 59
and strength, he'll go elsewhere and build

A better place.' His men were called 60
to cast him from the fortress walls.

61    See how bloodthirsty earth cast down
      the builder from his high design.

62    Long years he raised a palace; in
      a moment Fortune threw him down.

63    He kindled fire, himself fell in
      the smoke; climbed late, and fell low soon.

64    He raised it high—a hundred ells
      and more; did not his fall foretell;

65    He'd not—had he his grave foreseen—
      have bettered three ells by a span.

66    The throne's steps should not be so high
      that, when you fall, you'll broken lie.

67    From that high building Nu'mân's fame
      did cast its lasso round the moon.

68    Called 'mighty sorcerer' by the earth;
      by men, the Lord of Khavarnaq.


# 11

## Of Khavarnaq, and How Nu'mân Vanished from his Kingdom

1     When Khavarnaq, by Bahrâm's star,
      became a garden fresh and fair

2     Heaven called it *qibla* of the earth;
      earth judged it Chinese painters' work.

3     Hearing of it, from near and far
      flocked thousands just to gaze and stare.

4     All those who saw sang praises loud,
      and humbly at its threshold bowed.

5     Over its porticoes, in fair
      calligraphy, flowed verses rare.

6     Since Canopus lit Yemen's land,
      not moon nor sun had ever been

7     So praised. Like Aden's sea it strewed
      fair pearls; the land with light infused.

8     Yemen grew famed by its design;
      the world esteemed it like Iram.

9     It decked the world out like the Ram;*

still more, since therein dwelt Bahrâm.

When Bahrâm mounted to its top     10
(and Venus bore his festive cup),*

He found a round tower, the sphere's twin,     11
the moon without, the sun within.

Within, the sun in bright display;     12
without, the moon's light-giving rays.

The wind above blew ever fresh;     13
'twas safe from Autumn's cruel blast.

Beneath the castle walls, his gaze     14
roamed o'er a plain like Paradise:

On this side the Euphrates passed,     15
sweet as the Water of Life; on that

Sadîr, like Sidra,* throne-like, held     16
a village filled with oil and milk.

Before the plain, behind the mead,     17
whose soft airs musky perfume breathed.

Those royal heights one day Nu'mân     18
did climb to view; with him Bahrâm.

All round that vault, like Paradise,     19
he saw red tulips and green grass.

The plain a Shushtar carpet seemed,     20
where partridge plump and pheasant teemed.

Said he, 'Was e'er a spot so choice?     21
In such a place one should rejoice.'

The king's vizier was, in those days,     22
a Christian, practising just ways.

He said, 'To know one's God aright     23
is better than all-owning might.

Once you have found such wisdom fair,     24
your heart from worldly things you'll tear.'

That spark enkindled such a flame     25
that Nu'mân's hard heart soft became;

Since the sphere raised its seven forts,*     26
no such siege-engine plied its work.

Nu'mân came down from that high dome,     27
lion-like the desert waste to roam,

Abandoned wealth and sovereignty—     28
faith and world ill-assorted be—

29    His Solomonic state foreswore
     and, perî-like, was seen no more.

30    No more was he found in his place:
     behold, the ruler of his age!

31    Although Munzir in search did fly,
     his fortune's voice made no reply.

32    He greatly grieved—and it was due—
     his house smoke-darkened, black in hue.

33    He held great mourning, as was fit,
     and spent some days in pain and grief.

34    Since he could not flee crown and throne,
     he occupied himself with them:

35    Banished injustice, brought forth right,
     maintained the kingdom with his might.

36    His generals, who held troops and lands,
     gained state and fortune from the king.

37    Bahrâm he held dear as his soul,
     with father's love—nay, even more.

38    His own fine son, by name Nu'mân,
     had shared a wet-nurse with Bahrâm.

39    Companions, of an equal age,
     one from the other never strayed.

40    They grammar learned from the same slate,
     and, feasting, scattered pearls in spate.

41    Like sun and bright light, not a day
     was one from other far away.

42    The prince, within that lofty tower,
     was raised and taught for several years.

43    Save study he had no delight;
     to knowledge, reason was his guide.

44    The Persian, Greek, and Arab speech
     a Magian master did him teach.

45    Munzir, that skilled and loving king,
     knew well the heavenly reckoning:

46    The seven planets and twelve signs
     disclosed their secrets to his mind.

47    With geometric lines he worked,
     all problems solved, Mijistî-like.*

48    He had surveyed the Nile-blue sphere

in every part. From secret stores
Of far-seeing vision, he had gained          49
great wisdom through his keenest mind.

Finding the prince in judgement wise,        50
a student skilled in mysteries,
He gently slate and stylus* brought,         51
and Heaven's secrets to him taught.

Each secret notion that was hidden,          52
whether it spoke of earth or Heaven,
He joined together, one by one,              53
and taught the prince, until Bahrâm

Became so wise and learned that              54
he knew the truth of every art.
With true celestial reckoning                55
he took the veil from the unseen;

Then, setting up his style and slate,        56
unlocked the scheme of heavenly fate.
When he'd grown skilled in argument,         57
to learn the skill of arms he bent;

In weapons, riding, racing, bore             58
the ball from the polo-playing sphere.
He reached such heights of skill, he'd take  59
the claws from lions, sever wolves' necks.

Dawn's blade, at his spear-cast, threw up    60
the shield before his horsemanship.
His arrow pierced the granite rock           61
as though it were but silken cloth.

And when he shot his arrows forth,           62
a quiverful would hit the mark.
If with his sword he struck a stone,         63
it turned to water red as flame.

His lance would carry off a grain            64
of millet like a target-ring.
When he his marksmanship displayed           65
with hairs his well-aimed arrow played.

Or light or shade, whate'er he'd see,        66
he'd hit, however far away;
And even that which he saw not,              67
his fortune hit as it deemed right.

68    The lion-guards of the flock of men
      all boasted that he'd grown a lion.

69    Sometimes he would attack the pard,
      sometimes with fiercest lions played.

70    All talk in Yemen, near and far,
      was of him, hailed as 'Yemen's star'.*

# 12

## How Bahrâm Hunted and Branded the Wild Asses

1     When Bahrâm's fair Canopus bore
      rawness from Yemen's hide, Munzir,

2     Like Yemen's leather by its star,*
      was brightened by his grace. Therefore

3     Nu'mân, Munzir, from their esteem,
      a brother and a father seemed.

4     His loyal slaves in all affairs;
      of such relations say no more.

5     One vied with him in studying,
      one joyed with him in banqueting.

6     One strengthened him through learning's force,
      and one rode out with him to horse.

7     The prince's horsemanship so gained
      in skill, the skies gave back his name.

8     No pleasures save the chase had he,
      and wine; impassioned of his prey,

9     He hunted onager; how can
      the grave* be spurned by mortal man?

10    The arrow speeding from his bow
      dealt to his prey a deadly blow.

11    He had a swift-paced chestnut steed
      that galloped smooth, with faultless speed,

12    As if its hoofs had sprouted wings;
      it tamed the force of hurricanes,

13    And as its course it swiftly ran,
      bore ball and disk from moon and sun.

14    Accustomed to the sphere's swift pace,

it faster than the wind did race,
Its twisting tail like hundred snakes;          15
its hoofs for onagers dug graves.
To hunt, the king rode forth that steed;        16
for others had no wish nor need.
When saddled up, its speeding pace              17
earned it the swift wild asses' praise.
It outstripped other mounts, and caught         18
all onagers in swift pursuit.
Sometimes, when weary, Bahrâm would             19
saddle that lion-swift steed. Its hoofs
Would trace the hunting ground with forms       20
fairer than idols. More than stones
In weight, he'd fill the hillocks there         21
with heaps of onager and deer.
'Neath his steed's hoofs, the level plain       22
grew hillock-heaps of asses slain.
When he, on his hill-coursing steed,            23
which raised no dust with its great speed,
Took up his noose to hunt, he'd seize           24
a thousand onagers alive.
He felled most with his mighty arm,             25
or with his noose; but never harmed
(Though he a hundred felled) a one              26
under four years; for he'd foresworn
The blood of any onager                         27
that had seen less than four full years.
Upon its haunch he'd brand his name,            28
and let it once more roam the plain.
Whoever took a branded ass                      29
alive (one of a hundred beasts),
On seeing the king's brand thereon,             30
would turn his thoughts from any harm,
And, placing on the brand a kiss,               31
would free the beast's legs from the noose.
I, branded with the sultan's name,              32
should with more speed my thanks proclaim.
With such a king, in mount and plain,           33

the branded beast escapes all harm.

34   In the world's graveyard there's no ant
that has not felt oppression's brand.

# 13

## How Bahrâm Slew a Lion and an Onager
## with a Single Arrow

1   One day in Yemen's hunting-ground,
with Arab nobles all around,

2   The prince, who Bahrâm Gûr was called,
from sphere and Mars bore off the ball;

3   The sport made him breathe hard; Nu'mân
behind, Munzir before, were stunned

4   In admiration, lost, amazed,
at the fine form the prince displayed.

5   Suddenly dust rose from afar
and earth and sky as one appeared.

6   The young prince urged his chestnut steed
towards that dust, with torrent's speed.

7   A lion, drawing his cruel claws,
rode on the back of a wild ass,

8   To bring it to the ground. The king
waited in hiding, his bow drawn.

9   He sought a sharply pointed barb,
strung it and loosed it at the mark.

10   The shoulder of both beasts its struck,
pierced both, passed clean through both, and stuck

11   Deep in the ground. What use to have
armour or shield, with such a shaft?

12   Lion and onager fell dead;
the shaft was buried to its head.

13   The ruler who had loosed it, bow
in hand, stood there. His mighty blow

14   The Arabs saw, and all approved
he should rule Persia. All who looked

15   Upon that prey then kissed his hand
in homage. Thenceforth was his name

Called 'Lion-Strength', though as before    16
he bore the title 'Bahrâm Gûr'.

When they returned to town, the word    17
of lion and ass was widely spread.

Munzir then gave command to seek    18
skilled painters to record that feat.

In Khavarnaq they limned in gold    19
the lion above, the ass below,

The prince's shot, the bolt which found    20
both beasts, and lodged deep in the ground.

This work completed, all who saw    21
thought that it lived. 'May blessings fall',

They said, 'from Him Who made the world,    22
upon that prince so brave and bold.'

# 14

## How Bahrâm Gûr Slew a Dragon
## and Found a Treasure

One day, within his garden's heaven,    1
he launched his ship upon the wine.*

He quickly drained a few cups down,    2
and, drunken, set out for the plain.

He loosed his lasso for the prey,    3
and onagers pursued that day.

So many felled he, by his power,    4
the plain with bones was covered o'er.

A female onager appeared    5
at last, whose sight the whole world stirred.

A vision of the soul she seemed;    6
bright was her face, her forehead beamed.

Her back was streaked like golden money,    7
her belly daubed with milk and honey.

From head to hoof a musky line;    8
from hoof to head all spotted fine.

Her rosy mane, in housing's place,    9
a silken veil cast o'er her face.

Her form outdid all of her kind;    10

her haunches left her form behind.

11 A flame grown friendly with the grass;
a beauty garbed in beggar's rags.

12 Her legs like arrows, straight and long;
her ears two diamond daggers drawn.

13 Her breast was elegant and straight;
her ears stood high above her neck.

14 Like saddle bands, two stripes of black
adorned the curve upon her back.

15 From those black bands, her upper half
gained that which silver gains from black.

16 Fat sides and ruddy neck: the one
like pearls, the other carnelian.

17 Like wine-red silk drawn o'er her form
her red blood coursed through her neck-veins,

18 And, swiftly pulsing, her dark blood,
like a black drummer, beat and throbbed.

19 Her haunches neighbours with her tail;
hoof scratching neck, as if in play.

20 Seeing Bahrâm, the ass leapt forth;
Bahrâm Gûr followed the ass.

21 The ass was swift indeed, and young;
the hunter followed like a lion.

22 From break of day to setting sun,
that lion in train, the ass ran on.

23 He chased that *gûr*; turned not aside;
for how can one the grave avoid?

24 Ass-King* behind, the ass before:
*gûr*, Bahrâm Gûr, and no one more.

25 Until they reached a cave, remote,
where human kind had ne'er set foot.

26 Nearing his prey, the hunter saw
a dragon lying in wait before

27 The cave; a pitch-black mountain, coiled
in twisting loops against the foe.

28 When the king saw this dreadful sight,
he grew a dragon in his might .

29 Fear of the grave his pleasure drowned;
with hand on hip, he stood his ground,

And, marvelling, thought, 'What prey is this?  30
Why bring me here? What plan is this?'

He knew well, from the beast's alarm  31
She'd suffered from the dragon harm,

And sought the prince—whom just she knew—  32
to do her justice on the foe.

'If I call this a dragon, not  33
an ant, I'll be ashamed,' he thought,

'Even in death. I must requite  34
the ass, without fear for my life.

Let be what will be.' Then he sought  35
a swift, two-headed poplar shaft,

Placed it in his white bow, and shot  36
it at that dragon black as night.

The dragon opened wide his eye;  37
the prince his twin-barbed bolt let fly.

Both barbs within those eyes did light;  38
forever closed the path of sight.

The forged tips of the prince's barbs  39
sewed tight that pitch-black dragon's orbs.

The dragon in such straits, the king  40
attacked him like Leviathan.

Just as the lion claws the ass,  41
towards the dragon's throat he cast

His lance (six sides, eight feet in length);  42
the dragon's mouth and throat it rent.

The dragon gave a mighty cry,  43
and crashed to earth like a felled tree.

The king feared not its awful coils:  44
does the cloud fear low-lying hills?

With iron that demon's head he cut;  45
'tis best that foes be dealt with thus.

He cleft its form from stern to stem,  46
and found the ass's foal therein.

He knew for sure the vengeful beast  47
has summoned him revenge to wreak.

He knelt and gave his thanks to God:  48
the dragon slain, and he alive;

Then sought again his steed to mount,  49

and turn once more unto the hunt.

50   Seeing his restlessness, his prey
ran up and went into the cave.

51   Once more, to seize the ass, the king
entered that narrow opening.

52   When, with much toil, he'd gone some way,
he found a treasure; smiled with joy.

53   Many great jars were placed therein,
veiled like the perî-faced from men.

54   Bringing the Ass-King to that cave,
the wild ass left without a trace.

55   When the king found the treasure's key
and severed the dragon from it, he

56   Came out again from that narrow cave,
and found a guide to show the way.

57   His special guards, after a space,
seeking the king, followed his trace.

58   As one by one they joined the king,
around their lord they formed a ring.

59   The king gave orders to his men—
both bold and strong—to go within

60   The treasure-cave, bring out the hoard,
and load it up. That heavy load

61   Was borne away by camels, young,
of Bactrian race, sturdy and strong.

62   A king who to a wild ass gives
justice; imprisons in a grave

63   A dragon, finally, for his pains,
salvation and a treasure gains.

64   Returning to Khavarnaq, he
dispensed it with festivity:

65   Ten camel-loads of treasure sent
unto his father, Iran's king;

66   Ten more to Munzir and his son
he gave, with other precious things.

67   He spent it all, without the fear
that anyone might interfere;

68   And, having opened such a trove,

what dear was gained he cheaply gave.
Munzir then called a painter; him     69
he bade a painting new to limn;
The painter took his brush in hand,     70
painted the dragon and the king.
With all such feats Bahrâm performed,     71
the painter Khavarnaq adorned.

# 15

## How Bahrâm Saw the Paintings of the Seven Beauties in Khavarnaq

One day the prince, come from the plain,     1
through Khavarnaq did joyful range.
He saw a secret room, locked fast,     2
through which no servant ever passed,
Nor courtier nor treasurer;     3
the prince had never entered there.
'Why is this room locked fast?' said he;     4
'where is the keeper, and the key?'
The keeper came, gave up the key;     5
the door unlocked, what did he see?
A chamber like a treasure-store,     6
which turned to jewellers all who saw.
The pictures on its walls excelled     7
a hundred Chinese temples;* all
That finest art and skill could form     8
of pictures, did its walls adorn.
Seven beauteous images* there hung,     9
each one connected with a realm:
Fûrak, the Raja's daughter fair;     10
more than the moon's her beauty rare.
Yaghmâ-Nâz, daughter of the Khâqân,     11
charmer of Chîn and Turkestan.
Khwârazmshâh's daughter, Nâz-Parî:     12
a graceful, strutting partridge she.
The Slav king's daughter, Nasrîn-Nûsh,     13

|    | a Chinese Turk in Grecian dress. |
|----|----------------------------------|
| 14 | The Maghreb's princess, Âzaryûn, a sun like day-increasing moon. |
| 15 | Wise Qaysar's daughter, fair Humây, noble in name and nature she.* |
| 16 | Kisrâ's daughter, of Kaykâvûs' line, fair as a peacock, Durr-Sitî named.* |
| 17 | One hand had drawn these seven forms, by one cord in a circle hung, |
| 18 | Each, with a thousand beauties bright, kindled the gem of vision's light. |
| 19 | An image in the midst therewith— the others rind, this one the pith— |
| 20 | A belt of pearls circled his waist, and musky down his moon-like face, |
| 21 | Like a straight cypress rising tall, his form encased in silver; all |
| 22 | Those beauties gazed on him; each gave her heart to him in perfect love; |
| 23 | He on those idols smiling sweet, they all adoring, as was meet: |
| 24 | And o'er his head, in skilful script, the name of 'Bahrâm Gûr' was writ: |
| 25 | 'Such is the seven stars' decree, that such a conqueror come to be. |
| 26 | Seven princesses from seven realms shall he embrace, like single pearls. |
| 27 | Not we ourselves this seed have sown: what the stars showed us, we have shown. |
| 28 | We but the example show; 'tis God alone, we say, Who'll bring it forth.' |
| 29 | When Bahrâm had this legend read, at the sphere's spell he stood in dread. |
| 30 | Love for those princesses so fair his heart invaded, hair by hair. |
| 31 | Such fecund mares, a stallion bold: a lion-brave youth, and seven brides: |
| 32 | How should desire not fire his heart, and, waxing, not attempt the mark? |

Although surprised by that design,                              33
his joy increased a hundred times,
For to his life it brought resolve,                             34
and hope for his desire. For all
Which makes a man hope for completion                          35
aids him in finding moderation.
When the prince left that chamber, he                          36
locked the door; gave the steward the key,
And said, 'If I should ever hear                               37
that any one unlocks this door,
Within this room his blood I'll shed,                         38
and sever from his neck his head.'
In all that house no woman or man                             39
dared cast their eyes towards that room.
Sometimes, on drunken whim, the king                          40
approached that chamber, key in hand,
And, entering into Paradise,                                   41
on those angelic forms would gaze;
And like one who, near water, thirsts,                        42
would sleep, still moved by his desire.
Abroad, he but the hunt pursued;                              42a
at home, that room his sorrow soothed.

# 16

## How Bahrâm Heard of his Father's Death

When his informers brought the king                            1
reports about his son, Bahrâm—
'He lions takes with his bare hands                            2
(see that old wolf, and this young lion!);
In contest lions to him are dogs;                              3
he fells foul dragons to the dust;
Binds demons with his curving noose,                          4
and levels hills 'neath his steed's hoofs;
His diamond blade makes silk of iron;                         5
his iron makes paste of hardest stone'—
His father feared that fiery youth,                           6
and in his life saw his own death.

7    He feared that fiery-natured lion
     as lions fear the leaping flame.

8    He kept him distant from his sight—
     how dull the vision that lacks light!

9    Bahrâm still hunted night and day,
     now rode the wind, now drank in play;

10   Quick to the chase and to the wine,
     he, like bright Canopus, did shine.

11   From love for him, great Yemen's king
     made all bow down to his command.

12   The wise and competent Bahrâm
     he made the governor of his realm;

13   On him bestowed bright pearls, sharp blades;
     his life (if asked) would not have grudged.

14   All that he needed—treasures, gems—
     were his, without his toil or pain.

15   That favour he received abroad
     made him forget his father's land.

16   When some time had elapsed this way,
     the sphere a new game did display.

17   Yazdigird wearied of his throne—
     so all that rises must come down—

18   And his ancestral throne and crown
     did as it had to others done.

19   The throne once emptied of its king,
     his subjects called a gathering,

20   That none of his line might remain,
     no longer snakes and dragons reign.

21   Although Bahrâm was honoured still,
     and known for wisdom, strength, and skill,

22   His father's tyranny decreed
     his princely skills be set aside.

23   'We'll not consider him,' they said,
     'nor tell him of his father's death;

24   For he, by desert Arabs reared,
     for Persia's rule is not prepared.

25   He'd give the Arabs rule and wealth;
     the Persian-born would suffer ill.'

26   (But, though none wished him on the throne,

God willed it so; gave him the crown.)
An aged sage* they chose, and him                    27
Just Ruler of the World proclaimed.

Though not entitled to the throne                    28
he was of royal lineage sprung.

Upon his head they placed the crown,                 29
and gave the seven-eyed belt* to him.

When Bahrâm heard the news that Heaven               30
had brought one cycle to an end;

Begun another cycle, fresh,                          31
in opposition to the past;

His father had given up the throne                   32
and crown and, there being none to claim

Just rule, a stranger had stepped in,                33
and discord in the world begun;

He first held mourning rites, and clothed            34
his ruby form in turquoise robes.*

Then, like a lion, he resolved                       35
to draw the sword against his foes;

Extend his blade against them; make                  36
war on them, his revenge to take.

Again he thought, 'Why play the beast?               37
'Tis better to use wisdom first.

Though they've done me a grievous wrong,             38
and from me due respect withdrawn,

Into their hard hearts I can't see;                  39
'tis softness that will be the key.

With hearts like dogs, they are my prey;             40
the sheep-dogs in my pasture, they.

They creep about in their own wool,                  41
but all are in *my* cotton field.

Let them be faithless, hard of heart,                42
till in the end with shame they smart.

From treachery accrues man's shame,                  43
and brings him but regret and pain.

If not for shame, base things would be               44
but one more form of tyranny.

Unwisely, they've left my control;                   45
I, wise, will make them worshipful.

46     When man's impatient of his prey,
       his arrow quickly goes astray.'

# 17

## How Bahrâm Led his Army against Iran

1      Cease, sorcerer, word-weaver fine;
       how long old tales will you intone?

2      Breathe, like the rose, from mouth perfumed,
       its scent enough your words to tune.

3      From first my covenant was drawn
       with Him Whose pact is ever sound,

4      That what another poet spake*—
       though he lies sleeping, we're awake—

5      I would not make its thought my own;
       for evil ways I'll not be known,

6      But, while I can, like New Year's breeze,
       I'll never claim to mend old clothes.

7      Yet since the path to treasure's one—
       a single mark, though arrows twain—

8      Though in my task of stringing pearls
       I would not use another's words,

9      When repetition must be made,
       I silk from sackcloth can create.

10     The ancient coin has been made new,
       through alchemy of speech, by two:

11     That one from brass pure silver drew;
       *I'll* turn to gold that silver. You,

12     Who've seen brass equal silver, should
       not marvel when silver turns to gold.

13     The jeweller of this lofty throne
       his necklace thus together joined:

14     When Bahrâm Gûr became aware
       a stranger Persia's crown did wear,

15     In rage he girt himself to claim
       his Kayânid crown back again.

16     In his desire to claim his throne,

Nu'mân and Munzir aided him
With treasures more than can be told;          17
more jewels than any string can hold.

He raised a mighty army; grew                  18
sharp, as his anger was renewed.

From Yemen unto Aden's strand,                 19
a myriad horsemen fell in line,

In armour clad, for vengeance keen             20
to slay, take forts, and demons bind.

Each one in battle was a lion,                 21
his sword defender of a realm.

The cavalcade set on its way;                  22
its dust obscured both earth and sky.

Their wailing pipes and kettledrums            23
destroyed the courage of all men.

The drummers showered grievous wounds          24
upon their clamouring brass drums.

Their ferment caused both mount and plain      25
to boil up to the covering heavens.

Greater than locust swarms, ant hordes;        26
hot for revenge like Hell's own fire.

These, to secure the royal throne,             27
went to his capital from Yemen.

## 18

## How the Iranians Wrote to King Bahrâm

To the usurper came the news:                   1
A dragon raged with gaping jaws;

Heaven had turned towards the earth;            2
Canopus, risen, from Yemen shone forth;

The lion had spread its claws to take           3
its foe, like wild ass, to the grave,

To seize the throne and gain the crown;         4
to rule, and put disturbance down.

Nobles and generals all met                     5
before the king's gates. There they sat

6      In council, pondered well, and sought
       to set their differences at naught.

7      They wrote as reason did dictate,
       in veiled words, for safety's sake.

8      The letter done, they folded it,
       and set out to deliver it.

9      When they arrived, to the new king
       Fortune voiced praise. The chamberlains

10     Were sympathetic; granted them
       an audience. Then King Bahrâm

11     Gave orders to approach the throne
       more closely. Fearfully they came

12     Before his throne, bowed low, and gave
       thanks to the king, and offered praise.

13     He who was wisest of them kissed
       the letter and delivered it.

14     The secretary broke its seal,
       and to the conqueror read it all.

15     The name of God there held first place,
       Who guides the errant with His grace.

16     Of high and low Creator; He
       by Whom non-being comes to be.

17     From man to all that lives; from sky
       above, to mighty mountain high:

18     In Bounty's picture-house, it is
       His power which form to Being gives.

19     He knows no partner; for beyond
       that One, in sovereignty, there's none.

20     He looses all creation's bonds;
       the seal of praise is His alone.

21     Both space and time are in His hands;
       all men bow down to His commands.

22     His praise of the Creator done,
       the Persians' king addressed Bahrâm,

23     The sovereign prince, saluting him:
       'O you who've raised your head to Heaven;

24     Both king by *farr*, and a king's son,
       who chivalry and valour own:

25     How should I, Kisrâ's scion, be

bested by one less skilled than I?
Experienced, with virtue filled,                    26
honoured and praised throughout the world;
Fostered by Fortune: how can one                    27
less eminent gain crown and throne?
*I've* gained them through nobility;                28
no base man can be raised so high.
Yet, though I rule an earthly realm,                29
lead both the fairy race and men,
My kingship no contentment brings;                  30
'tis honey that is laced with bane.
So great my wealth and riches were,                 31
and ever young my fortune's star:
Would I had been content with that;                 32
high places are with danger fraught.
The Persians, with both force and shame,            33
softened me with cajolings warm;
Made me determined to be king,                      34
and raise myself to throne and crown.
I guard the realm from ruin; am                     35
no sovereign, but a guardian.
How apt the well-known proverb: "When               36
desire's your foe, the world's your friend."
Of such a world you nothing know;                   37
you rule a different world. To you
Roast onager is sweeter than                        38
the thousand bitter woes of kings.
A drop of wine, sweet music sung,                   39
excels all else that's under Heaven.
You have no cares but hunt and wine,                40
no headache from the pains of Time.
If truth you want: own of the world                 41
enough that you be no one's churl;
Spend eve and night in hunt and feast;              42
now drink deep, now enjoy your rest:
Not day and night, like me, bereft                  43
of joy; by men's affairs hard pressed;
Sometimes concerned with my friends' woes,          44
sometimes made anxious by my foes.

45    My least trial that, from such a king
      as you, I must defend a crown.

46    O you who've been on pleasure reared,
      from you such troubles have been far.

47    Would I were so employed; for then,
      things would be easy. I would spend

48    All of my life in sweet pursuits;
      caress my soul with wine and lute.

49    From kingliness you're not remote;
      you know of faith and statecraft both.

50    The kingdom's heir in truth you be,
      its rule your royal legacy.

51    But all your father's tyranny
      has banished you from sovereignty.

52    For ne'er his subjects did he treat
      in ways that did not raise complaint.

53    All marvelled at this sinful man,
      and called him "Sinner"* for his crimes.

54    So much did he, for bloodshed's sake,
      show sometimes harshness, sometimes haste,

55    That no one now will praise his seed
      or plant within that ground. Indeed,

56    Since no one wishes you to reign,
      'tis better you forsake this claim;

57    For if you boil, you'll find fierce heat;
      hammer cold iron* if you beat.

58    I myself, from my secret treasure,
      will give you riches without measure;

59    Whatever state that you ordain,
      to spend on it will be my gain.'

# 19

## How King Bahrâm Gûr Answered the Iranians

1     The letter fully read, a flame
      leapt up from deep within Bahrâm;

2     But with a hundred efforts, he

did keep his patience, cleverly.
Despite his heat, he hastened not,                    3
but answered after patient thought:
'What in this letter scribes have writ,               4
I've heard as they did read me it.
Although the scribes did lack in skill,              5
it indicates the speaker's will.
What lofty judgement it conveys                      6
I laud, for it deserves my praise.
I, to whom earth and silver are                      7
as one, to world rule don't aspire;
But 'twould be treason to consign                    8
to others, the kingdom that is mine.
My father claimed to be a lord;                      9
*I* God, Who wisdom gives, adore.
How different are the flesh and blood               10
of who loves lordship, and loves God.
I am excused of every crime                          11
that I did not commit; for I'm
Far from my father's sins; if he                     12
was hardest rock, a pearl am I.
From dark night comes the shining morn;             13
pure rubies from base stones are born.
Speak no more of my father's sins,                   14
for God's delivered you from him.
If he did ill, now that he rests                     15
in peace, speak no ill of the dead.
Where reason guides, who evil speaks                 16
does so from heeding evil speech.
Though he was evil-natured, and bad                  17
is said of him, 'tis worse to heed.
Pass o'er my father's crimes, and my                18
lack of experience; if the Eye
That's evil does not bar my road,                   19
I'll seek forgiveness for his deeds.
If once I slept in negligence,                       20
I've now foresworn my heedlessness.
The favoured man whom Fortune aids                   21

sleeps only till 'tis time to act.

22  'Tis better that the eye not fight
with sleep; but when the time is right

23  Awake. Although my sleep was deep,
my wakeful fortune watch did keep,

24  And, vigilant, it aided me
and from my slumber wakened me.

25  Hereafter all my acts shall be
improved; my heart of laxness free;

26  Nor bent on idle pleasures; now
I'm ripe, my acts shall not be raw.

27  Pious opinions I'll respect,
and serve the public interest.

28  I'll overlook each person's faults;
not seek his head, nor crave his wealth.

29  I'll not recall past sins, but find
joy in the fortune of the time.

30  I'll deal as I should deal with you,
and take from you but what is due.

31  I'll broach no person's treasure; spend
the wealth that from my foes I gain.

32  Good judgement won't be strange to me;
evil, bad counsel, banished be.

33  Good men alone shall me advise,
and evil teachers be despised.

34  All favouritism I'll avoid
in judgement; act in shame of God.

35  Men's children, wives, and wealth shall be
safer than shepherd's flock with me.

36  The bread of no one will I seize
by force, but with more bread increase.

37  Desire's demon will not lead
me from the path; desire I'll pledge

38  'Gainst sin; nor show to any eye
that which my Maker would decry.'

39  When the king finished, minds were swayed;
the oldest priest arose and said,

40  'In kingly wise, you both bestow
wisdom on us, and wisdom show.

The wisdom which your words impart    41
inscribes its judgement on our hearts.

Your loftiness your kingship marks;    42
you must be shepherd of this flock.

Sovereignty to your nature's wed;    43
the crown is ours, but on your head.

Who else will Gushtâsp's Zand revive?    44
bring to the Kayânids new life?

In you the seed of King Bahman    45
and Darius its image finds;

You, the new fruit of Siyâmak;    46
scion of Ardashîr Bâbak;

To Kayûmars, with throne and crown,    47
your lineage, king by king, goes down.*

'Tis you were chosen for this realm;    48
the whole world knows no other king.

The priests do all agree upon    49
this matter, whether old or young.

But we are servants, and constrained,    50
our will by pact and oath restrained.

With him who now sits on the throne,    51
our covenant now grips us strong,

To seek no other crowned head,    52
nor turn our faces from his gate.

Now we must have a proof that's firm    53
to free us from our oath and bond,

That we be not shamed in our faith,    54
nor break our pact, nor be disgraced.'

When King Bahrâm this answer heard    55
he gave the answer it deserved:

'Your plea is not allowed,' said he;    56
'wise men must shun disloyalty.

This rebel who your throne has seized,    57
your elder, is a child to me.

Though harming not a hair, the crown    58
from off his head I shall bring down,

E'en though my rule does not depend    59
on caution or excuse. I am

The king—to Jamshîd goes my line—    60

and in all ways heir to the realm.

61 Both crown and throne are tools; not rule,
which has no need of any tool.

62 He who is crowned and enthroned,
earth is his throne, Heaven his crown.

63 Farîdûn's crown and Jamshîd's throne:
both vanished now; but he who owns

64 True substance raises high his head;
both crown and throne for his sake made.

65 I know the way to crown and throne;
with sword I'll make them both my own.

66 Although a traitor holds my place,
his spider's web spun o'er the cave,

67 A dragon to the cave door's come;
seeks audience with the spider. When

68 Was ant of Gabriel's kind, or gnat
the equal of the elephant's foot?

69 So bravely cries the onager
that it drowns out the lion's roar.

70 The sun's light, when in Aries: can
it equalled be by hundred lamps?

71 I, suffering, among strangers live,
my own house in the hands of thieves;

72 My foe on honeyed sugar fares,
I on my heart and liver. Sword

73 And dagger set all pain at naught:
dagger in belly, sword at neck.

74 All Persia's realm my treasure, yet
my stable's 'mongst the Arabs set.

75 Now Munzir sends to me a feast;
now Nuʿmân offers up his life.

76 The givers of my bread are kings,
but those who eat it full of sin.

77 I conquer realms like a young lion:
how can an old fox take my throne?

78 Royal am I; how shall my foe
take crown, or taxes to *me* due?

79 Kayânid scions deserve the throne;

it can't be held by some unknown.
*We* are the king, all others slaves;          80
*we* full of merit, empty they.
A king must raise an army; but             81
does one lone horseman raise much dust?
The wine, the Magian elder's labour,       82
should ought but his own offspring savour?
You know well that, in what I say,         83
I seek both right and truth; but by
Good covenant and pact, not through        84
rebellion and despotic rule.
I'll do as you see fit; 'tis best          85
to seek to satisfy your wish.
When you say there must be a proof         86
by which this pact may be dissolved,
This is the proof: the share will fall     87
to him who, 'twixt two lions, is bold.
Tomorrow, let their keeper bring,          88
starved of all food, two roaring lions,
Savage and fierce, with sharpest claws,    89
their fiery breath emitting smoke,
To the arena; let troops surround          90
the place, in ranks all gathered round.
Then lower down the royal crown;           91
set it between those two fierce lions.
Whoever seizes it shall be                 92
worthy of crowning on that day.'
When he had spoken—courteous words,        93
pleasing, and deep in their import—
He sealed the letter with his seal         94
and thus conveyed his plan to all.

# 20

## How Bahrâm's Letter Reached Iran

When the supporters of the king            1
his kindness saw, and heard those fine

2      And precious words, they went their way
       homewards, his image in their eyes.

3      His kindness in each one inspired
       devotion to his kingly *farr*.

4      They all averred, 'Bahrâm is king,
       sovereign in nature and in name.

5      He cannot be opposed; how can
       one hope with mud to hide the sun?

6      That warrior bold's a raging lion,
       who dragons with an arrow hunts.

7      When the bold lion spreads his claws,
       none can resist him. He will seize

8      The crown and throne by force, and bring
       the mighty to their knees. Such flames,

9      Now quenched, should not be newly lit;
       'tis best that we not test his heat.

10     This tale of lions, a crown that's seized:
       of such a test he has no need;

11     But this condition is a proof
       which tells the foxes from the wolves.'

12     They went to court, and told the king
       the king's conditions; read to him

13     The letter and explained its words;
       and added nought to what they'd heard.

14     The crown-worshipping old man put down
       the crown, and sat below the throne.

15     'I'm weary of this throne and crown
       for which I'll fall prey to a lion.

16     Better to live below the throne
       than to be killed between two lions.

17     A clever man's not rash enough
       to snatch food from a lion's mouth.

18     The kingdom's heir, by cup and sword,
       is King Bahrâm, no other lord.

19     Give to the kingdom's heir the throne;
       a young king's better than an old.

20     I've given up this job; I am
       no king, but worship the true king.'

21     The nobles their reply adorned:

'O king of kings, of kings the crown,
We chose you as our ruler for 22
that very wisdom you now show.
Since by our order you did sit 23
upon the throne, now abdicate.
Now Bahrâm's made the lion a test, 24
'twere rashness if you should persist.
To seize the crown from them's no sport; 25
who knows what tricks the night brings forth.
In our own way we'll meet his terms: 26
tie up the lions, present the crown.
If he's afraid, the ivory throne 27
is yours; if he is killed, the crown.
But if he's skilled; seizes the crown, 28
exacts just taxes from the realm,
Then he deserves both throne and praise 29
(though difficult will be success).
In sum, we do conclude (though loath): 30
we may not violate our oath.
Tomorrow, when the day is born, 31
the king will hunt the fearsome lion.'

# 21

## How Bahrâm Seized the Crown from between Two Lions

At daybreak, when the gold-crowned sun 1
raised golden footstool, ivory throne,
The officers and nobles, strong 2
in judgement and in mighty arm,
Arab and Persian, riding, came 3
towards those two ferocious lions.
The keeper let the lions loose 4
against their mark (man-eaters both);
Lion 'gainst lion was pitched in war; 5
they dug a grave for Bahrâm Gûr.
A lion-keeper—courageous man!— 6
then placed the crown between the lions.

7        Between black lions a golden crown;
         like, in two dragons' jaws, the moon.

8        The moon escaped that cloud, shone forth,
         as it was freed by Bahrâm's sword.

9        Those vicious lions lashed their tails
         upon the ground, like dragons fell,

10       As if to say, 'Who'll seize this crown?
         Who'll rob a dragon, or a lion?'

11       They knew nought of that fearless man
         who hunted dragons and slew lions.

12       In range of those fierce lions, from fear,
         no one would dare to venture near.

13       It was decided that Bahrâm,
         lion-hearted, should first dare the lions.

14       If he should seize the crown, he'd own
         crown, golden cup, and ivory throne;

15       If not, ill fortune would be blamed,
         and he'd return to whence he came.

16       Bahrâm did not this compact broach,
         but from the plain the lions approached.

17       There was no height in vale or plain
         on which he had not lions slain.

18       But two-and-twenty, he had flayed
         the manes from hundred lions' heads.

19       He who a hundred lions felled:
         how could two lions his courage quell?

20       He fixed his belt around his waist,
         and, like the south wind, swift made haste

21       Towards them; shouted at the lions,
         and from between them stole the crown.

22       Like warriors stout they rushed at him,
         with daggered claws and sword-like fangs,

23       To seize the crown-bearer's hand, and make
         things strait for him who'd the throne take.

24       The king devised a way to tame
         the beasts; the heads of both cast down,

25       Then rent their claws and tore their fangs,
         and from them saved both head and crown.

26       Then, crowned, he mounted to the throne;

so Fortune aids the fortunate man.
He seized the crown from those two lions:     27
brought down the foxes from the throne.


## 22

## How Bahrâm Ascended the Throne in his Father's Place

The ascendant of his throne and rule     1
auspicious showed, through his goodwill.
Before this deed, astrologers     2
had sought his fortune from the stars.
They'd seen the Lion on the throne;     3
a stable portent, likewise firm.
The sun at apogee, well met     4
with Mercury; while Venus sat
In Taurus, Jupiter in the Bow,     5
each house like Paradise. And lo,
The moon in tenth, in sixth house Mars,     6
feasting with sword and cup; the Scales
Were weighed (they said) by Saturn's hand;*     7
their treasures reached from earth to Heaven.
When, with this happy portent, King     8
Bahrâm ascended to the throne,
From pearls and rubies scattered wide,     9
the ship of fortune overflowed.
Innumerable treasure-hoards     10
wealth upon wealth from tribute poured.
The former king, who'd first enjoyed     11
subjects' and warriors' loyalty,
Seeing the splendour of Bahrâm,     12
by which both crown and throne grew famed,
Of great and small, became the first     13
to call him king of Heaven and earth.
The priests called him king of the world;     14
the nobles termed him supreme lord.
Thus everyone, abroad, at home,     15
praised him according to his own

16  Degree. When Bahrâm rose so high,
    his loftiness surpassed the sky.

17  He gave his speech of justice; strewed
    bright pearls from rubies fresh. He said,

18  'God's given me the crown; and may
    God's sacred gift rejoice in me.

19  Great praise and thanks to God I give;
    may he who thanks his God be praised!

20  I shall not disregard His gifts,
    but show my thanks; why not? To seize

21  The crown from two lions' jaws—this was
    the work of God, not of the sword.

22  Since I've gained crown and lofty throne,
    I'll act in ways that will please Him.

23  God willing, I shall do no harm,
    in all my deeds, to anyone.

24  With me, O nobles of my court,
    be straight and true, like my own course.

25  'Tis best from crooked ways you turn,
    and rightness from right conduct learn.

26  If you grasp not right rule, your left
    ear will be wearied by complaint.

27  I'll rest some days, then open wide
    the door of equity and right.

28  My duty calls me to requite
    ill deeds with ill, and right with right.

29  Till the blue sphere endures, may there
    be blessings on the dead; but more

30  Than all things else, for live souls be
    good tidings and security.

31  May I do naught but good and right;
    who likes it not, let nought rejoice!'

32  When the king made his justice clear,
    there bowed to him all who did hear.

33  A while he sat upon the throne,
    and then retired to be alone.

34  He justice did, commanded right,
    God and men pleased with him alike.

Sat with the noble and the great, 35
and trusted those who were upright.

## 23

### How King Bahrâm Gûr Administered Justice
### in his Reign

When by Bahrâm both crown and throne 1
were honoured, and with glory shone,
The seven–eyed belt he girded on 2
and sat upon the seven-stepped throne.\*
In Chinese silks as fine as skin, 3
and Rûmî robes with gold adorned,
His beauty tribute took from Rûm, 4
and nightly levied tax from Chîn.
Like Jamshîd's his four–cushioned throne; 5
his fanfare raised above the sun.
He fostered justice in the world, 6
and raised it high; supported those,
Throughout the world, who cherished right, 7
humbled those who abused their might.
The key that opened suffering's lock, 8
where'er he went he brought good luck.
He caused the world to prosper; freed 9
the air, that every soul might breathe.
The barren cow quickened and bore; 10
the water in the streams grew more;
Ripe fruits hung heavy on the trees; 11
new coins were minted with fresh dies.
Binding and loosing, he spread right 12
throughout the world. Division's blight
Forsook the realm. On every side 13
princes in his fair state took pride.
The kingdom's income, at his gate, 14
poured out in e'er-increasing spate.
Proud seneschals gave up the keys 15
and treasures of their forts. Thus each

16  Man wrote anew his own life's page;
to the king's seal his soul did pledge.

17  In matters of the state, he gave
each honour fitting to his rank.

18  The poor man's state he ordered; and
brought back all those who'd fled the land.

19  He freed the sheep from the wolf's fang,
and made the falcon the dove's kin;

20  Cured mischief's head of drunkenness;
shortened the reach of grasping hands;

21  Destroyed the strength of all his foes,
his friends made lords of all the world.

22  In rule he practised manliness;
virtue will e'er oppression best.

23  Chastising enemies, he ten
might kill, but would not one man wrong;

24  Better, at time of punishment,
to kill a man than him torment.

25  He saw this earthly camping place
brings nought but sorrow's dust. He kept

26  Himself content with love, maintained
his life with pleasure sweetly gained;

27  Knew worldly rule unstable; sought
in love's domain his firm support.

28  One day on state affairs he spent;
the other six on love was bent.

29  Who has no sign of loverhood?
He who loves not, is not alive.

30  His essence by love's die was stamped,
and lovers were his dearest friends.

31  His lofty business reached the sky;
the world 'neath his command did lie.

32  In pleasure he devoured the world;
did pleasure justice. Treasures flowed

33  Throughout his capital, gained by
his sword and whip, his conquest's prize.

34  But, though the realm through him grew green—
for he traversed it like the sun—

35  Men, proud of wealth and comfort, put

faith in a year which plenty brought.

They failed to thank God in their hearts,   36
divorced compassion from their breasts.

Whene'er God's creatures fail to give   37
thanks for the bounties He provides,

That plenty will be turned to none,   38
their daily bread to iron and stone.

## 24

## About the Year of Famine and Bahrâm's Compassion

One year the blades produced no grain,   1
and nowhere could it be obtained.

Dearth had so straitened food that men,   2
like beasts, ate grass; and everyone

Grew so distressed at that great dearth   3
that bread, though light, gained noble worth.

They brought the news to King Bahrâm:   4
'The world's by famine overrun.

Like wolves do men on others feed:   5
sometimes the quick, sometimes the dead.'

Seeing the price of grain had soared,   6
the king unlocked his royal stores.

To every town in which some grain   7
was stored, he issued his command:

That those in charge should meet before   8
the storehouse, and throw wide its doors;

Sell to the rich at market rate;   9
give freely to the destitute;

And any grain remaining should   10
be given the birds in time of need;

So that, in those times, none might die   11
from lack of food. What chivalry!

Everyone took whatever grain   12
the royal storehouses contained.

From foreign lands, time and again,   13
his camel caravans brought grain.

He spent great effort and much wealth,   14

striving to save the lives of all.

15 Thus four years without harvest passed;
men's daily bread came from his stores.

16 Such were his deeds when he attained
the throne; thus he true kingship gained.

17 His subjects' lives the king preserved,
save for one man who died from dearth.

18 At that man's death the king's heart grew
as strait and cold as ice; unto

19 His God he turned, and sought, in pain,
forgiveness for his shortcoming.

20 'O You Who grant all sustenance;
unequalled in Your providence;

21 By virtue of Your divine power,
You make much little, little more.

22 I cannot, though I labour long,
feed one gazelle that roams the plain.

23 You are He Who, triumphant, gives
to every man his daily bread.

24 If, out of dearth, one wretched man
perished, that was no crime of mine;

25 I had no knowledge that he lived;
what gain to me news of his death?'

26 When the king's plea to God was done,
a voice spoke to him from within:

27 'God, from your good intent, has given
a space of time out of your reign:

28 Since for four years, in wisdom, you've
one death from hunger not approved,

29 For four years more 'tis His command
that death be absent from your land.'

30 For four years in that realm, I heard
that, great or small, no person died.

31 Happy that king who, with kind gifts,
keeps from his subjects dreaded death.

32 All who were born, lived. Ever best
is income that's without expense.

33 With people filled, no mount or plain
without inhabitants remained.

From Isfahan to Rayy, I've heard, 34
house followed house, like jointed reeds.

From roof to roof, the blindest man 35
could pass from Rayy to Isfahan.

(If you think this unlikely, then 36
the fault's the author's, and not mine.)

Many were those who comforts found; 37
comforts more numerous than men.

When palm-branch joins to palm-branch, then 38
the crop of dates will pass all bounds.

Food becomes scarce when men are few; 39
more people can produce more food.

People, secure in plain and mount, 40
in pleasure sported, group by group.

For two long leagues there stretched a line 41
of fine musicians of all kinds;

A pool of wine near every stream, 42
a merry party in each lane.

Each man bought wine and sold his sword, 43
tore up his mail and sewed brocade.

All put their weapons by; forgot 44
the sword and arrow. He who'd got

The means for pleasure, took his joy 45
in merriment and luxury;

While he who lacked, the king commanded 46
that with his luck he be contented.

To each he gave some task to do, 47
and gave a share of pleasure too.

He ordered each day split in twain: 48
one half for work, one half for wine.

He cancelled taxes for six years, 49
uprooted seventy years of tears.

Six thousand masters of all arts, 50
puppeteers, dancers, minstrel bards,

He gathered in from everywhere, 51
and gave each district its fair share,

That everywhere that they might go 52
they'd entertain, be happy too.

Taurus, ascendant, paired his sway 53

with Venus, ruler of the age.*

54    In such an age, when Venus reigns,
how should adversity obtain?

## 25

## The Story of Bahrâm and his Slave-Girl

1    One day the king a hunt ordained
through hill and desert. Towards the plain

2    His swift-paced chestnut stallion flew;
he havoc wreaked, wild asses slew.

3    Jupiter's house is in the Bow:*
*his* bow left Jupiter below.

4    His soldiers, ringed around the plain,
beat forth the game towards the king.

5    The king, lion-like, in centre stood;
the stallion danced beneath his lord.*

6    His hand pearls from the bowstring flung:
the thumbstall emptied, arrows strung.

7    His bolts of tempered steel hurled down
now fire, now game, upon the ground.

8    With haunch of game, and purest wine,
it wants a fire to roast the chine.*

9    Did then the royal spear strike fire
for this, while slaying onager?

10   His lance's heat, with grisly wound,
cooked well the prey he brought to ground,

11   While those that fled he swift pursued,
and living snared, or fiercely slew.

12   With him a moon-like maid did ride,
clever and quick, her lord beside.

13   Fitna her name,* of thousand lures;
the king's temptress, he charmed by her.

14   Bright-faced like spring in Paradise;
quick as the wind o'er meadow's grass.

15   Like oil and honey mixed was she,
as sweet and smooth as *pâlûda*.*

16   She played and sang with elegance,
and was quick-footed at the dance.

When to the lute she joined her song,        17
the birds from air to ground would throng.

Most often, at the hunt or feast,        18
the king her sweet songs would request.

The harp her weapon, the king's the bow:        19
she struck up tunes, he game laid low.

From the plain some wild asses neared;        20
the king his steed towards them spurred,

And, overtaking those swift beasts,        21
the raging lion his crossbow seized,

An arrow in the thumbstall placed,        22
then drew the bow and loosed his grasp.

It struck the onager's broad haunch,        23
and his prey did obeisance.

Thus in a moment, of that prey        24
so wondrous, he would seize or slay;

But that slave-girl, from wilful whim,        25
restrained herself from praising him.

The king stood patiently a while,        26
until a wild ass came in view.

'Say then: do not those narrow eyes        27
know how such skills as mine to prize?

Yet how should such abundant prey        28
be compassed by such narrow sight?

This new beast: tell me, how shall I        29
attack it? where·my arrow try?'

The sweet-lipped maid, as was her wont—        30
a woman she, and idle-tongued—

Said, 'If you'd kindle praise, then join        31
its hoof to head, with arrow bound.'

When the king heard her twisting words,        32
for her ill will he sought a cure.

His sling so swift he first took up,        33
and nocked a ball within its cup.

Quick to the quarry's ear, the ball        34
sped sure, and set its brain aboil.

The wretched beast drew hoof to ear        35
the offending ball therefrom to clear.

Like lightning flashed the royal bolt:        36
stitched hoof to head at but one stroke.

37  The king then asked the maid of Chîn,
    'What think you of the feat you've seen?'

38  She said, 'The prince is quite well versed
    in this; what's hard that's oft rehearsed?

39  Whate'er a man's by teaching trained
    to do, though hard, is always gained.

40  Your royal bolt the hoof transfixed
    through practice, not by strength unmixed.'

41  These words the king's wrath did incite;
    the tall tree felt the axe's bite.

42  He felt no pity for that moon;
    his rage was clear in every limb.

43  When bent on vengeance, kings should wait:
    slay only when in better state.

44  'Gainst young gazelles one does not ride,
    nor make a fur coat from dogs' hide.

45  'Leave her (he thought) and she'll make trouble;
    but kill her—that's dishonour double!

46  For lion-brave warriors do not slay
    weak women; they're unequal prey.'

47  An officer of noble line—
    fearsome as wolf and bold as lion—

48  He summoned secretly, and said,
    'Go you, and rid me of this maid.

49  She has disturbed our stately court:
    death to disturbers* reason supports.'

50  The honest warrior swift removed
    that fairy-face to his abode.

51  He sought to do the king's command:
    to snuff her like a candle's flame.

52  With brimming eyes the beauty cried,
    'Do not condone this evil deed;

53  And, if you love yourself, do not
    take on your head my guiltless blood.

54  I am the privileged consort of
    the king, his choice all else above;

55  His sole companion at the chase
    and feast am I; none takes my place.

56  If my unbridled tongue made me

sport for some demon, so it be:
In heat the king my death decreed;      57
so slay me not with undue speed.

For several days your hand restrain;      58
then tell the king that I am slain.

If at that news the king is pleased,      59
slay me; of guilt you are released.

But if my death doth make him grieve,      60
in soul and body both you're safe:

You freed from vengeance, I from death;      61
this cypress will not fall to earth.

A day will come when, though I'm nought,      62
your service to me I'll requite.'

She spoke, and then her chain unclasped;      63
laid seven rubies in his grasp,

Each worth a kingdom's ransom; twice      64
the value of all Oman's price.*

The officer, at these honest words,      65
forbore to shed that idol's blood.

'Beware,' he said, 'and shun repose;      66
to no one this affair disclose,

But say, "I am a servant in      67
this house," and your work so ordain.

I to the plans that must be wrought      68
will turn, if time give us respite.'

They swore a binding oath; thus one      69
escaped wrongdoing, the other harm.

When, in a week, he waited on      70
the king, who asked him of that moon,

'The Moon to Dragon I've given',* he said,      71
'and slain; with tears her bloodwit paid.'

To the king's eyes sharp tears did start;      72
the man grew easy in his heart.

The officer owned fertile lands,      73
estates far from the eyes of men;

A palace there rose towards the sky,      74
beaten by waves from Heaven's sea.

A tower sixty steps in height      75
was crowned by a fair place to sit;*

76 That maiden too did dwell therein;
   to precious ones high place is given.

77 Meanwhile, one day a cow brought forth
   a comely calf. Each day thenceforth

78 That lovely world-illuming maid
   the calf across her shoulders laid,

79 And standing firm beneath him, bore
   him daily up the lofty tower.

80 The Sun does bear the Calf in spring;*
   who's seen a moon do such a thing?

81 That silver-limbed gazelle would bear
   daily that calf from house to tower.

82 Day after day she did not quit
   this practice, but continued it,

83 Until—the calf an ox become
   of six years' age—her task was done:

84 That rose-limbed idol still could bear
   the ox from palace grounds to tower.

85 Its burden troubled her no whit,
   for she had grown quite used to it;

86 And as the ox increased in weight
   her own strength ever grew more great.

87 One day that maiden, sore at heart,
   with her protector sat apart;

88 From her bejewelled ears four gems
   that hourî loosed, then said to him,

89 'Go, take and sell these precious things,
   and quietly the money bring:

90 Buy sheep and incense, attar rare,
   and candles, fruits and wine prepare;

91 Array a Paradisal feast,
   with incense, wine, sweet fruits, and meat.

92 When the king to the hunt shall ride,
   like victory, do not leave his side,

93 But to his service dedicate
   yourself; his reins a moment take.

94 King Bahrâm is by nature kind;
   of gentle habit, noble mind;

95 And when he your entreaty hears,
   he'll seek to raise you o'er your peers.

Upon this star-girt prospect, we     96
will milk and honey to him feed;
And if this deed will bring us gain,     97
we both will high degree attain.'
The officer the gems disdained,     98
for on him God had treasures rained.
He went, and from his secret treasure,     99
prepared a feast for Bahrâm's pleasure:
The finest foods fit for a king:     100
fish and fowl, mutton and lamb;
Wine and sweet basil for the feast,     101
and victuals for a banquet meet.
He readied all against the time     102
Bahrâm should choose to hunt again.

# 26

## How Bahrâm Came from the Hunting-Ground to Feast with the Officer

One day the king rose from his throne     1
and made towards the hunting-ground.
Before the king could hunt or slay,     2
his victim made the king her prey.
When he passed through that village where     3
the officer had his lofty tower,
He saw a splendid pleasure-ground,     4
all green on green, and shaded round.
'Whose are these lands,' he asked, 'and where     5
the owner of this village fair?'
The officer, who rode beside     6
the king, and heard, humbly replied.
He kissed the ground, and homage made:     7
'O gentle king, your humble slave,
Owns this fair village by your gift;     8
of your rich wine the merest drop.
And if the king will will it so,     9
and honour to his servant show,
Without constraint, as is his wont,     10
and as his judgement wise may prompt,

11  Let him go in this narrow gate,
    and raise his slave to lofty state.

12  The king's largesse to me has given
    a tower that rises to the moon,

13  By gardens girdled, served by Heaven,
    Eden its pupil. If the king deign

14  To drink, atop it, the stars will bow
    before its gate; his dust will fill

15  The house with scent; my flies will make
    sweet honey, and my bulls give milk.'

16  When the king heard these honest words,
    this noble speech: 'Command is yours,'

17  He said; 'then go now and prepare,
    until I from the hunt repair.'

18  The officer bowed low; made haste
    to cleanse that mirror of its rust;*

19  With Paradisal carpets decked
    the prospect, and fine ornaments.

20  When the king came from the hunting-ground,
    his royal eagle reached the moon.*

21  His host the finest folded stuffs,
    of Chinese make and Grecian weave,

22  Carpet on carpet, rare and fine,
    whose brilliance cheered the heart and mind,

23  Cast 'neath the king's swift Turkish steed,
    and scattered pearls before his feet.

24  Mounting the sixty steps, the king
    found there a vault lofty as Heaven,

25  As fair as Khavarnaq in form;
    its carpet was the azure dome.*

26  The host brought all that was required:
    incense, rose-water, drink, and food.

27  When the king finished this repast,
    he called for wine, made joyful feast.

28  When he had drunk a glass or three
    sweat dewed his rosy face. Said he,

29  'Host of this golden palace, your place
    is pleasant, your provisions great;

30  But these high sixty steps of yours,

which the sky grasps within its noose:
Your age is sixty years or so;                          31
how can you climb them? Tell me now.'
His host said, 'May the king live long,                 32
his sâqîs angels, Kawsar his wine;
'Tis not amazing; I'm a man;                            33
how could I fail these steps to climb?
The wonder is, a maid, moon-fair,                       34
supple and soft, like silks and furs,
Carries upon her back an ox,                            35
that's like a mountain, here to graze.
She climbs these sixty steps at once,                   36
quickly, nor stops at any one.
An ox? what ox! more elephant,                          37
that cannot bear its own great weight.
By God! no man in all this land                         38
could ever raise it from the ground.
But when a woman brings it here,                        39
up sixty steps, is this not rare?'
When this was told, the king, amazed,                   40
did bite his fingers in surprise.
He said, 'How can such a thing be?                      41
It can't; or else, it's sorcery.
I won't believe what you have said,                     42
till my own eyes have seen this feat.'
He then requested that his host                         43
should prove his claim. On hearing this,
His host descended, there to tell                       44
the ox-bearing maid the lion's tale.
The silver-limbed one had foreseen                      45
this time, before she made her plans.
She donned Chinese adornments; gave                     46
to rose narcissus' langourous gaze;
Strewed musky curls over the moon;                      47
taught loving glances magic's charms
With eyes made dark with kohl. Deceit                   48
disguised reproach with manner sweet.
Tulip-like cheeks her cypress dyed                      49
a rosy hue; below, a reed.

50  She decked with pearls her cypress form;
    bound Pleiads' necklace to the moon.

51  Rubies her lips, rare pearls her teeth;
    her chin a lover's apple cleft.

52  Her curls, a crown of amber, swept
    from head to ears, and graced her neck.

53  (A king whose throne's of ivory formed
    cannot dispense with crown and throne.)

54  Her Hindu mole and Ethiop curls
    were ranged as if prepared for war.

55  Her jet-black mole on ruby lips
    an Ethiop's seal on fresh dates set.

56  Her wimple's glittering seed-pearls bound
    a veil of stars around the moon.

57  The beauty of her jewel-hung ears
    kindled both ardour and desire.

58  She bound her moon in a veil of white,
    like a Syrian rose amid jasmine bright.

59  This fortnight's moon, when, by love led,
    her seven adornments* had arrayed,

60  Like a full moon drew near the ox:
    the Moon finds strength in Taurus' house.

61  She bent her head and raised the ox:
    see what a jewel adorned that beast!*

62  Step by step she sped to the roof,
    drew near the foot of Bahrâm's couch.

63  Bearing the ox, she stood erect;
    seeing the Bull, the Lion leapt up.

64  He stood amazed: what might this mean?
    some gain?—yet he knew not *what* gain.

65  The Moon set down the ox, and said
    unto the Lion, with toss of head:

66  'This gift of mine, which I alone
    present you, by my strength was done.

67  Who in the world, through power or plan,
    could bear it from this tower again?'

68  The king replied, 'This is no power;
    you've practised this feat long before,

69  And, year on year and bit by bit,

through constant striving, mastered it:
Till now, without apparent stress,    70
you balance in your scales this beast.'

The beauty, silver-limb'd, bowed low,    71
with salutations as were due,

And said, 'The king a great debt owes:    72
"practice" the ox—not the wild ass?

Am I, who to the roof have borne    73
an ox, for "practice" to be known?

Why, when *you* shoot a wild ass small    74
should no one *your* deed "practice" call?'

At her reproach, he knew the maid,    75
his Turk, and humbly to her sped;

Raised the moon's veil, and, seeing her,    76
upon that moon rained pearl-like tears;

Embraced her, begged her pardon; she    77
poured rose-water from narcissus eyes.

He cleared the house of bad and good;    78
spoke sweetly to that lovely maid.

'If in this house you've been in prison,    79
a thousand times I beg your pardon.

If I, headstrong, kindled a fire,    80
'twas I was burned; you have survived.'

When from disturbers the place was free,    81
he made 'Disturbance' seated be.*

Fitna sat down, her speech began:    82
'O king, who sets disturbance down,

Whose separation caused my death,    83
whose love has brought me back to life.

This sorrow that has made me waste    84
away, would mountains turn to dust.

My loving nature nearly caused    85
my life to end; and all for love.

When the king, hunting onager,    86
with arrow joined hard hoof to ear,

At such a loosing of his bow    87
not earth, but sky as well, bowed low.

I, who was slow to praise, thereby    88
did keep from him the Evil Eye;

89  For what man's eye has worthy found,
    the harmful Eye is sure to wound.

90  To the Sky-Dragon,* who falsely showed
    my love as hate, my crime is owed.'

91  These words so moved the king, they pierced
    his soul as they shot through his heart.

92  'Indeed, you speak the truth,' said he,
    'and much does prove your loyalty:

93  A love so great when all began,
    such fine excuses at the end.

93a Praised be that pearl a thousandfold
    whose nature doth such merit hold!

94  This pearl were shattered by a stone,
    had it not been for that brave one

95  Who guarded it.' He summoned then
    the officer, and gladdened him,

96  Embraced him, splendid gifts bestowed:
    a thousand pearls for that one owed

97  Exchanged; and gave him the control
    of Rayy, with other gifts as well.

98  Joyful, he headed for the town,
    and scattered sugar at his own

99  Great wedding feast. He summoned priests,
    and made that moon his lawful wife.

100 He lived with her in love and ease,
    until a long, long time had passed.

# 27

## The Invasion of the Khâqân of Chîn
## and Bahrâm's Victory

1  When Bahrâm's fame had risen high,
   from Fish to Moon,* for kingship wise,

2  The hearts of noble men grew strong;
   through him their fame new life put on.

3  The evil in dark corners died,
   and perished, drowned by death's black flood.

4  There was a sage, Narsî by name
   (King Bahrâm's brother bore the same),

In judgement strong, whose reason kenned    5
the ins and outs of everything;

Descended from Darius, great king    6
(a fact not hidden, but well known).

Alike a minister and friend,    7
the king was never far from him.

He had three sons, each one of them    8
a world of virtue on his own.

The oldest of them, Zarâvand    9
(so was he by his father named),

The king a hundredfold increased    10
in worth, and made him his chief priest.

He bore the goal in mind, and knew    11
the way; his faith was boundless, too.

The second taxes oversaw,    12
collected imposts on the roads.

His just decisions caused the king    13
to give him charge o'er all the land.

Most trusted member of the court,    14
The third controlled both town and troops.

The king left them to do their work,    15
and they were loyal to their tasks.

They worked each day; while he made bright    16
with flowing wine the feast each night,

And, like a mill which takes and grinds,    17
dispensed the wealth that came to him.

Throughout the world this news grew known,    18
and cutting blades were sharply honed.

All said, 'Bahrâm doth drunken sup;    19
trades faith for wealth, and sword for cup.

He drinks unceasing with his friends,    20
consumes but wine, and reaps the wind.'

Each one was filled with high desire,    21
and to the kingdom did aspire.

The Khân of Khâns marched out from Chîn*    22
to seize the world-ruler's domain;

Like fearsome dragons, in his train    23
three hundred thousand archers strong.

They seized by force the ruler's lands    23*a*
held in Transoxiana; then,

24　The Oxus crossed, they hurried on,
　　and havoc raised in Khurasan.

25　Bahrâm learned of that Turkish raid;
　　his army's state left him dismayed.

26　He saw that all, on pleasure fed,
　　the ways of war had laid aside.

27　Their leaders too, he found, had slight
　　devotion to maintain his rights.

28　Each one by hidden routes had sent
　　a spy to seek out the Khâqân;

29　They bore ill-feeling towards the king,
　　and sought to save their wealth and lands.

30　'We're your well-wishing slaves,' they said;
　　'advance: we're dust upon your road.

31　Advance with pride; *you* rule the world;
　　Bahrâm's incapable of rule.

32　'Gainst him we'll draw the sword, should you
　　so wish; or give him up to you

33　In chains.' A lettered spy did bring
　　this diresome news unto the king.

34　He lost hope in Iran; bequeathed
　　his kingdom to his deputies;

35　Concealed himself; one cannot wage
　　a war with weapons such as these.

36　The news spread far and wide: 'The king
　　has hid himself from troops and realm;

37　Has fled, not man enough to face
　　the Khâqân and his troops, disgraced.'

38　When the good news reached the Khâqân:
　　'The king has from his throne come down;

39　*Your* fortune royal belt and crown;
　　advance, and take both crown and throne.'

40　And when the Khân of Khâns had heard:
　　'Bahrâm has vanished from the world,

41　Has left off sword and sword-play both,
　　and sits to drink in leisured sloth,

42　Recks not the foe, and drinks his wine,
　　and does that which should not be done,'

43　What in his foe he'd not approved

he did; that foe to laughter moved.
Bahrâm went hunting every day; 44
his messengers sped every way.
News of the Chinese chief he sought; 45
his courier brought a true report:
'He thinks him safe, of easy mind.' 46
The king was pleased at this good sign.
From all his army mustered were 47
three hundred horsemen; nothing more.
All warriors skilled in warfare they, 48
dragons on land and sharks at sea.
Like the pomegranate (its hundred seeds 49
all in one house), of single heart.
The king then played a crooked game; 50
juggled with balls, but hid his own.*
His foe sought fire; he gave him smoke, 51
and so deceived him with false hope.
He loosed his arrow towards that mark, 52
for he knew well his foe's mistake.
He launched a night attack; the sphere 53
his armies' dust made dark and drear.
In the deep blackness of a night 54
which, like a snake, devoured light;
A night which quenched all lamps; when plain 55
and hill were blacker than crow's wing;
As if a drunken Zangî horde 56
ran to and fro with brandished sword;
And men in fear of that black foe 57
opened their eyes, and nothing saw;
And the bright sphere, in blackest silks, 58
was like a wine-jar smeared with pitch:
On such a night of amber pure, 59
Bahrâm waged his Bahrâmian war.*
He rushed upon the Chinese horde, 60
now with his spear, and now with sword.
Where'er he aimed his arrow, true 61
it sped, and pierced its target through.
His granite-piercing arrows put 62
his enemies' watchful eyes to sleep.

63    They saw the wound, no arrow found;
      they arrows saw, but ne'er a wound.

64    'What trick is this', they asked, 'to find
      wound without shaft, shaft without wound?'

65    Till, out of dread, no one would come
      a league's length from that battleground.

66    He, like a cloud, rushed here and yon,
      from plain to hill, from hill to plain;

67    So many with his shafts did slay,
      that earth from blood became as clay.

68    Life fled, in unbecoming haste,
      each body that his arrow pierced.

69    When morning drew the sun's bright sword,
      the sphere disclosed a bowl of blood.*

70    How should the sword lack bowl and blood?
      With sword and basin, blood abounds.

71    From all that blood, red rivers flowed,
      and bore off heads like polo balls.

72    So many limbs sharp blades had hewed,
      that men, from fear, bile's poison spewed.

73    Sharp lance had pledged to sword its tongue
      to smite the dragons: bring them on!

74    Like leaping snakes the arrow shafts;
      there's danger in the snake that leaps.

75    King Bahrâm held the centre; loosed
      his slender arrows. If he smote

76    With blade a warrior's crown, he'd split
      him like a melon to the waist;

77    Or, threatening with a sideways blow,
      he'd cleave him at the waist in two.

78    With such a sword and shaft, 'twas right
      that the foe fear his dreadful might.

79    The Turks, at his swift Turk-like raid,
      and those grave wounds left in his wake,

80    All for swift flight good reasons found:
      their swords grown dull, their running honed.

81    When the king's iron strove so well,
      the Turkish horde, in chaos, fell.

82    The king saw victory's rising star;

he loosed his shafts and cast his spears.
With mighty blows he scattered them 83
as clouds before the wind are driven.
Victorious, he called his men: 84
'Behold our luck! our providence!
Strive yet again to strike off heads, 85
and tear the centre from its place.'
As one they launched a strong attack, 86
with lion-like mounts, and dragon blades.
The right retreated, the left fled; 87
the centre towards the vanguard poured.
The king held victory in his grasp; 88
vanquished the centre and its chiefs.
A troop more numerous than the sands 89
had been destroyed at Bahrâm's hands.
The mighty claws of his black lions 90
pounded the feeble swordsmen's brains.
Arrows, like Zahhâk's serpents, struck 91
bold warriors to the ground. The dust
Of Turkish armies, as they fled 92
the sharp blades, reached the Oxus' edge.
The king took jewels and treasures fine, 93
beyond the treasurer's reckoning.
When he victorious returned, 94
then to his subjects' care he turned.
He sat in triumph on the throne; 95
renewed the New Year's feast; to him
All bowed in salutation; then 96
great praises of that victory sang.
The minstrels, versed in Persian song, 97
sang heroes' tales to the harp's strains;
The Arab bards* sang poems that shone 98
like lustrous pearls, to rebec's tones.
The well-versed king their verse assayed; 99
gave them more wealth than could be weighed.
Skirtfuls of pearls, hatfuls of gold 100
o'er the fire-temple's priests he poured.
So much largesse did he bestow 101
that no one living remained poor.

## 28
## How Bahrâm Rebuked his Generals

1  One day, with smiling fortune crowned,
   King Bahrâm Gûr sat on his throne.

2  Princes and kings from everywhere,
   who gave men crowns, or crowns did wear,

3  All, at the foot of Bahrâm's throne,
   were ranged like stars before the moon.

4  The king unsheathed his tongue's sharp blade:
   'O generals bold, and leaders brave:

5  Both peace and war need armies; man
   would otherwise be like a stone.

6  But which of you, in any fray,
   has shown his manly bravery?

7  My chosen warriors of this age:
   what battles have I seen you wage?

8  Who among you such deeds has shown
   as from the brave and bold should come?

9  What harm did fall on any foe
   from your swords' points, in time of woe?

10 Which of you have I seen advance
   to quell a foe, conquer a land?

11 Boasts one, "I'm of Îraj's line;"
   one, "Ârash's skill is nought to mine."

12 One speaks of Gîv, one of Rustam;
   others from lions take their name.*

13 But when the time to act had come,
   not one did battle; every one

14 Preferred to secret sessions creep,
   and say, "Alas! our king's asleep;

15 Heedless of all, he quaffs his wine;
   no one can stomach such a king."

16 Though I drink wine, 'tis not so great
   that I lack care for the world's state.

17 Though I may drink a pool of wine,
   my sword's not far from bloody streams.

18 Like lightning when the cloud pours rain,
   one hand grasps sword, the other wine.

19 I drink wine, and the feast adorn,

yet still the sword's work never scorn.
My hare's sleep* is a secret ploy;                              20
though sleeping, I yet see the foe.
My laughter and my drunkenness                                 21
are lion's grin and elephant's must.
The grinning lion sheds blood; who'd not                       22
flee from the drunken elephant?
Only fools drink and lose their wits;                          23
quite otherwise are those with sense.
Whoever does not lack for wit                                  24
drinks wine, but is not drunk from it.
When I determine to drink wine,                                25
I tread upon great Qaysar's crown.
When I am keen for wine, I pour                                26
its dregs upon my lowly foes.
What then do my supporters think?                              27
That Heaven's stars but idly blink?
Though I may sleep, my luck's awake;                           28
I drink, but it's about its work.
With such a drunken sleep, see how                             29
I've spoiled the Khâqân's rest; in so
Pursuing error, how I've borne                                 30
away the Hindu robber's things.
He is a dog who, weak and frail,                               31
does not, to guard his trust, sleep well.
Though dragons in their caves may snore,                       32
the lion won't enter through the door.'
When the king's tale was fully said,                           33
the nobles' faces blushed as red
As roses; bowing low in awe,                                   34
they gave their feeble, weak reply:
'The king's fair words unto his slaves                         35
are an adornment to the wise.
We've made of them a talisman                                  36
for soul and body; service's ring.
'Tis God Who crowned the king; all men                         37
contrive is nought but empty wind.
Those princes proud who with you vied                          38
in vain to equal you did strive;
But none was equal to you, none                                39

became the head; all were cast down.

40 We slaves have seen the king perform
deeds none has ever seen: he's bound

41 The demon, burned the dragon, killed
the elephant, the rhino felled;

42 Let alone lions (common game);
all birds and beasts his arrows claim.

43 Who else but he can hunting ride,
and twist wild asses' necks aside?

44 Now aims he at the leopard's spots;
now draws teeth from the mouths of sharks.

45 Now furrows India's brow; now smites
the Chinese foe in Indian night.

46 Now takes his tribute from Faghfûr;
now gathers taxes from Qaysar.

47 Though many men have lions smote,
and strained their brains out through their mouths,

48 That lion-man he who, with three hundred
men, has three hundred thousand bested.

49 Of former kings the tale is told
who were in love and warfare bold:

50 If any of them fame did win,
'twas with great armies, over time;

51 No one could do what he has done
in battle with but some few men.

52 When kings are reckoned up, 'tis he
who'll as a thousand counted be.

53 Each has his sign; but he alone
the whole world holds. When he brings down

54 His sword on any head, it splits
like two halves of a dome; and if

55 His arrow towards the hard rock flies,
like pebbles, stone in pieces lies.

56 His lance, like snake-stone, heals; he takes,
with dragon steed, the venom'd snake.

57 All his opponents, candle-like,
are melted down by fiery fate.

58 Each head which rises 'gainst his sword
is tainted by the scent of blood.

His drunkenness a sign of sense;    59
his sleep no sleep, but vigilance.

And when to wine he turns his thoughts,    60
he drinks; but 'tis his foes who're drunk.

Most learned of all men, he holds    61
most perfect power o'er good and ill;

The most sagacious of the age,    62
who needs not any other sage.

As long as earth 'neath Heaven lie,    63
may he reign o'er the lofty sky,

The earth in his protecting shade,    64
the heavens beneath his throne arrayed.'

When those wise men had said these words—    65
next to his rubies strung jet beads—

King Nu'mân rose up from their midst,    66
and with his praise adorned the feast.

'Wherever goes the monarch's throne,    67
be it the Fish,* it scrapes the moon.

What man is able to confirm    68
or doubt the justice of his claim?

God on your head has placed the crown;    69
may ever verdant be your throne.

We, servants of your court, are raised    70
to eminence by your crown's shade.

All that we have is by your grace;    71
you govern all that we possess.

Arabs and Persians, all your slaves,    72
at your command our heads we'd give.

For long, with all my skills, I've served    73
the king. Since in his court I've earned

Great rank and station; in his sway    74
have found provision for my way,

If he'll consent and give me leave,    75
I will go home, to take my ease

And rest a little from my pains,    76
and then, should he command, return;

If not, so long as I shall live,    77
full loyally his throne I'll serve.'

The king then gave the order that    78

|    | the treasurer for him weigh out |
| 79 | Jewels and wealth; bring royal gifts: |
|    | Egyptian, Moorish, Omani work. |
| 80 | The porters then grew busy; poured, |
|    | load upon load, a treasure hoard: |
| 81 | Musk-sacs in bushels, loads of gold, |
|    | and troops of slaves, both youths and girls; |
| 82 | Elegant stuffs for precious robes, |
|    | many more times than can be told; |
| 83 | Fine Arab horses, Persian-bred, |
|    | who deep seas swam and mountains trod; |
| 84 | Davidian mail and Indian swords; |
|    | his largesse launched a second Ark.* |
| 85 | Rubies and pearls whose worth was more |
|    | than sellers of pearls and rubies know; |
| 86 | A jewelled crown from his head; a robe |
|    | worth more than Shushtar's income. So |
| 87 | He gave, till Nuʿmân beamed; and then |
|    | gave lands from Aden to Yemen. |
| 88 | With bounty from the court, Nuʿmân |
|    | withdrew, like Venus from the moon. |
| 89 | The king, grown tired from bitter fight, |
|    | bent him towards joy and love's delight. |
| 90 | He ordered everyone's affairs; |
|    | then to his own he made repair. |

# 29

## How Bahrâm Sought the Princesses of the Seven Climes

| 1 | He sat to pleasure, eased in mind; |
|   | his foes subdued, took up the wine. |
| 2 | He then recalled that master who |
|   | limned that description, and that room |
| 3 | In which the seven portraits hung; |
|   | the Artang of the Seven Climes. |
| 4 | Love for those hourî maids had cast |
|   | the seeds of love into his heart. |
| 5 | His furnace ceased its boilings seven |

when those elixirs* came to hand.
The first maid, of Kayânid stock 6
(whose father was no more), he sought
With countless gifts of greatest price, 7
and gained a pearl of his own race.
To the Khâqân his envoy sped, 8
and, mixing love with threats, conveyed
His wish: for daughter, treasure, crown, 9
and seven years' tribute. The Khâqân
Gave to him tribute, daughter, and 10
a load of gold, a hoard of gems.
Then, Turkish-wise, he raided Rûm, 11
and kindled fire throughout the land.
Fearful, the Qaysar tarried not: 12
his daughter gave, and pardon sought.
Then to the Maghreb's king he sent, 13
with Barbary gold, and crown, and throne,
And gained his daughter too; just see 14
what cleverness the king displayed!
When from that garden he obtained 15
that cypress, to India he went;
With reasoned words he sought and gained 16
the princess; his desire attained.
His envoy from Khwârazm did seek 17
a beauty worthy of a feast;
He wrote to Siqlab, seeking then 18
a beauty bright as water. When
He'd from the Seven Climes' rulers gained 19
those pearl-like beauties, then he turned
From worldly things, and pleasure sought; 20
did justice to good life and youth.

# 30

## How Bahrâm Feasted in Winter;
## The Building of the Seven Domes

One day, with victory's light aglow, 1
the sky unveiled its radiant brow—
Auspicious, brilliant, happy day! 2

for long may it remembered be!—

3   With sages learned and wise, the king
     arrayed a beauteous gathering.

4   The first of winter, 'twas a day
     for house, not for the garden's play.

5   The garden's blooming torches out;
     the gardeners' things all gathered up;

6   The crows had robbed the nightingales
     of song. 'Stop thief!' Their cries assailed

7   The garden. Crows black as Hindus be;
     no wonder they're, like Hindus, thieves.

8   The morning wind, a painter, limned
     upon the water, chain-like rings.

9   The burning cold outshone the fire,
     made water swords, the sun's blades water.

10  The snowstorm's lustrous file pierced eyes,
     and froze the springs to bitter ice.

11  Fermented milk became like cheese;
     the blood within the veins did freeze.

12  The hills wore ermine, earth did wear
     white robes; the sphere donned miniver.

13  Predators ambushed kine; tore off
     their skins to make themselves warm robes.

14  Plants huddled 'neath the earth; and all
     that grew, withdrew. The bi-coloured world,

15  By alchemy, had hid within
     the hearts of stones, fire's ruby flame.

16  Wise roses in the furnace hid,*
     crucible-clay above their heads.

17  Mercurial drops in streams had turned,
     layer on layer, to silver pure.

18  The winter chamber* of the king
     the four seasons' nature still maintained.

19  The scents of many rare perfumes
     made temperate the snowy wind.

20  Like elixir, its fruits and wines
     wakened the heart, and lulled the mind.

21  Sandal and aloes fed the fire,
     smoke-girt, like Hindus at their prayer:*

A fire which supported pleasure;              22
a mine of red Magian sulphur.

It seemed like blood that boiling had         23
congealed; or like silk steeped in blood.

Its jujubes were a nutty colour,              24
its mercury braised cinnabar.

A hollowed apple, rosy red,                   25
all stuffed with pomegranate seeds.

A rebel wakened from his sleep                26
and, washing, in red grape juice dipped.

Like ambergris that's dyed with pitch;        27
a brilliant sun all veiled in musk;

Darkness caught in light's throat; or else    28
a tulip sprung from houris' locks.

A fair Turk from Greek stock it seemed;       29
'The Joy of Hindus'* was its name.

The torch of Jonah, Moses' lamp,              30
the feast of Jesus, Abraham's

Rose garden.* Round it coals, like musk,      31
seemed like a shining mirror's rust.

One agate, one cornelian; like                32
a mine of rubies in the dark.

Upon its gems the eyes did feed:              33
like jacinth, yellow, blue, and red.

A blooming bride with sparks adorned,         34
embracing coal, amber-perfumed.

Gilt bridal tent and banquet hall:            35
one grenadine, one gold sandal.

Its yellow flame within the smoke             36
was golden treasure 'neath black snake.

Famed as both Hell and Paradise:              37
a Hell of heat, a Heaven of light.

A Hell for unbelievers; Heaven                38
to those who're to that Garden bound.

Hymned by Magian Zand; its priests,           39
like moths, had pledged their robes to it.

It made the frozen ice perspire:              40
alas! why should it be called Fire?

Above the fire, familiar friends,             41

doves danced, grey feathers poured on flames.

42  Around that silk-hung banquet house
    flew plump, ringed francolin and grouse.

43  The room more green than cypress shade;
    the wine more red than pheasant's blood.

44  The dove-grey sky rained from above
    its plump ring-doves, from them their blood:

45  In the crystal cups that wine was poured;
    say, frozen water with wet fire.

46  Beauties with wild-ass eyes drank there,
    and roasted joints of onager.

47  With his companions, King Bahrâm
    in regal fashion drank his wine.

48  Wine, sweetmeats, music, company,
    good friends, and confidants had he.

49  The rosy wine was cooked, all smiles,
    by living fire, like rose pastilles.

50  Sweet music made the brain grow warm,
    and hearts grew soft as wax therefrom.

51  Each worthy, from his store of wit,
    said something to his status fit.

52  When words had followed words, speech passed
    to one most eloquent: 'These heights',

53  He said, 'to which the king has soared;
    this just rule over which he's lord,

54  No one has known, not hid nor plain,
    in all the world, from any king.

55  Thanks to his blessed *farr*, we owe
    all to his most auspicious rule:

56  Security there is, and health;
    both straitened enemies and wealth.

57  Health, safety, and sufficiency:
    these true wealth, all else vanity.

58  With body clothed and belly full,
    what need for rubies or for pearls?

59  We, who have one like you as king,
    in having you have everything.

60  Would that, with this, there were a way
    to hide you from the Evil Eye:

That moving stars and turning sphere 61
might gaze on this good fortune here;
That joy's auspicious star not stray; 62
such pleasure not be swept away;
That the king might rejoice forever, 63
and wind not steal his store of pleasure.
The king should lead a happy life; 64
so be it, though we be sacrificed.'
When he had done, all there were stirred, 65
and gave their hearts unto his words,
Which drove away the icy storm, 66
and were approved by everyone.
There was with them a man of worth, 67
freeborn, upright, of noble birth,
Named Shîda, brilliant as the sun,* 68
who all things, black or white, adorned.
A master of design was he, 69
surveyor famed. Geometry,
Physics, astronomy: all these 70
were like wax in his hands. And he
A master-builder was as well, 71
and painted images with skill;
His brush and chisel, used with art, 72
stole Mânî's soul and Farhâd's heart
Away. Reason's apprentice he; 73
Simnâr had his first master been.
In Khavarnaq, at that rare task, 74
he'd helped his master. When he saw
The king, rejoicing, in that feast— 75
fluent of tongue, fire in his breast—
He kissed the ground and praised the king; 76
His homage done, he sat again,
And said, 'If the king give me leave, 77
I'll keep the Evil Eye away.
For I can weigh the sky, and know 78
the stars; my wit their work does show.
In painting, building, you would say 79
God's art inspires me. I will make
A likeness of the heavenly sphere, 80

that it not bring him harm; and nor,

81   While he dwells in earth's picture-house,
need he have fear of Heaven's stars.

82   He'll dwell protected all his life;
on earth he'll govern like the sky.

83   To do this, I will build for him,
like seven strong forts, seven fair domes,

84   Each of a different hue, and all
than hundred fanes more beautiful.

85   The king has seven idols fair;
each one a country's banner bears.

86   Each clime is firmly governed by
its sister planet. Every day

87   Within the week, as all know well,
is by one planet clearly ruled.

88   On such auspicious feast-days, let
him in a dome his pleasure seek;

89   Don robes of that dome's hue; drink wine
with the fair bride who dwells within.

90   If with my words the king complies,
he'll raise himself above the skies.

91   As long as life endures, he'll gain
enjoyment of his life.' The king

92   Replied to him: 'Were I to build
an iron-gated house of gold;

93   Yet, in the end, since all must die,
why go to all this trouble? Why

94   Build me these domes as you advise;
adorn a palace in such wise?

95   These are but castles of vain pleasure;
where is the house of the Creator?

96   Though I may praise them all, where should
I seek their Maker?' Then he said,

97   'I've erred in this; why should I speak?
The place of the Creator seek?

98   He, Whom in no place can we see,
in every place can worshipped be.'

99   He said these words, and then fell still,
his brain from this desire aboil.

For in Simnâr's design\* he'd seen          100
that which the seven brides explained.

And now those fairy-forms he held,          101
as, in his casket, priceless pearls.

These words had deeply moved the king;      102
he saw therein a secret scheme.

To answer them he did not haste,            103
but held his peace for several days.

When some days passed after these words,    104
he summoned Shîda to his court.

He bade him do as he'd proposed;            105
all necessary things disposed:

Prepared a treasure, readied goods,         106
that he might labour if he would.

Then for that work, upon a day              107
by Bahrâm's aspect\* graced, Shîda,

Who knew the stars' connections, bent       108
his mind to choose a fair portent;

On an ascendant fortunate                   109
the palace's foundations laid;

In two years such an Eden wrought           110
that men from Eden knew it not.

When the dome-builder with such skill       111
those precious Seven Domes had built,

The nature, ruling star, of each           112
was as Shîda had first decreed.

The king observed the seven spheres         113
joined hand in hand in love, and heard

How all men spoke, both near and far,       114
of Nu'mân's dealings with Simnâr;

How all wise men expressed their blame      115
that he that wondrous man had slain.

That Shîda might rejoice, he gave           116
all Amul to him; then he said,

'If Nu'mân sinned when he did wreak         117
injustice on a friend, I seek,

Through justice, pardon; though my deed's   118
not generous, nor was his, greed.

So does the turning world ordain:           119

| 120 | to one man loss, another gain.<br>One burns with thirst; another drowns<br>in water. Thus the world confounds |
| 121 | All men in their affairs; and they<br>no remedy but silence see.' |

# 31

## Description of the Seven Domes; How Bahrâm Took his Pleasure therein

| 1 | When Bahrâm raised Kayqubâd's crown,<br>and Kaykhusraw's, up to the moon, |
| 2 | In that realm he a palace built<br>that put to flight all Farhâd's skill; |
| 3 | In that seven-columned Bîsitûn<br>against the sky raised seven domes; |
| 4 | In those sky-joining ramparts reared<br>a rampart 'gainst the lofty sphere. |
| 5 | Within that fort, the Seven Domes<br>the seven planets' natures* owned. |
| 6 | The hue of each the star-knower weighed,<br>against each planet's cast assayed. |
| 7 | The dome of Saturn, as was fit,<br>was veiled in musky black; while that |
| 8 | Of Jupiter, just as it should,<br>received the hue of sandalwood. |
| 9 | The one that Mars encompassed clasped<br>red as its emblem; as for that |
| 10 | The Sun informed, bright bands of gold<br>made its hue yellow. That which hoped |
| 11 | For Venus-like adornment blazed<br>as bright and white as Venus' face. |
| 12 | That one sustained by Mercury<br>was turquoise-hued, like victory; |
| 13 | While that towards whose tower the Moon<br>went forth, was clad in verdant green, |
| 14 | Like Bahrâm's fortune. Thus were raised<br>those domes whose forms the planets gave. |

The Seven Climes to them were tied,    15
the seven princesses their brides.
Each one, in colour and in mode,    15a
had made one dome her own abode,
And everything within it made    16
the selfsame hue the dome displayed.
The happy king, day after day,    17
in one fair palace held his sway:
Saturday when that day's lot fell,    18
the others as was right and well.
When his wise judgement so ordained    19
that he should feast in any dome,
To drink his cup of wine, he'd don    20
robes the same colour as the dome.
The bride would sit with him therein,    21
displaying charms of every kind,
So that she might entrance the king,    22
and he her sweetness might consume.
She'd tell him tales that made love grow,    23
and fuelled the ardent heart. Yet though
He built him such a fortress, he    24
could not escape death finally.
Nizâmî, flee the rose garden:    25
its roses are but sharpest thorns.
In such a realm, a two-days' rest,    26
see what befell Bahrâm at last.

# 32

## How Bahrâm Sat on a Saturday in the Black Dome: The Tale of the Princess of the First Clime

When Bahrâm pleasure sought, he set    1
his eyes on those seven fair portraits;
On Saturday from Shammâsî temple went    2
in Abbasid black* to pitch his tent;
Entered the musk-hued dome, and gave    3
his greetings to the Indian maid.
Till night he there made merry sport,    4

burnt aloes-wood, and scattered scent.

5   When night in kingly fashioned spilled
black grains of musk on whitest silk,

6   The king from that Kashmiri spring
sought perfume like the dawn breeze brings:

7   That she might loose some women's words,
sweet stories, from her store of pearls,

8   Those tales for which all hearers long,
and soothe to sleep the drunken man.

9   That Turk-eyed, Hindu-born gazelle
loosed fragrant musk, her tale to tell.

10   Said she, 'May the king's fanfare play
above the moon's high throne; and may

11   He live as long as turns the world;
may all heads at his threshold bow.

12   May he gain all his wishes; may
his fortune never flag.' This prayer

13   Concluded, she bowed low, and loosed
from sugared lips sweet aloes-wood.

### The First Tale

14   She told (her eyes cast down in shame)
a tale unmatched by anyone:

15   When young, a kinswoman told me
(clever and quick of thought was she),

16   A lady of the palace—a place
like Paradise; she gentle, chaste—

17   Each month would come unto our house,
in robes of blackest silk all dressed.

18   'From what deep fear or dread', they asked,
'hide you your silvery form in black?

19   'Tis best you share your tale with us:
whiten this blackness; now, you must

20   Tell us, from your goodwill, the truth:
what means the marvel of this black?'

21   She, seeing no escape from truth,
said, 'Since you will not leave untold

22   The tale of this black silk, I'll give
the story, that you may believe.'

## The Lady's Tale

I served a certain king (now dead)—      23
said she—with whom I happy lived.

One great and fortunate, who kept      24
his flock in safety from the wolf.

He'd suffered much, and striven long,      25
and dressed in black from suffering wrong.

The sphere, at his unhappy fate,      26
called him 'The King Who Dressed in Black'.

The robes he used to wear at first      27
were red and yellow,* of great worth.

He, like the rose, of guests was fond,      28
smiled on them like the red rose-bud.

He kept a guest-house, well disposed,      29
which from earth to the Pleiads rose;

With feasts prepared and carpets spread,      30
servants to kind affection bred.

Whoso arrived was made to stay;      31
and he himself the host would play.

When they had laid a fitting feast,      32
and entertained him as was meet,

The king would ask the guest his tale,      33
of home and travels, good and ill.

Whatever wonders he had seen      34
he then recounted to the king.

In such wise the king spent his days      35
lifelong, and never changed his ways.

A while he vanished from our sight;      36
hid himself from us, Sîmurgh-like.

A while of him we had no news;      37
he hid, like the 'Anqâ, from view;

Then suddenly, one day, returned,      38
through Fortune's favour, to the throne.

Robe, crown, and shirt: his form was clad      39
from head to toe in black. He ruled

Wisely thereafter, ever dressed      40
in mourner's black, without a loss.

He dwelt in blackness, like the Stream      41

of Life; none asked, 'What does this mean?'

42     One night, with love and sympathy,
    I waited on that *qibla*; he

43     Reclined upon my lap; complained
    of what the stars had brought to him.

44     'See what a Turkish raid Heaven made;
    what games with such a prince it played.

45     It banished me from Iram's green;
    made my black lot* a legend seem.

46     None asked, "Where is that region? Why
    does black upon your silver lie?"'

47     I thought how best to answer; pressed
    my face against his feet, and said,

48     'O best of rulers, who supports
    all those who sorrow: who on earth

49     Has power to attempt the task
    of scraping Heaven with an axe,*

50     Seeking to know a hidden tale?
    you know it, you alone can tell.'

## The King of Black's Tale

51     When my lord found me worth his trust,
    he pierced his rubies, loosed his musk,

52     And said: Since I, in sovereignty,
    did practise hospitality,

53     All men I met, both good or ill,
    I'd ask each one to tell his tale.

54     One day a stranger came from the road;
    all black his turban, shoes, and robe.

55     When I'd seen to his needs, I then
    called him to me, and honoured him.

56     'O you whom I know not,' I asked,
    'why are your garments all of black?'

57     'Leave off this talk,' he said; 'for none
    knows where the Sīmurgh may be found.'

58     'Tell me,' I begged; 'make no excuse;
    tell me of pitch-pot and of pitch.'

59     'You must excuse me; this affair
    cannot be told,' the man declared.

'None knows the secret of this black,    60
save he who wears it on his back.'

I strengthened my cajolery    61
(both skilled in bargaining were we),

But nought could make him lift the veil;    62
my blandishments did nought avail.

When past all measure grew my pleas,    63
he grew ashamed at my unease,

And said, 'In China's land there lies    64
a realm adorned like Paradise.

Its name, the Land of Lost Wit-Lack;    65
the mourning-house of those in black.

Its folk, fair-featured as the moon,    66
all, like the moon, black silk put on.

Whoever feasts his eyes upon    67
that land, it makes him black robes don.

Whose fate lies there, his tale, unknown    68
though it may be, is wondrous strange.

Now, though you shed my blood for it,    69
I will not tell you more than this.'

He said this, and prepared to leave,    70
closing the door upon my need.

Thus, having lulled me with that tale,    71
the story-teller went away

From me; him gone, the tale unknown,    72
I feared I would go mad. Though on

And on about that tale I pried,    73
and played my pawn on every side,

His powerful queen did not allow    74
my king to take that castle.* Though

I tricked my mind with patience feigned,    75
within my heart no patience reigned.

Open and secret, all about    76
I asked, but no one told me ought.

Finally, I forsook my realm,    77
leaving a kinsman as its king.

Sufficient robes, with wealth and gems,    78
I took, to ease the anxious mind.

I long that city's name enquired;    79

I went, and found what I desired:

80 A town like Iram's garden decked,
where all a banner raised of musk.

81 As white as milk the face of each,
all dressed in garments black as pitch.

82 I settled in a house, and piled
therein my rich stuffs, bale on bale.

83 A year I sought that city's tale,
but none its secret would reveal.

84 When long the matter I had pondered,
an honest butcher I encountered,

85 A fair, refined, and gentle man
who spoke no ill of any one.

86 His goodness and sound judgement made
me seek a way to be his friend.

87 When I had met him, I prepared
ways to deceive him, unaware.

88 I gave to him abundant treasure,
and fresh-faced coinage without measure.

89 His worth I added to each day;
his iron with gold did overlay.

90 Him utterly my prey I made:
now silks bestowed, now silk-faced maids.

91 The butcher, at this golden shower,
was, ox-like, led unto the slaughter.

92 I so inveigled him with gold,
he groaned beneath that weighty wealth.

93 One day he took me to his house;
prepared a more than lavish feast.

94 He decked a tray, brought food, expressed
devoted service to his guest.

95 That feast contained all things required
except his guest's longed-for desire.

96 When we had sampled every plate,
we sat and talked of this and that.

97 The feast concluded, my good host
offered me countless precious gifts;

98 And all I'd given him he brought
before me, and my pardon sought.

'So many precious gifts', he said,    99
'no jeweller has ever weighed.

I'm happy with the slightest gain:    100
what cause on me these gifts to rain?

What recompense does this deserve?    101
declare it, so that I may serve.

I've but one life; but if it were    102
a thousand, it would still fall short.'

I said, 'What servitude is this;    103
what rawness? show more ripened wits.

In the scales of such a learned man,    104
what weight or worth has this humble one?'

Then to my well-trained, knowing slaves,    105
winking, a secret sign I gave,

To hasten to my private store    106
and bring back golden coinage pure.

I gave him, of that precious coin,    107
more than that which before I'd given.

He, heedless at the snare I'd laid,    108
abashed at my affection, said,

'My debt to you before this night    109
I have not managed to requite;

Once more you precious gifts bestow    110
which cause me shame; what may I do?

I have not laid your gifts here at    111
your feet, for you to take them back;

But such a treasure must be earned    112
through toil and effort. I was shamed

When you on treasure treasure heaped;    113
though you're content, I'm ill at ease.

If I can be of help, then say;    114
if not, take all your gifts away.'

When his support thus heartened me,    115
his friendship I could clearly see.

My lengthy tale I told to him:    116
about my kingship and my realm;

Why I had to this region come,    117
abandoning my royal throne,

That I might learn why all within    118

|       | this city suffer, without pain; |
| 119 | Why all, in sorrow, dress in black. |
|       | My words took the good man aback, |
| 120 | And, like the sheep who fears the wolf, |
|       | affrighted, he his silence kept. |
| 121 | A while he stood in mute alarm, |
|       | and closed his eyes as if in shame. |
| 122 | 'You've asked what is not right to say; |
|       | but I will tell you what I may.' |
| 123 | When night o'er camphor amber poured, |
|       | and men left their accustomed roads, |
| 124 | He said, ''Tis time you be apprised |
|       | of what you wish to know. Arise, |
| 125 | And I the secret will unveil; |
|       | the form of the unshown reveal.' |
| 126 | He said this; left the house, and led |
|       | me towards the way. He went ahead, |
| 127 | While I, the stranger, followed on; |
|       | with us there was no other man. |
| 128 | Fay-like, he bore me far from men, |
|       | and led me towards a ruined land. |
| 129 | When we that ruined place had reached, |
|       | like perîs we were veiled by it. |
| 130 | Tied to a rope, a basket lay; |
|       | he went and brought it quietly— |
| 130a | A rope around the basket bound: |
|       | a dragon, round snake's basket* wound— |
| 131 | And said, 'Sit here a while; display |
|       | yourself to Heaven and earth; this way |
| 132 | Perhaps you'll learn why those who lack |
|       | the will to speak, wear robes of black. |
| 133 | What good or bad remains concealed |
|       | nought but this basket can reveal.' |
| 134 | The basket looked to be quite sound; |
|       | I stepped into it and sat down. |
| 135 | The basket (once I settled there) |
|       | became a bird, took to the air. |
| 136 | By some strange trick of rings, it bore |
|       | me up to the ring-juggling sphere.* |

The man pulled the rope magically;　137
I, wretched, did rope-dancing try.
The rope stuck like a candle wick　138
to me; clung tight to my frail neck.
A captive by bad fortune bound,　139
the rope around my neck was wound,
And choked me. Fortune's donkey had　140
bolted, taking the rope. And though
That rope wound round my body tight,　141
it was my only thread of life.
A column stood there, rising high,　142
so tall one craned the neck to see.
The basket reached the column's top,　143
the rope its end; it fell from off
My neck, and helped to set me loose.　144
I cried aloud, but 'twas no use.
Above, below, I cast my eyes,　145
and found myself up in the skies.
On me the sky had cast a spell;　146
I, like it, hung aloft; that peril
Made me think that my life was o'er;　147
my eyes were blinded by my fear.
I dared not look above, and yet　148
lacked courage to look down; I shut
My eyes in terror; gave myself　149
to helplessness and dread. I felt
Repentance for that tale of mine,　150
and longed to see my home and kin.
That penitence brought me no gain　151
but fear of God and prayers to Him.
When some time passed, as there I stood　152
atop that lofty column, a bird
Of mountainous size alighted there,　153
and made me desperate with fear.
So huge from head to foot—a column,　154
you'd say, that from its place had fallen.
Wings like the branches of a tree,　155
feet like a throne's legs; massive beak,
Like a tall column in Bîsitûn,　156

mighty without, a cave within.

157  Examining itself, it scratched
continuously; each feather root

158  It scratched poured out, like oyster-shells,
a copious shower of shining pearls.

159  Each precious feather that it preened
scattered a musk-bag on the ground.

160  It went to sleep above my head;
like one who drowns I then despaired.

161  'If I should grasp his foot,' thought I,
'he'll clutch me to him like his prey;

162  If I stay here, this place is full
of peril both above, below.

163  That faithless man, unchivalrous,
has put me in this dreadful pass.

164  Why has he so tormented me,
rendered me helpless in this way?

165  Did my wealth lead him from the path,
that he's delivered me to death?

166  Better to grasp the bird's leg, and
escape this peril, if I can.'

167  At cock-crow, when the sun came up,
and birds and beasts all started up,

168  That great bird's heart was heated too;
it flapped its wings, and off it flew.

169  Trusting in God, I raised my hands,
and grasped its leg; it spread its wings,

170  Drew feet together, swift flew high,
and bore this earth-born to the sky.

171  From early morn until midday
I travelled, filled with great dismay.

172  When the sun's heat became intense,
and o'er our heads the sky had passed,

173  The bird then longed for cool and shade,
and, drifting slowly down, he made

174  His way, until he reached a spot
but a mere lance's throw to earth,

175  O'er ground as green as silk, with scents
of rose-water and ambergris.

I blessed that bird a hundredfold; 176
let go my grasp; like lightning fell,
With heart aflame, and came to rest 177
on tender flowers and soft grass.
A while I lay there where I fell, 178
my heart consumed with thoughts of ill;
Then, rested, gave thanks to my Lord, 179
and felt myself somewhat restored.
I looked around, myself again, 180
and scanned that place before, behind.
I saw a garden untouched by 181
the dust of men; its earth the sky.
A myriad flowers blossomed there, 182
its water sleeping, grass aware.
Each flower was of a different shade; 183
the scent of each for miles did spread.
The lassos of the hyacinths 184
bound up the tresses of the pinks.
Jasmine bit roses' lips; deep grass 185
silenced the flowering Judas-trees.
The dust was camphor, ambergris 186
the earth, sands gold, the stones all gems.
Streams flowed like rose-water, and hid 187
pearls and carnelians in their midst;
A spring from which our turquoise fort* 188
begged both its hue and lustre bright.
The fish in those bright streams did play 189
like silver coins in mercury.
Girt by a mount of emerald hue, 190
where cypress, pine, and poplar grew,
Its stones were all of rubies red, 191
its poplars with their colour dyed;
Sandal and aloes everywhere; 192
with them the breeze perfumed the air.
It seemed of hourîs' forms devised, 193
who taxes paid from Paradise.*
'Heart's-ease' its name by Iram given, 194
and by the turquoise sphere called Heaven.
I, finding it, was filled with joy, 195

like one who treasure-hoards puts by.

196   Its beauty left me all amazed,
and for its sake great God I praised.

197   All up and down I wandered it,
that garden that so soothed the sight;

198   I ate of its delicious fruits
and thanked God for its benefits.

199   At last, in joy, I rested me
beneath a cypress, like it free.\*

200   Till eve I moved not from my place,
nor would had I a thousand tasks.

201   I ate a little, slept a bit,
and always uttered thanks, as fit.

202   When night adorned itself anew—
put crimson by, took on kohl's hue—

203   A wind, more restful than a breeze
in spring, came and dispersed the dust

204   From the road. A spring-like cloud then passed
and sprinkled pearls upon the grass.

205   The road, thus swept and dampened down,
grew filled with idols like a shrine.

206   Far off I saw a myriad lights,
which made my patient calm take flight:

207   A world with radiant forms ashine,
all bred with grace, like fragrant wine.

208   Each idol fresh as early spring,
grasping another by the hand.

209   Their ruby lips, like tulips, shamed
the sugar-cane of Khuzistan.\*

210   Their limbs were decked with chains of gold;
their necks and ears wore lustrous pearls.

211   They kingly candles bore, which lacked
trimmers or smoke, or circling moths.

212   Graceful and charming, they advanced,
with myriad beauties. On their heads

213   Those hourî forms bore carpets, thrones
like those of Paradise. They then

214   Spread carpets, set up thrones, and stole
my patience quite away. A while

Went by; and then it seemed 215
as if a moon came down from Heaven.

A brilliant sun came from afar 216
whose light made Heaven disappear.

Those hourîs, perîs, round her were 217
like to a myriad morning stars.

A cypress she, those maids her mead; 218
they jasmine, she a rose of red.

Each maid a candle in her hand; 219
sugar and candles are well joined.*

The garden filled with cypress forms, 220
all brilliant jewels, with shining lamps.

That Fortune-favoured queen approached; 221
bride-like, sat on her royal couch.

When she sat down, the quiet world 222
was on all sides to turmoil stirred.

She sat a moment, then removed 223
her veil, and bent to doff her shoes.

A queen came forth from her palace dome, 224
Greek troops before, Ethiops behind.*

Her Greeks and blacks, like two-hued dawn, 225
set Ethiop troops 'gainst those of Rûm.

Narrow of eyes, not miserly; 226
others of earth, of pure light she.*

Rose-like she sat a while, head bowed, 227
and kindled fire throughout the world.

A while elapsed; she raised her head, 228
and to a maiden near her said,

'It seems to me an earthly wight 229
has trespassed here, without the right.

Rise, swiftly round this compass wind, 230
and bring whomever you may find.'

That perî-born maid rose, and, like, 231
a perî, flew to every side.

On seeing me she stood amazed, 232
then seized my hand in friendly wise.

'Arise,' she said; 'like smoke we'll go; 233
the queen of queens has ordered so.'

I added nothing to her words, 234

for I had hoped for them. I sped
235    Crow-like, with that peacock, and came
to the bride's throne. I hastened then
236    Towards her; humbly kissed the ground
before her—I, an earth-born man.
237    She said, 'Arise; 'tis not your place;
such servitude is but disgrace.
238    With such a loving host, the guest
should not have rind; the pith is best;
239    Especially a handsome friend,
by a skilled master duly trained.
240    Come to the throne, sit next to me;
Pleiads and Moon well-mated be.'*
241    'O angel-natured queen,' I said,
'do not speak thus to me, your slave.
242    No place for demons, Sheba's throne;
'tis fit for Solomon alone.'
243    'Make no excuses; 'tis no avail
to show a sorceress your wiles.
244    This place is yours, beneath your sway;
but you must sit and rise with me,
245    So that you may my secret learn,
enjoyment of my love to earn.'
246    'Your shade's your only peer,' I said;
'my crown is dust at your throne's foot.'
247    'Now by my head and life,' she cried,
'you must a while stay by my side.
248    You are my guest; and one must show
a worthy guest all honour due.'
249    Since I saw nothing but to serve,
I rose before her like a slave.
250    A servant kindly took my hand,
set me upon the throne, and then
251    Retired. Seated thereon, I saw
a moon, and seized it in my snare.
252    With sweetest blandishments she spoke
to me. Then she commanded that
253    A tray be brought, upon it heaped
more food than can be told. A feast

Those Paradisal treasures set,    254
whose foods diffused sweet amber's scent.

A turquoise tray, a ruby bowl,    255
which nourished both the eyes and soul.

Whatever fancy could conceive    256
the cook brought forth. When we had ceased

To eat hot victuals, and consume    257
fresh, cooling draughts, the minstrel came,

The sâqî passed the cup. Then mirth    258
could not excuse itself. Fair pearls

Unpierced, bored precious pearls of song,    259
as those maids sang of love. Dance then

Opened a square, a circle closed,    260
gave wings unto the feet of those

Who joined. Dancers like tapers stood    261
erect, with candles on their heads.

Then, when they rested from the dance,    262
against the wine they made advance.

The sâqî swiftly poured the wine;    263
it rent the barrier of shame.

I, strong with love, with wine's excuse,    264
behaved as one who's drunk too much;

That sweet-lipped one, in sympathy,    265
made no objection to my play.

Seeing her friendly towards my suit,    266
I fell like curls before her feet.

I kissed her hands; she cried, 'Desist!'    267
The more she begged, the more I kissed.

The bird of hope lit on the branch;    268
I thought my pleas would have a chance.

I sought, with kisses and with wine,    269
to make that precious beauty mine.

'My love,' said I, 'what will you? Fame    270
you surely have; what is your name?'

She said, 'A lissome Turk I am,    271
Turktâz the Beautiful my name.'

'In harmony and accord,' I said,    272
'our names are to each other wed.

How strange that Turktâz is your name,    273

for mine—Turktâzî—is the same.

274 Rise; let us make a Turkish raid;*
cast Hindu aloes on the flames.

275 Take life from the Magian cup;
with it, on lovers' sweetmeats sup.

276 We've sweetest fruits and bitter wine;
let's serve the fruits, take wine in hand.'

277 Her glances, actions, gave me leave
all distance 'tween us to remove.

278 Her glance said, ''Tis your time to play;
come; Fortune smiles on you this day.'

279 Her smiles encouraged me to seek
sweet kisses, for my love was weak.

280 Admitted to that treasure-trove—
I sought one, she a thousand gave—

281 I warmed as one who's drunk with wine,
clasped tight my love (things out of hand).

282 My blood boiled in my heart; the sound
soon reached the ears of that fair moon.

283 She said, 'Make do with kisses now'
tonight; strive not for any more.

284 Beyond this nothing is allowed;
true lovers should show gratitude.

285 Caress my curls while you are calm;
steal kisses, bite my lips; but when

286 You reach the moment when you can
no more from nature turn the reins,

287 From all these maidens—each a moon,
the dawn of lovers' night—she whom

288 You find most pleasing to your sight,
and on her your desire lights,

289 Bid me detach her from my band,
and bring her under your command,

290 That she may serve you lovingly
within a private chamber; be

291 Both bride and servant; steal your heart
and give you hers; with loving art

292 Put out your burning flame, and seem
like coolest water from my stream.

If, the next night, you should require 293
a new bride, I'll grant your desire;

Each night bestow a precious pearl, 294
and yet another, if you will.'

Her speech done, she then treated me 295
with kindness and with sympathy.

She looked covertly at her maids; 296
that one who gifts of love displayed

She summoned, gave to me with love; 297
'Rise, and do what you will,' she said.

That moon, thus given, took my hand; 298
I at her moon-like beauty stunned.

With charm, seductiveness, and grace, 299
she was for love a worthy mate.

She went; I followed, by her curls 300
enslaved, and by her Hindu mole,

Until we reached a chamber fair; 301
she waited, while I went before.

Once in that private palace, we 302
accorded like sweet harmony.

I saw, upon a high-placed couch, 303
a sleeping-place of finest silks.

Bright candles on the carpet shone, 304
with amber smoke and ruby flame.

We laid us down, embracing, on 305
the pillow; clasping her, I found

A harvest like red roses in 306
white willows, slender, soft, and warm.

She was a shell whose door was sealed; 307
I took the seal from her jewel.

She lay with me till morning's dusk, 308
my bed all camphor and sweet musk.

At dawn she, like my fortune, rose, 309
prepared my bath; an ewer brought

For me to wash, all set about 310
with gold, and crimson gems. I washed

Myself in rose-water, and bloomed 311
just like the rose, in belt and crown.

Out of that treasure-house I came; 312

the stars were scattered o'er the heavens.

313   I crept into an empty spot,
  and offered up my thanks to God.

314   Those idols, brides of Turkestan,
  had all departed, every one.

315   Exhausted, like a yellowed rose,
  by a cool spring, on meadow's grass,

316   Wine-dazed, I laid my head upon
  dried roses, with moist curls. From dawn

317   To dusk I slept, my fortune yet
  awake, the lord asleep, content.

318   When musk was loosed by night's gazelle,
  the musky sphere was filled with pearls.

319   I raised my head from languorous dreams,
  and sat, like verdure, next the stream.

320   That cloud, that breeze, came as before:
  one scattered pearls, one perfume bore.

321   The breeze did sweep, the cloud did shower;
  one jasmine sowed, violets the other.

322   When amber-scented grew the plain,
  it filled with sweet rose-water streams.

323   The sportive maids again drew near;
  the sky became a puppeteer.*

324   They brought a throne—a slab of gold,
  its covering with jewels made.

325   When that high couch had been arrayed,
  and on it silken carpets laid,

326   A royal feast was then set out,
  and with bright lights was decked about.

327   The world was in a tumult; from
  all sides those beauteous maids did come;

328   That Turkish bride was in their midst,
  who patience stole from lovers' hearts.

329   She settled on that golden throne;
  from her it took the hue of spring.

330   Again, she bade them find me; clear
  my name from the roll of those not there.

331   I came; they bade me mount the throne,
  and, as their custom, sit thereon.

Then, like the day before, they laid 332
a tray with food upon it, spread
With victuals to delight the heart, 333
a worthy feast, which joy imparts.
They did all that was fitting; then, 334
when all had finished eating, wine
Was brought; they played the harp, and smote 335
the strings with sweet and loving blows.
Sweet cupbearers, refreshing wine: 336
love's market grew increasing warm.
Intoxication filled the brain 337
as love and wine worked hand in hand.
My Turk was merciful; displayed 338
compassion to her Hindu slave.
Her wish to favour me increased; 339
her kind attentions never ceased.
With glances at her friends she signed, 340
until they left us quite alone.
Such privacy, a love so fine: 341
my heart's hot fire assailed my brain.
Like twisting curls I grasped her waist, 342
and lover-like my love embraced.
'Beware; 'tis not the moment now 343
for hastiness, or breaking vows,'
She said; 'enough my sugared lips, 344
that you may freely bite and kiss.
For he who's with contentment pleased 345
will ever find a life of ease;
But he who makes desire his friend 346
will be a beggar in the end.'
'For God's sake find some remedy,' 347
I cried; 'I drown; pain pierces me.
Your pitch-black curls are twisting chains, 348
and I a madman bound by them.
Chain up your door, I tell you, lest, 349
like madmen, I should lose my wits.
The night is over; dawn is near; 350
but there's no end to this affair.
Slay me; my life is yours; my head 351

is here, and there the sharpened blade.

352 But why all this resistance feign?
The rose smiles not before the rain.

353 I seek the water of your stream;
though earth, sweet perfumed water bring.

354 To him who thirsts, by your love bound,
give water, and he'll do the same.

355 But if you won't—live long, and see
my honour dust beneath your feet.

356 Think me a clod by water borne;
a thirsting man drowned in the stream.

357 Let not an atom thirst, but give
a drop to one who thirsts. Believe

358 Me but a date that's drowned in milk,
a needle* in the midst of silk.

359 If it be other, I shall rise
and cast dust in desire's eyes;

360 Think it a bird which lit and flew,
and not an ass which lost its load.'

361 She answered, 'Be content tonight,
e'en though love's flame be burning bright.

362 Put off this fancy for a night,
and you will gain eternal light.

363 Don't sell the well for a mere drop;
one sting, the other honey sweet.

364 On this one craving shut your door,
and laugh with joy forever more.

365 Take kisses, and caress my curls,
but play your game with other girls.

366 Don't seek to leave; the garden's yours;
don't seek milk from the captured bird.

367 You've pleasure and enjoyment; why
then turn your hand to treachery?

368 Tonight be patient; do not fight,
but seek the duty of last night.

369 When I descend from this degree,
I will be won, though late it be.

370 Each garden's rose-bud boasts a shield;
but different the carnation's field.

From the sweet water you will gain 371
a fish; later, the moon obtain.'

Finding her slow that game to play, 372
I calmed myself, feigned to agree.

I set my heart on kisses sweet, 373
and fasted from all other meat.

In amorous vein I quaffed the wine; 373*a*
patiently watched the heated pan.

By wine and kisses sweet renewed, 374
again my fevered passion grew.

When my fair Turk saw once again 375
my heart consumed by blazing flame,

She with another maid conspired 376
to quench the flames of my desire:

A mate such as the heart might wish 377
(the heart wills all in measure fit).

Who finds his love's a happy man; 378
may every love be like that one.

I went that night, like that before; 379
that night my joy was even more.

I supped on sugar sweet till dawn; 380
with that fay-maiden joined my hand.

When day had bleached its robe to white 381
and night, that dyer, broke its pot,

Those colours which bewitched the sight 382
forsook the carpet of delight.

I sat beneath a cypress tree, 383
no confidant or company,

Hoping that when night came again 384
I'd drink with those fair maids of Chîn;

Wind Turkish tresses round my waist; 385
clasp a sweet charmer to my breast;

Now drink a cup with lips full sweet; 386
now gain my wish from rose-red cheeks.

When night fell my desire was met, 387
my throne above the Pleiads set.

For some while more, with lute and wine, 388
each night unending joys were mine:

Gazing on light as night began, 389

a hourî with me at its end.

390   By day I in the garden dwelled,
by night in Paradise, mid soil

391   Of musk, a golden house; I reigned
over the clime of joy; the sun

392   I held by day, at night the moon;
lacked for no wish; my fortune e'en

393   Was as it showed. Yet since I was
ingrate, for blessings in excess,

394   Joy's words I from my pages washed,
for I sought more than more. At last

395   When thirty nights the moon had seen,
night covered up the stars, and turned

396   The world to black; Heaven's amber locks
grasped the moon's curls in fond embrace.

397   That cloud and breeze which came before
their fresh appearance made once more.

398   Again the world their tumult stirred;
the sound of ornaments was heard;

399   And as before those maidens' hands
held apples; pomegranates their breasts.

400   They came, set up that throne, then formed
a circle, and gave voice to song.

401   That sun-like moon came too; her locks
poured o'er her breast, and scattered musk.

402   Candles before, behind, as ere
her wont; nay, candles came before.*

403   With all her beauties, charm and grace,
she went unto her feasting-place.

404   The minstrels tuned their instruments,
the singers on their songs intent.

405   The cupbearers, to the harp's strain,
began to pour the crimson wine.

406   Their queen those sweet-lipped beauties bade,
'Go, quickly bring to me my mate.'

407   Those beauties led me gracefully,
and to my queen delivered me.

408   Seeing me bent on love, she rose,
and set me on her right; I bowed,

409   And greeted her with joy; and then

my past wish came to mind again.

They laid the accustomed feast, and brought 410
rare dishes beyond count. We ate

Our fill of that fine fare. Then wine 411
arrived to make the banquet shine.

The sâqîs' generous hands poured pearls 412
(wine's bubbles) from the mouths of shells.

Wine flowed like song, and sweeter than 413
the honeyed syrup of Nihavand.*

Drunken with passion, once again 414
I took her rope-like curls in hand;

Again my demons 'scaped their bonds, 415
and me, the madman, firmly bound.

I, spider-like, played with her locks, 416
and learned that night rope-dancing tricks;

Mad as an ass for grain; struck down 417
in fits, as if by the new moon.

A-tremble like a thief who spies 418
a treasure-hoard, I clasped her waist;

Caressed pure silver; passion grew 419
more hard to bear, I weak. She saw

My state—that beauteous moon—and placed 420
her hand on me with love, then kissed

My hand—cruel hourî!—so that I 421
would take it from the treasure. 'Ah,'

She said; 'touch not the treaure sealed; 422
the grasping hand will miss the goal.

One cannot take the seal away 423
that guards the mine; it cannot be.

The date-tree's yours; now patient wait, 424
and do not haste to reach the dates.

Drink wine; the roast will come anon. 425
The sun will rise; regard the moon.'

'Sun of my garden, source (said I) 426
of light, light-giver to my eyes:

Your face's morn like roses blooms; 427
my own light fades, by yours consumed.

You show sweet water to a youth 428
who thirsts; then tell him, "Close your mouth;

Drink not!" Sweet reason, at the sight 429

of your fair face, goes mad, fay-struck.

430    When you display your pearl-hung ear,
you cast my iron\* in the fire.

431    Can I resist the moon's night raid?
Or with a mote the bright sun shade?

432    How stay my hand, when you are here?
I know no grief when you are near.

433    You are earth-born, and so am I;
but I'm a man, if you're a fay.

434    How long, then, bite my kips in pain,
and swallow disappointment? Find

435    Some way—for grief o'erwhelms me—that
I gain my heart's desire tonight.

436    Support my fortune; let us work
together; make me fortunate.

437    You say, "Grieve not; I am your friend;
continue; I will be yours soon."

438    When was there a calamity
like this? I need you! Set me free!

439    O fair gazelle I hold so dear:
how long false promises? I fear

440    That ancient wolf, with fox-like wiles,
will soon his nature base reveal;

441    Attack me as one would a lion,
and fell me like a leopard. I'm

442    Impassioned with you; let me now
obtain what I desire from you.

443    If you against my love shut tight
the door, I'll be consumed tonight.

444    Indulge me, for sultans and kings
indulge their guests in everything.'

445    Seeing my patience once more fled,
'I *shall* do; stay your hand,' she said.

446    'I'll favour you, at life's own cost;
if you're a Turk, I am your black.

447    What matter if I sacrifice,
for such a guest, my humble life?

448    But that desire for which you long:
you'll find it late, but seek it soon.

When Paradise grows from a thorn, 449
by me shall such a deed be done;
When sandal scent from willow comes, 450
then shall I such an act perform.
Take from me what you will, save that 451
one wish, which has not ripened yet.
My lips, my cheeks, my breast: all yours; 452
save one pearl, all my treasure's hoard.
If you're content with this, you'll gain 453
a thousand nights like that to come.
Now that your heart's inflamed by wine, 454
I'll give a sâqî like the moon,
That you may take your pleasure's fee 455
from her, and loose your grasp from me.'
But that fair queen's beguiling words 456
I heeded not, although I heard.
I strove a while for calm and shame, 457
my fire ablaze, my iron aflame.
'You fool,' my fortune said; '*beyond* 458
*this Abadan there is no town*.'*
Thus I, unripe, from seeking more, 459
fell into less.—I still implored,
'O you who make things hard for me, 460
who've stolen all my peace away:
Thousands of men have died of love, 461
when none has found the treasure-trove.
How shall I stay my hand, who've gained 462
this treasure, though I suffer pain?
While I have breath, I have no power 463
to stay my hand from your dark hair.
Kindle my lamp upon this throne, 464
or nail me like a plank thereon.
Rise up upon the mat* and dance, 465
or shed my blood upon this place.
My heart and life, my wit and sight: 466
how can I live without you? Might
I, heart-enslaver, gain my goal, 467
I'd give my life for it. For who
Would not buy such a hoard for nought, 468

nor pay for such desire with life?

469    Your honeyed lips aren't marred by flies;
no thorns surround your rose-like face.

470    Who would not eat rose-honey sweets?
Let him who would not, never eat!

471    Now kindle me like candle's flame,
since like a lamp I burn with pain.

472    Lamp-like I burn; love gives me life,
else I would perish from love's spark.

473    For if the blazing sun did not
revolve, mankind would lack for light.

474    'Tis not my own desire I seek;
'tis but a dream of which I speak.

475    No doubt my brain's asleep. What then?
Dead or asleep, 'tis all the same.

476    But had my eyes your face not seen,
how would they then have known such dreams?

477    Be quick, if you would shed my blood,
for speed's required for such a deed.'

478    Then, blood aboil and brain afire,
I set upon that blossom rare.

479    I quickly grasped the treasure's door,
its ruby with jacinth to bore.

480    With sweet lament she, patient, sought
a brief respite; I listened not.

481    'The treasure shall be yours,' she swore;
'tonight hope, tomorrow your desire.

482    Since, in your suit, you've borne this plight
from day to day and night to night,

483    Tonight make do with hope of treasure;
tomorrow night you'll take your pleasure.

484    To wait one night you can endure;
'tis but one night, and not a year.'

485    She spoke; but I, like dagger honed,
clasped tight her waist, and blindly clung—

486    Her plea but whetted my desire
for her a hundredfold, and more—

487    Until my quickly grasping hand
prevailed upon that close-tied band.

When she perceived my harshness, my 488
impatience, my anxiety,

'A moment close your eyes,' she said, 489
'till I unlock the sugared hoard.

When I disclose that which you prize, 490
embrace me; open then your eyes.'

I, at her sweet pretext, shut fast 491
my eyes against her treasure. At last,

After a brief respite, she said, 492
'Open your eyes,' and so I did,

Prepared at last to seize my prey, 493
to clasp that bride in my embrace.

But when I looked towards my bride, 494
I found me in that basket tied,

No man nor woman near; alone, 495
my sole companion sighs and groans;

Without light's radiance, like a shade, 496
a Turk, far from that Turkish raid.

Thus troubled, 'neath the column I felt 497
the basket give a sudden jolt.

My friend came and unloosed the rope 498
which bound my basket to that vault.

My fortune, sated with this game, 499
brought down my basket to the ground.

He who'd avoided me, and fled, 500
embraced me and, repentant, said,

'A hundred years I might have told 501
this tale; you'd not have grasped its truth.

You went and saw what was concealed; 502
to whom could it have been revealed?

I too from that hot passion burned, 503
and dressed in black at being wronged.'

I said, 'Like me, you've been oppressed; 504
I find that your decision's best.

I, wronged, in silence, have no choice 505
but to wear black; go now, and fetch

Black silks.' He went, and quickly brought 506
the very blackness of the night.

I donned those silken robes of black; 507

     began that night the journey back,
508  And, mantled all in black, returned,
     heart filled with sorrow, to my land.

509  Thus I, who am the King of Black,
     like black clouds now bewail my lack:
510  That my desire, so nearly gained,
     was, through my rawness, unattained.

                    ❧

511  When my lord had his tale revealed,
     and told me that which was concealed,
512  I, who was but his concubine,
     made that which he had chosen mine.
513  With Sikandar, to mourn the lack
     of Life's bright Stream, I entered black.

                    ❧

514  The moon in blackness shines forth bright,
     king-like, 'neath parasol of night.*
515  There is no better hue than black;
     fish-bone's less prized than fish's back.*
516  Black hair's a sign of youth; and down
     of black the youthful face adorns.
517  The eye's black pupil views the world,
     and robes of black are never soiled.
518  The moon—if night's fine silks weren't black—
     would a fit bridal chamber lack.
519  Seven colours 'neath the seven thrones:
     no colour beyond black is known.*

                    ❧

520  When to Bahrâm the Indian maid
     her tale in full had thus displayed,
521  The king upon her words rained praise;
     embraced her; slept in joyful ease.

## 33

### How Bahrâm Sat on a Sunday in the Yellow Dome: The Tale of the Greek King's Daughter

1    When morning's scales had filled with gold
     the mountain's collar, the plain's robe,

On Sunday, like the sun, the world-　　　　2
illuming lamp was veiled in gold.

He grasped a golden cup, like Jam;　　　　3
sun-like, a golden crown put on,

And bound on, like the yellow rose,　　　　4
his signet ring, amber and gold.

Towards the gold dome, scattering gold,　　　5
he went; his joy grew hundredfold.

He joy's foundation laid with wine　　　　6
and music's strains; and when night came—

Not night; love's bridal chamber, veil　　　7
of lovers, by its dark concealed—

He bade that sugar-scattering torch　　　　8
join ruby lips to sweet discourse,

And make, from the sweet strains of song,　　9
sweet music in that golden dome.

Swiftly to his command she bowed　　　　10
(excuses do not please the proud).

The Chinese-adorned bride of Rûm　　　　11
said, 'Lord of Rûm, Taraz, and Chîn,

Ruler of kings, who give them life;　　　　12
exalted be your victory.

The heads of those who serve you not　　　13
are trodden 'neath your mighty foot.'

When she had paid her homage meet,　　　14
she made her breath as incense sweet.

## The Tale of the Slave-Selling King

She said: A town in Iraq's land　　　　15
boasted a world-illuming king,

A brilliant sun, without a peer,　　　　16
as beautiful as spring's New Year.

All skills which can be reckoned up;　　　17
all the accomplished man might hope

To have, he had; and with all that,　　　18
with solitude he was content.

For in his horoscope he'd read　　　　19
he'd dwell in conflict if he wed;

Because of this he sought no wife,　　　20
so that he might not suffer strife.

21  So for a while he dwelt alone
    in solitude; was close to none.

22  To ease his pain, he hoped to find
    a loving maid who suited him.

23  Though many lovely slaves he bought,
    none served him in the way he sought.

24  Within a week or so, each one
    o'erstepped her limits, and put on

25  Fine airs, like ladies, asking for
    the treasures of Qârûn,* and more.

26  The palace held a hunchbacked crone
    who baited fools; a stupid woman.

27  Each slave the king might buy, that crone
    found idle talk worked to her gain.

28  Each newly purchased maid she'd hail
    as 'Rûmî queen' and 'Turkish belle',

29  And so increased that maiden's pride
    that she from service turned aside.

30  How many meddlers have their friends
    thus taught their masters to disdain.

31  She called one maiden 'David's spouse',
    another one, 'Mahmûd's Ayâz'—*

32  A jewel-bedizened mangonel,
    who ruined homes, and wives beguiled.

33  Despite the efforts of the king,
    no maid would keep her place; each one

34  For whom he'd sewn love's garment, lacked
    true love; and so he'd sell her back.

35  So many slaves he bought and sold,
    that he 'the slave-dealer' was called.

36  All judged the matter from without,
    and no one knew the inner truth.

37  From searching long the king grew tired;
    burned at not finding his desire.

38  He married not, from hostile fate,
    nor could he find a fitting mate.

39  He washed his hands of those whose skirts
    were tainted; a pure beauty sought.

40  One day, the slave-trader informed

the king's slave-buyer: 'There has come
A merchant from fair-templed Chîn,      41
a thousand hourîs in his train.

With many fair and untouched slaves      42
from Turkish Khallukh and Cathay.

Each face a candle world-illuming,       43
inspiring love, lovers consuming.

Among them is a fay-like maid            44
who puts the bright sun in the shade:

An unpierced pearl, this slave, whose price   45
this pearl-seller would set at life.

Her coral lips enclose fair pearls;      46
she's sharp of answer, sweet of smile.

When from her smile she sugar pours,     47
she makes the earth grow sweet for years.

Although her tray is full of sweets,     48
it sorrow brings to him who eats.

I, who pursue this trade, am dazed       49
by those dark curls, that mole, that face.

If you that beauty and allure           50
observe, you'll praise it too, I'm sure.'

The dealer was enjoined to bring         51
those slaves to that slave-knowing king.

He brought them; the king looked them over,   52
and then conversed with the slave-seller.

Though each was lovely as the moon,      53
she who was told of was a queen;

She was more lovely to the eyes          54
than all the informant had described.

The king said to the dealer, 'Say,       55
what is the nature of this maid?

If I should find her fitting, name       56
your price.' The Chinese merchant then

Unleashed his tongue: 'This fresh young maid,   57
with lips of honey, has,' he said,

'As you can see, all you require         58
of looks and charm, and sparks desire.

She's but one fault, and it is grave:    59
he who would bed her, she'll not have.

60   Whoever buys her, filled with joy,
        returns her to me the next day;

61   For when he seeks to slake desire,
        she brings the lover to despair;

62   And he who most importunes her
        soon seeks his own destruction. For

63   Her nature can't be pleased; and you
        (as I have heard) are like that too.

64   She thus, you thus—forget her; how
        could this work out, things being so?

65   Say that you've bought her from me, and,
        like others, given her back. Refrain

66   From buying her; that's best; and see
        which other girl best suits your need.

67   Whoever pleases you, I'll send
        at once (no charge) to your harem.'

68   Of all those perî-maids the king
        observed, he wanted to buy none;

69   Except that first maid, fairy-faced,
        his heart to none became attached.

70   He stood amazed: what should he do?
        how play the game with one so raw?

71   Nor was he tired of her, nor could
        he boldly buy her, with that fault.

72   At last love turned his head, and threw
        dust in the eyes of patience; so

73   He paid her price in silver; gained
        with silver coins those silver limbs.

74   On one desire the door he barred;
        the snake slew, was from dragon freed.

75   Within his harem, that fair maid
        did honest service for her lord.

76   A tender rose-bud she resembled;
        with harsh demean her love dissembled.

77   Save intimacy, whose door she closed,
        she shirked no service: kept the house,

78   Preserved the harem's trust; with kind
        concern, ordered all one by one;

Though by the king like cypress raised, 79
she served him humbly as his shade.

That ancient crone her wiles arrayed, 80
and sought to bend that supple reed.

She cried out 'gainst that wicked crone 81
to call her nought but slave. The king,

Seeing her protest, grasped full well 82
the matter of the other girls.

He drove the woman from the place; 83
enmeshed in spells that sorceress.

So dear to him did grow that maid 84
that by her love he was enslaved.

Although her Turkish wiles enflamed, 85
he kept his passion tightly reined.

Until one night it so transpired 86
that both of them by love were fired.

the king lay by that lovely's side; 87
of furs and silks their couch was made.

Her fort was girt by watery moat, 88
his mangonel was fired up hot.

When sharp flames heated the king's blood, 89
he said to that moist-petalled rose,

'My luscious date, my own soul's eye, 90
my own eyes' life: the cypress tree

Next to your stature is like grass; 91
the moon draws water for your face.

I make but one request of you: 92
that what I ask, you'll answer true.

If your reply is—like your height— 93
upright, I too will deal aright.'

Then, for that purpose, sugared words 94
from lips fresh as the rose he poured.

'Bilqîs, like Venus in sextile,* 95
sat once with Solomon. In all

The world they but one son possessed, 96
crippled in hand and foot, helpless.

"O prophet-king," said Bilqîs; "both 97
of us are sound from head to foot.

98    Why is our son afflicted so,
      his limbs unsound? Someone must know

99    A remedy for his great pain;
      when known, a cure can be obtained.

100   When Gabriel descends to bring
      some message, tell the tale to him;

101   When he returns, he may discern
      the secret from the Tablet.* Then,

102   When he has found the cause, he'll show
      the remedy, my king, to you.

103   Perhaps this child will once again
      be sound; his former health regain."

104   Solomon with these words was pleased;
      he waited, hoping, for some days.

105   And then, when Gabriel spoke with him,
      he told his wish. The angel went;

106   Returned, with tidings of good cheer,
      from Him Who made the azure sphere.

107   He said, "Two things provide the cure;
      and those two things are very dear:

108   That when your wife sits with you, both
      must to each other speak the truth.

109   From speaking truth (you must believe)
      the child's pain will be relieved."

110   Bilqîs rejoiced these words to hear:
      the house would prosper with an heir.

111   She said, "Ask what you will of me,
      that I may answer truthfully."

112   That lamp of life enquired of her,
      "Fair one, of all eyes cynosure:

113   Did ever you desire to lie
      with any in the world but me?"

114   Bilqîs replied, "The Evil Eye
      be far from you! who far outshine

115   The sun's bright fount. In beauty, youth
      and rank, all others you outdo.

116   Good nature, lovely face, and kind;
      Heaven your feast, and you Rizvân.*

117   You rule o'er all, both hid and clear;

your prophet's Seal protects the world.
Despite all this—your youth, fair face,     118
your sovereignty, and your success—
Whenever I a young man see,     119
from base desires I am not free."
When the child heard this secret told,     120
he˙stretched his hand to her, and said,
"Mother, my hand is cured; no more     121
will I depend on others' care."
When she looked on her child and saw     122
that her truth had his strength restored,
She said, "O lord of dîv and fay,     123
like wisdom skilled, like virtue fair:
Before the child some secret show;     124
he's hands from me; give legs from you.
I'll ask (don't take my words amiss):     125
With all the treasures you possess,
Does ne'er the longing you assail     126
to wish for someone else's wealth?"
The pious prophet said, "What none     127
in all the world possess, I own:
Wealth, treasure, and unequalled reign;     128
all these I have, from Fish to Moon.
Yet, with such perfect wealth, when I     129
see someone come to honour me,
I secretly glance at his hands,     130
to see what gifts he bears in them."
The child (this tale once truly told)     131
then moved his legs; rose from the ground;
Cried, "Father, see: my legs can move;     132
your judgement's let me grace the world."
Since truthfulness within God's shrine*     133
thus banished from those limbs all pain,
'Tis best therefore that we too be     134
truthful, and shoot straight at the prey.
Tell me, O peerless lover, why     135
has your love grown so cold, when I
Suffer so greatly from desire,     136
yet look on you but from afar?

137    Why, with such beauty, have you grown
       accustomed to aversion?'

138    The supple cypress by the pool
       approved no answer but the truth.

139    She said, 'Our humble race has found
       a quality which each one owns:

140    Whoever gives a man her heart
       dies at the time of giving birth.

141    Since any woman dies who bears,
       how should we give in to desire?

142    Why give up life for pleasure; eat
       poison in honey? Far more sweet

143    Is life to me, than that I give
       it up to what endangers it.

144    I love life, not a lover; now
       I've laid my secret bare for you.

145    Now that the mystery's revealed,
       keep me or sell me, as you will;

146    But since I've not concealed my mind,
       and told you of my case, I find

147    Some hope that you, world-ruling king,
       will not hide from me anything:

148    Why do you tire, year after year,
       of slave-girls than the sun more fair;

149    Why do you give your heart to none?
       Spend not a month with any one?

150    Treat one with great care like a lamp,
       and, candle-like, snuff out again;

151    Raise one in love and ease to Heaven,
       then cast her down to earth again?'

152    'This is because no one (said he)
       has breathed a word of love to me.

153    All cared but for their own affairs;
       were bad, though they appeared so fair.

154    Grown used to ease, they then forsook
       the yoke of service. Each one's step

155    Matches his height; not all can eat
       hard bread; one needs a stomach made

Of iron, that its mill may grind                    156
all that it eats. A woman, when
She sees a man who's open, spins                    157
a plan for both herself and him.
Don't trust a woman; she's a straw                  158
the wind bears any way it will.
When she sees gold, like scales she'll tilt         159
towards one who is of lesser worth.
For when the pomegranate's full,                    160
it's ripe with rubies, not with pearls;
Woman's like grapes, a child so pure,               161
white when raw, black when mature.
A household's women are called gourds;              162
they're raw when ripe, and ripe when raw.
A woman chaste her mate adorns;                     163
the dark night, when it finds the moon,
Is beautiful. From all my maids                     164
I witnessed nought but self-display.
In you I see that, now and then,                    165
you show more than your task demands.
Thus, though you won't fulfil me, yet              166
without you I can find no rest.'
The king loosed several subtle shafts              167
like this at her; none hit the mark.
The saucy girl clung fast to her                   168
excuse; his arrows ever erred.
So he continued to traverse,                       169
burdened by grief, that stony pass.
Thirsting before sweet water, he                   170
was patient, and the days sped by.
The old crone, whom the kingly maid                171
had put out of the palace, heard
The tale: the patient king had found               172
no way to her for whom he longed;
And how that newly ripened lass                    173
had made that strong man powerless.
She thought, 'My time has come; perchance          174
I'll lead that fay a demon's dance;

175     Effect a breach in the sun's throne,
       destroy the fortress of the moon;

176     So that no more will a straight shaft
       strike an old woman's bow-like back.'

177     Witch-like, she sought to see the king
       in private; used her wiles on him.

178     In vengeance 'gainst that radiant sun
       she cast her spell upon the king;

179     Said, 'If you wish that untamed colt
       beneath your saddle not to bolt,

180     Saddle a tame mount twice or thrice
       before her; stroke it gently; thus

181     Horse-tamers who break colts can bring
       wild mounts to bridle, bit, and rein.'

182     This seemed a clever trick to him;
       the bricks made in her mould showed sound.

183     He bought a witty, graceful girl,
       with lips like honey, wondrous skilled

184     In sport, in harem ways well trained,
       and from birth one by nature tame.

185     Her clever and flirtatious ways
       showed in each game an artist's grace.

186     The king feigned love for her, and cast
       his lance with great pretence and craft.

187     In love for one he case his hook;
       at time of need the other took;

188     Dallied with one, with the other slept;
       here pierced a pearl, and there his heart.

189     He thought this way to gain his will,
       and pierce at last the unbored pearl.

190     Though the king's plan had cast the dust
       of jealousy on that moon's face,

191     She did not loyal service quit,
       nor change from what she'd been a whit.

192     'What art is this?' she thought; 'this storm
       was cooked up* by that aged crone.'

193     But patiently she held her peace
       (patience in love brings no increase),

194     Until one night, in private, she

could seize her chance. Then, lovingly,
She said, 'O angel prince, who rule            195
the realm with faith and justice: you
Have championed truth and fairness; pray,      196
don't leave the path of truth with me.
Although each day which sees the light         197
begins with morn and ends with night,
You—may your days never grow less,            198
and may your nights sweet union bless—
Who once, like dawn, but sweetness brought,    199
why now bring bitterness, like night?
Even if you, without a taste,                  200
are sated of me: why then cast
Me in the lion's mouth, to die                 201
from grief; show dragons to my eyes?
If that my death is clear decreed,             202
come, slay me then with your own blade.
Who guided you along this way?                 203
Instructed you this game to play?
Tell me, for I have lost my wits;              204
my heart is near to taking flight.
By God and by your life, I vow,                205
if you unlock this secret now,
I'll break the lock of the pearl-treasure,     206
and give myself to the king's pleasure.'
The king (for he was in her thrall)            207
trusted her oath, and told her all;
From that kind moon he nothing hid,            208
revealing all that could be said:
'My passion for you kindled fire               209
in which I burned from my desire.
My pain all patience cast away;                210
my body lost all power to stay,
Till that old woman found the cure             211
to heal me. With deceit, she urged
This trick upon me; and that dish,             212
untasted, brought me gain. I lit
A fire from my burning heat                     213
to soften you with harsh deceit.

214 'Tis fire alone makes water hot;
  'tis fire alone makes iron soft.

215 Were not my heart set on you, sure
  your suffering were my best cure.

216 You kindled fire in my heart,
  and that old woman made it smoke.

217 When, like a candle, you were straight
  with me, the smoke did dissipate.

218 Now, when my sun knows joy in spring,
  why then recall old winter's sting?'

219 Many such soothing words he said;
  that lovely maiden loving heard.

220 The untamed Turk, seeing things thus,
  gave way to lily-sweet cypress.

221 The nightingale perched on the bud's throne,
  it opened, and the bird grew drunk.

222 A peacock saw a tray heaped high,
  and scattered sugar on it; no fly

223 Buzzed there. Into the pool he cast
  his fish; threw into milk his dates;

224 Marvelled at that sweet fluency
  which made his dates more sweet. When he

225 Took off her silken veil, and breached
  the sugar-casket's lock, he reached

226 A treasure worth much gold; he made
  her yellow, with bright gold arrayed.

❦

227 Yellow's the source of joy; 'tis that
  makes saffroned *halvâ* taste so sweet.

228 Don't look at saffron's yellow; hail
  the smiles it brings. A yellow veil

229 Makes bright the candle's flame; the Calf
  of Gold* from yellow gained its worth.

230 Bright yellow, gold's the source of cheer;
  for this is yellow ochre* dear.

❦

231 When Bahrâm heard this tale, he clasped
  the maiden tightly; happy, slept.

34

# How Bahrâm Sat on a Monday in the Green Dome: The Tale of the Princess of the Third Clime

When Monday came, the prosperous king          1
raised his green parasol to the moon.

Lamp–like, in brilliant green he shone          2
like green–clad angels in the heavens.

Towards the emerald dome he went,          3
and gave his heart to merriment.

When Heaven's garden strewed starry flowers          4
of spring upon its emerald bowers,

He begged that cypress robed in green          5
to loose wise words from her sweet tongue.

That perî, bowing low, revealed          6
to him those secrets closely veiled:

'O you whose life makes mine rejoice          7
(may all lives be your sacrifice!):

Fair Fortune dwells within your tent,          8
and crown and throne before your gate;

The crown ennobled by your head;          9
the throne by your court firmly set.

Your noble lineage crowns your rule;          10
all men to your just court appeal.'

When she had praised the lofty throne,          11
her ruby lips let sweet words flow.

## The Story of Bishr and How He Fell in Love

In Rûm there lived a gentle man,          12
as sweet as honey, pure and kind.

All virtues men should have, he owned,          13
and all his worth by goodness crowned.

In virtue and in wisdom, he          14
preferred to practise chastity.

'Bishr the abstinent' his name          15
among his fellows—well-earned fame!

He strolled, for pleasure's sake, one day          16
along a smooth and level way.

17      Love launched a Turkish raid on him;
        temptation set his wits aspin.

18      A moon-like figure, darkly veiled
        in cloud-like silks, his heart assailed.

19      Heeding him not, she passed him by;
        just then a quick breeze stole away

20      Her veil; the breeze, temptation's guide,
        that moon through its black clouds displayed.

21      When Bishr saw this his legs grew weak;
        the straight-shot arrow found its mark.

22      That form, with its seductive charms,
        would cast all chaste vows to the wind:

23      A heap of roses, cypress-straight,
        her face both fair and ruddy bright;

24      Her languorous, bewitching glance
        stole sleep from all whom it entranced.

25      Her lips were like the dewy rose,
        whose petals nectar sweet enclose.

26      Her eyes, two languid lilies, held
        temptation in their drowsy spell.

27      Beneath black locks her bright face gleamed,
        like eagle's breast beneath dark plumes.

28      Her mole more musky than her curls;
        her dark eyes yet more infidel:

29      Those locks, that tempting mole, did rob
        the patient heart from all who saw.

30      Bishr cried out, unknowing, like
        a child who's bitten by a snake;

31      And at his cry the wandering moon
        made fast her fluttering veil again,

32      And hastening on her way, she sped,
        with such a murder on her head.

33      When Bishr's wits returned, he found
        his house in ruins, the thief long gone.

34      He thought, 'To follow her is wrong,
        though she's brought patience to an end;

35      Yet only patience can begin
        to heal this wound; all else is sin.

36      Though passion has led me astray,

I am a man; I will not die
Of grief; 'tis pious to renounce     37
this passion, and choose abstinence.

I'd better leave this city; turn     38
my face towards Jerusalem,

That God, Who knows both good and evil,     39
may grant me ease from this sore peril.'

He made his preparations; turned     40
and hastened towards the holy shrine;

From fear he fled unto his God,     41
and to His stern command he bowed,

That He might guard him from the devil,     42
and save him from temptation's evil.

When he had worshipped long, he turned     43
homewards, and left the holy shrine.

His company on his return,     44
who irked his passage like a thorn,

Was one who cavilled at all things,     45
and talked at length on anything.

Whatever Bishr might mention, he     46
would seize the bit between his teeth,

And say, 'That's so! this may be true;     47
no idle words on that will do.'

Bishr was dumbfounded by this talk,     48
like someone drugged, who's quite forgot

The art of speech. 'Come, tell me then',     49
the fellow said, 'your proper name.'

'This humble slave of God', he said,     50
'is Bishr; pray, what are you called?'

'You're Bishr, who brings bad news to men;*     51
I'm Malîkhâ, chief of the learned.

All that the heavens and earth comprise,     52
all that man's judgement can surmise,

Through perfect reason I know well;     53
what's lawful from what's not I tell.

I'm better than a dozen men;     54
in every art I'm fully learned.

Forest and river, mount, plain, sea:     55
all that exists 'neath the blue sky:

56　　I know the source of each full true;
　　　how this began, and that one grew.

57　　I know the secrets of the sky,
　　　although I've never reached so high.

58　　Any event, in any region,
　　　I see with my unfailing vision:

59　　I know a kingdom will decline
　　　full fifty years before the time;

60　　If grain will yield up less or more,
　　　I tell of it a year before.

61　　The leech's art I know so well,
　　　that fever's pain I can dispel.

62　　When I employ my magic's might,
　　　amber I turn to ruby bright.

63　　My alchemy turns stones to gems;
　　　base earth is gold within my hands.

64　　The magic spells breathed from my lips
　　　turn plaited ropes to speckled snakes.

65　　Each treasure-mine that God has wrought,
　　　I set its talisman at nought.

66　　All that men seek, in Heaven or earth,
　　　I give forth knowledge of them both.

67　　In all abodes where learning lies,
　　　there's none more skilled or learned than I.'

68　　Such boasting talk gave Bishr pause;
　　　that idle speech left him amazed.

69　　A black cloud o'er the hill appeared;
　　　when Malîkhâ at that cloud peered,

70　　He asked, 'Why is one cloud black as pitch,
　　　another white as milk?'—'It is

71　　God's will that does such things,' Bishr said,
　　　'as you well know.'—Malîkhâ cried,

72　　'Leave off! such pretexts go astray;
　　　the arrow should strike the target; say,

73　　Rather, the dark cloud's burning smoke;
　　　that's rational; while that like milk,

74　　All filled with pearls, which brings the rain,
　　　has purest moisture mixed within.'

75　　A wind arose, a hidden wind;

see what this know-it-all said then!

'Say, why does the wind stir? do not pass 76
your life confused, like ox or ass!'

Bishr answered, ''Tis God's will again; 77
nothing is done save He command.'

'Let wisdom guide you,' Malîkhâ railed; 78
'how long recount such old wives' tales?

The earth produces wind, that's sure; 79
'tis the earth's vapours make it stir.'

He spied a lofty mountain; asked, 80
'Why is this grander than the rest?'

Bishr said, 'Again, 'tis God's decree 81
that one is low, the other high.'

'One more to proofs I am constrained: 82
how long this talk of Plan and Pen?*

When the clouds make fierce floods pour down, 83
they wash the hills to lower ground;

But that whose peak is higher yet 84
from the flood's passage is remote.'

Bishr cried out, his brain aboil: 85
'Strive not so much against God's will!

It's not that I am ignorant; 86
I am more learned than you; and yet

None can construe things as he likes, 87
nor ease the way with fancy's works.

We mortals, who can't pass beyond 88
the veil, read the designs thereon.

To follow error is no learning; 89
we can't rely on such false readings.

I fear that when this veil is raised, 90
those who've misread will be sore tried.

'Tis better, with this high-branched tree,* 91
the hand of all should not make free.'

Though Bishr thus exorcized him, 92
that garrulous demon stayed in trim.

They travelled on for several days; 93
that loudmouth's chatter never stayed.

In desert hot and waterless, 94
their brains aboil from sleeplessness,

95  They ran about; they wailed and screeched,
    till, in that burning waste, they reached

96  A sturdy tree which towered high,
    all fresh and green against the sky.

97  Beneath it, like green silk, the grass
    made hot and weary eyes rejoice.

98  An earthen jar was buried there,
    with water in it, sweet and clear.

99  When that boor did the water spy,
    like sweetest herbs among dry clay,

100 He said to Bishr, 'O lucky friend,
    I ask you now: say, to what end

101 This wide-mouthed jar of clay has been
    buried in earth up to its brim?

102 How deep the water it contains?
    No foothills here, but barren plains.'

103 Bishr said, 'In hope of heavenly gain,
    someone's done this (many the same),

104 And, lest some blow should shatter it,
    has buried it deep in the earth.'

105 Malîkhâ scoffed, 'Oh, don't go on!
    All answers of this sort are wrong.

106 Oh yes! men for the sake of others
    bear water on their backs! What bother!

107 Especially in a such a place
    where, from the heat, there is no trace

108 Of water. 'Tis a trappers' den
    here, the abode of hunting men.

109 They've made the water of this jar
    a trap; when goats, gazelle, or deer,

110 Or onager, eat the bitter herbs
    that grow in desert wastes, and thirst,

111 They, seeking water in this waste,
    will hasten to this watering-place.

112 The hunter, having barred the way,
    bow drawn, lies waiting for his prey,

113 And as it drinks, will strike it dead,
    and roast the wounded game for food.

114 Thus do you solve all mysteries,

that all who hear may utter praise!'
Said Bishr, 'O you who can discern     115
the secrets of the world: each man
Has his own view: both of us scan,     116
within each person, what within
Ourselves we bear. Do not think ill     117
of things beforehand, lest after all
Ill thoughts may evil ends bring forth.'     118
When by that pool they ate and drank—
Water indeed for the thirsting meet,     119
so pure and cold, so clean and sweet—
Malîkhâ shouted suddenly,     120
'Get up; move off a little way,
That I may dive into that pool,     121
and cleanse my limbs in water cool.
These salty rivulets of sweat     122
have sullied me from head to foot.
I'll wash this dirt off of my limbs,     123
and set out fresh and clean again;
Then shatter this jar with a stone,     124
and save wild beasts from further harm.'
Bishr said, 'You fool! Abandon that;     125
don't stain the water in this vat!
With joy you've drunken deep of it;     126
why soil it with your body's dirt?
He that's drunk deep of water sweet     127
does not spit in it. Mirrors can't
Be cleansed with vinegar; nor do     128
men taint pure wine with dregs. So you
Must leave it, that if someone comes     129
here thirsting, it may succour him.'
That erring man heard not his words;     130
his evil nature now appeared.
He stripped, and bundled up his clothes;     131
bending, into the jar he dove.
But lo! 'twas no jar, but a well     132
whose watery depths he could not tell.
He could not argue with his death;     133
he struggled much, but was not saved.

134     He flailed about, much water drank,
but in the end was drowned and sank.

135     Bishr sat apart; wept bitter tears
for that pure water. 'See once more

136     How this crude, ill-begotten lout
has turned my friendly words to nought.

137     I fear this dirty-natured churl
will bring pollution to the pool;

138     Stain its pure water with his dirt,
then with a stone shatter the vat.

139     Such evil-thinking comes from those
who're evil, not the pure and wise.

140     May all be spared from such a friend;
may such a base man only drown!'

141     Thus to himself he mused; and when
a long time passed, and still the man

142     Did not appear, he went to find
him, unaware that he had drowned.

143     He saw the drowned man, cold and dead,
his empty head on the jar's edge.

144     He stood amazed—what could this be?—
then seized a branch of that stout tree,

145     And, like the sharp head of a spear,
with hands and nails he stripped it bare;

146     Then like one who surveys the sea,
lowered it down, the depths to see.

147     No jar was there! he found a well
built up with bricks, too deep to tell,

148     With half a jar on top of it,
that wild beasts might not swim in it.

149     He pulled the drowned man out; transferred
him from his watery grave to earth,

150     And, covering him with dirt and stones,
he sat above the grave and mourned:

151     'Where now your cleverness and wit?
Those tools with which you loosened knots?

152     Where all your claims to artful schemes
with beast and dîv, perî and man?

153     You said, "I'll catch within a snare

the secrets of the seven spheres."
Where's that claim to a dozen arts,                     154
that manliness, O unmanned corpse?
You boasted, "My quick wits foretell                    155
all matters that the future holds."
But when a pit appeared before                          156
your eyes, what could your foresight do?
And what of all those things we said                    157
about this water: good or bad,
Though our opinions had some worth,                     158
neither of us hit on the truth.
All that we guessed, each in his turn,                  159
kindled a fire in which we burned.
That Plan was of a different sort;                      160
not you nor I could reckon it.
Its thread was knotted by the sphere;                   161
no one could find its end. Whate'er
We said about that Plan was wrong;                      162
mistaken so, now you have drowned,
And I escaped; for you forgot                           163
your debt to God, but I did not.
You thought it was a hunter's snare,                    164
and like a beast were trapped in there;
While I, in goodness, thought it good,                  165
was right, and so my life was saved.'
He said these words, then rose and sought              166
Malîkhâ's things from left and right,
Gathered them all up one by one:                        167
his Egyptian stuffs, his linen turban.
When he opened the seal of his box of clothes,         168
a purse fell out from among their folds,
With a thousand coins of Egyptian gold,                169
sound ancient coins from days of old.
He replaced the seal, stilled his desire,              170
and left it sealed up as before.
He said, 'I must collect his clothes,                  171
his turban, ornaments, and gold,
And keep them safe until I can                          172
deliver them unto his kin.

173    I'll ask about the place wherein
    he dwelt, and give them to his kin.

174    Although I could not give him aid,
    I'll not betray his trust,' he said.

175    'If I should do as he has done,
    my fate and his should be the same.'

176    He travelled till he reached the town,
    and saw his family and kin.

177    When he had rested some days there,
    enjoying sleep and decent fare,

178    He showed that turban all around,
    in hopes its owner might be found.

179    A worthy man, who knew it, said,
    'From where you are, walk on a bit:

180    In such a quarter, you will spy—
    seventh house—a kingly mansion high.

181    Knock at the door, for it is his;
    doubt not that that man's house it is.'

182    Bishr, with turban, clothes, and gold,
    went to the house that he was told.

183    He knocked; a sweet-lipped lady came,
    and opened up the door to him.

184    'Tell me your business and your need,
    that I may do what is required.'

185    Bishr said, 'With me I have some goods;
    where is the lady of the house?

186    Permit me to come in, and tell
    a truthful tale, of what befell

187    Malîkhâ; what Fate brought upon
    that Heaven of learning, with its games.'

188    The woman brought him in, and bade
    him rest upon a cushioned seat.

189    She, her face veiled, then asked him to
    tell the whole tale, and tell it true.

190    Bishr told the details, one by one,
    to her of moon face, silvery limbs:

191    How they fell into company;
    how Malîkhâ his acts displayed;

192    How, like a drunk, he grew inflamed,

and on all subjects made great claims;
Would think the worst of everything,                193
and every good with badness stain;

How he for others dug a pit;                        194
how he himself fell into it.

How, like the billowing sea, he foamed             195
with boasts, and in the end was drowned.

When he'd recounted what he'd seen                 196
and learned about that godless man,

He said, 'He's drowned (may you live long!);       197
his place the earth, your place this home.

His corpse, by water washed, I gave                198
unto earth's treasure-house, the grave.

I gathered his belongings and                      199
now have them here within my hand.'

At once the clothes and gold he lay                200
before her; showed his honesty.

The woman, worldly-wise and rare,                  201
perused his page and read it clear.

A while distracted by that speech,                 202
she wept a bit; and when she ceased,

Said, 'You, of kingly acumen,                      203
God's servant, and an upright man:

Blessings upon your lawful birth,                  204
your gentleness and honest worth.

Who'd ever show such chivalry                      205
as you have done, to helpless me?

The righteous man is not the thief                 206
who steals from bees their honey sweet;

For he whose deeds are truly good,                 207
is he who's not deceived by gold.

Malîkhâ's dead and laid to rest;                   208
his soul's gone to what place is best.

And what you said: that he approved                209
of nought, was true a thousandfold.

His deeds were nought but tyranny,                 210
and faithlessness and cruelty.

Women and men he wrongly served,                   211
and what he got he well deserved.

212    A rancorous Jew in his belief,
       unholy dragon, subtle snake:

213    Long years I suffered at his hands,
       and nought but evil did I gain.

214    While I was by soft words misled,
       he forged about me lies. I spread

215    A shield, like mist, against his wind
       and his sharp sword, like lightning drawn.

216    Since God has driven him from me,
       I'm freed from his calamity.

217    Now, good or bad, he's disappeared;
       one should not speak ill of the dead.

218    He's vanished from our midst; and now
       all between us is changed; for you,

219    Who showed concern for my affairs,
       I choose as husband. I have here

220    Both wealth and land, and beauty chaste:
       where will you find a better mate?

221    Now, for that wedding God's decreed,
       go order my affairs with speed.

222    I'll have you as my spouse, for I
       have seen your boundless chivalry.

223    If you will have me, let me claim
       to be your slave. The story's done;

224    Here's how things lie; with wealth I'm blessed,
       and now you'll see my beauteous face.'

225    So saying, she unveiled her moon;
       unsealed her moist carnelian.

226    When Bishr her lovely face espied—
       her magic mole, her tempting eyes—

227    It was that fairy-face he'd seen
       that first day, world-illumining.

228    He cried out as he swooned away,
       the slave of her who was his slave.

229    That sweet-lipped one, on seeing this,
       quickly brought scent, restored his wits.

230    The senseless man, revived, blushed red
       with burning shame. 'If I', he said,

231    'Seem by a perî's love distraught,

think not that I'm by demons caught.
Who sees a demon dies; but I                          232
have seen a lady born of fays.

The love you see's not born anew                      233
today; for long I've burned for you.

On such a path, on such a day,                        234
the rude wind snatched your veil away.

I saw you; lost control; without                      235
the wine of union, I was drunk.

I burned for you in secret grief;                     236
for love of you lost hope of life.

Though you were never absent from                     237
my thoughts, I would reveal to none

My secret; then, my patience spent,                   238
I fled; towards God my footsteps bent,

Till He, with grace and mercy, caused                 239
all my desires to come to pass.

Since I, like sensual men, did not                    240
covet another's lawful wife,

Fortune, which wealth and beauty gave,                241
brought not forbidden, but lawful trove.'

When his true love the lady saw,                      242
her own desire grew ten times more.

She treated him with love and care;                   243
he went and ordered the affair.

The bride-price* settled, they were joined;           244
he gave thanks for that blessing found.

His fay-like lady he enjoyed,                         245
and made spells 'gainst the Evil Eye.

Thus from a Jew he saved a queen,                     246
and rescued from eclipse a moon.

He washed the yellow from her silks;                  247
green jasmine leaves grew in their place.

Since like an angel she did seem,                     248
he sewed a dress of heavenly green.

❧

Better than yellow robes are green;*                  249
green well befits the cypress' form.

Green is the field of healthy corn;                   250

in green the angels are adorned.

251   Green, above all, is the soul's choice;
green verdure makes the eyes rejoice.

252   The growing plants are green of hue;
green is the colour of all that grows.

253   Her story done, the king embraced
that moon whose beauty graced his feast.

## 35

### How Bahrâm Sat on a Tuesday in the Red Dome: The Tale of the Princess of the Fourth Clime

1   One dark and dull December day
(short as the nights are in July),

2   A day which other days outstrips,
Tuesday, the navel of the week,*

3   The day of Mars, of martial hue,
Bahrâm, of both the namesake true,

4   Adorned himself in red on red;
at dawn to the red dome he sped.

5   The ruddy-cheeked fair Slav princess—
flame-hued, with water's gentleness—

6   Prepared herself to serve; that moon
is pleasing which adores the sun.

7   When night raised up its standard dark,
and rent the veil of the sun's vault,

8   The king a pleasant tale did seek
from that fair maid with apple cheeks.

9   That lovely did not disobey;
poured pearls from ruby lips, to say:

10   'O you before whose court the sphere
is threshold, the sun's disk your fair

11   Consort; than any pearl that's bored
more precious; better than any word

12   Can say; none can approach your state:
may he be blind who's blind to that!'

When she had thus her homage given,    13
she brought pure rubies to the mine.*

### The Tale of the Princess Guarded in the Castle

In Russia's* far-off lands (she said),    14
there was a city, like a bride,

Made prosperous by its king, who had    15
a daughter reared with love; a maid

Tall as the cypress, rosy-faced,    16
seductive, with enchanting eyes.

Her beauteous face the moon outstripped;    17
sweeter than sugar were her lips.

Her suitors all were dazed with awe;    18
sugar and candles to her bowed.

Her sweet, small mouth made sugar less    19
than the slim circle of her waist.

Musk envied her dark locks; the rose    20
was by her basil sweet brought low.

Her fresh face sweeter than the spring;    21
fairer than idols' her colouring.

The narcissus langourous for her love;    22
the beauteous eglantine her slave.

Her stature like the cypress straight,    23
her face than any lamp more bright.

Rose-water kissed her feet; the rose    24
girded itself her slaves to serve.

Her beauty and sweet smile apart,    25
she wore the ornament of art.

She'd every mode of wisdom learned;    26
of every art a page had turned;

Perused all books of magic; read    27
of sorcery and all things hid.

Her face with her dark locks she'd veiled,    28
at plans to marry had rebelled.

How can one peerless in her time    29
agree to wed? And when her fame

Had spread throughout the world—that from    30
far Paradise a hourî'd come;

31    The sun and moon had born a child;
      Venus had given her Mercury's milk—*

32    Each one's desire for her was warmed;
      from each side soft entreaties came.

33    One strove with gold, and one with might;
      but she her gold with strength did hide.

34    Her father, from those suitors famed
      (from whom that fair withheld esteem),

35    Was helpless: What to do? How play
      *nard* with a hundred adversaries?

36    That lovely, solitary maid,
      seeing her suitors thus arrayed,

37    Sought out a mountain, towering high,
      as far from harm as the turning sky.

38    She ordered built a mighty fort,
      as if a mountain had sprung forth

39    From deep within that mountain's heart;
      asked leave, and readied to depart.

40    Her loving father, though he grieved
      at her remoteness, gave his leave,

41    That, honey-like, the hive once left,
      bees would not swarm through door and roof.

42    When treasure's in a fortress kept,
      the watchman will not fear its theft.

43    That strong-held beauty, for her ease,
      ordered her fortress's affairs.

44    When it was strongly fortified,
      she, like a treasure, dwelt inside.

45    So settled, she of silvery limbs
      'The Lady of the Fort' was named.

46    That iron keep all thieves did thwart,
      a fortress like the Brazen Fort.*

47    She, like a Slav princess, therein;
      no fort of such a one e'er dreamed.

48    She'd barred the way to all who came,
      and thwarted those who'd pleasure gain.

49    In every art that skilful maid
      was clever, quick of thought; she'd read

50    The temper of the starry sphere,

and all the elements compared.
Of nature's elements fourfold                        51
their mysteries she all controlled:
With wet and dry what might be wrought;               52
how fire grows cold and water hot.
What are the qualities of men,                        53
and how the stars may work on them.
Whatever learning useful finds,                       54
and gives assistance to mankind,
She all encompassed, she in form                      55
a woman, but in essence, man.
Patient, she ordered her design;                      56
divorced her heart from all mankind.
Upon the road, from clever plan,                      57
she set up several talismans.*
Of iron and stone the form of each,                   58
each holding in its hand a mace.
All those who trod that fearsome path                 59
were severed by those blades in half.
Helpless all travellers on that road,                 60
except for one, the fortress' guard;
And even he, who knew the way,                        61
would count his paces carefully:
If of a hundred one was out,                          62
his head would have been swiftly cut
By one of those machines' sharp blades;               63
his life's bright moon eclipsed by clouds.
The gate of that sky-scraping fort                    64
was well concealed, like Heaven's gate.
A builder in a month would ne'er                      65
have found it, more than Heaven's door.
That fortress-dwelling maid knew well                 66
the Chinese temple-painters' skill;
Designing with her pen, she drew                      67
pictures as fair and fresh as pearls.
With pen as black as hourî's locks                    68
she painted shadow upon light.
When in that tower she made her home,                 69
the tower found favour from her moon.

70  She took her brush and drew upon
    a piece of silk her own fair form,

71  From head to foot; and over it
    she wrote, in finely crafted script:

72  'Tell him who would possess me (girt
    by such a fort) that, like the moth

73  Which gazes at the light, he dare
    to enter; not speak from afar.

74  A true man can this stronghold gain;
    the unmanly cannot pass therein.

75  He who desires this prey must have
    not one life, but a thousand lives;

76  Must tread the road with firm resolve,
    and four conditions—tests—must solve.

77  The first condition is his good
    repute, and beauty, if he would

78  Wed me. The second test is that
    he loose these talismans by wit

79  And judgement; and the third, that when
    he's broken all the talismans,

80  He must reveal the fortress gate;
    by door, not roof,* must be my mate.

81  If this condition be fulfilled,
    let him go to the city, till

82  I come there, to my father's court,
    and question him on every art.

83  If he gives answers fitting, I
    will be his wife, most loyally;

84  That worthy man alone I'll wed
    who can accomplish all I've said.

85  But he who fails these tests, his blood
    will surely be on his own head.

86  He who fulfils them will possess
    the elixir of happiness;

87  But he who does not heed them, though
    he noble be, will be brought low.'

88  When she had finished with that page
    she gave it to a messenger; said,

89  'Arise; go now, and take this sheet;

remove the cover from this plate.
Go up beside the city gate; 90
fasten the sheet to the gate's vault,
That all who wish a bride like me 91
(though citizen or soldier he)
May set out, this bold aim to try: 92
to be the fortress' lord, or die.'
The messenger departed; passed 93
through twisting ways; above the gate
He fixed the portrait of that moon, 94
that lovers might regard it, and
That whoso wished might rise, and shed 95
with his own hand his precious blood.
And when, to every crowned head 96
enthroned, word of this tale had spread,
Men came from everywhere to hear 97
more of that tale that sparked desire.
Each one, by youth and ardour driven, 98
did cast his life upon the wind.
Those who set out towards that maid 99
reaped but destruction from those blades.
No striver's wit nor clever plans 100
could loose the castle's talismans;
And though one might display some wit, 101
his spells at last fell short of it:
Though he some talismans might best, 102
he could not overcome the rest.
His ignorance and lack of sense 103
made plain his failure in the end.
Thus failing to attain their goal, 104
some fine youths perished. None at all
Escaped that deadly path; along 105
it lay the forms of headless men.
Each of those severed heads was set 106
up high atop the city gate,
Until so many had been cut 107
that head on head was piled up.
Throughout the world, where'er you look, 108
nothing but walls do cities deck;

109   That perî-face, that hourî cruel,
adorned the town with heads, not walls.

110   How many heads rose high above
her gate, not having reached its shade!

111   There was, of noble, princely race,
a highborn youth of comely face,

112   Clever and strong, courageous, true;
both lions and onagers he slew.

113   He passed the town one day, intent
on hunting, that like spring he might

114   Bloom fresh; that honey'd sheet saw on
the gate, with flasks of poison round:*

115   A portrait on black silk; a form
which pleased the eye and the heart charmed.

116   A face so lovely and so fair,
it stole his patience quite away.

117   'Praise be', he said, 'upon that pen
from whose tip comes this fair design.'

118   Around that portrait lay, from head
to foot, a hundred heads. He said,

119   'This pearl that's round a shark's neck hung:
how shall I flee it? I'm undone,

120   Should I renounce this tale of love,
'twill shatter all my fortitude.

121   Yet if this passion does not leave
my heart, still hot, I'll lose my head.

122   Though that silk bears a lovely form,
dragons guard treasures, dates have thorns.

123   So many heads have fallen in
that game; would something had been gained!

124   Say mine is cut off too: what gain?
An earth-born man the earth will stain.

125   If I do not let go this thread,
'twill bind and sever my own head;

126   But if I'm bold in facing death,
how can I bid farewell to life?'

127   Again he thought: 'This painted silk,
that suitors charms, is fairies' work.

128   Against the spell of such a fay,

save magic's charms, there is no way.
Till I that fairy's spells can best,                              129
let me not act with undue haste.
I need a plan, not small, but great,                              130
my sheep from the wolf's jaws to save.
Whoever some hard task assays,                                   131
his plans may often go astray;
In such a task, do not think small,                              132
that a great loss may not befall.
Dance to the tune the world plays; take                          133
things lightly, give back hard. My heart
Is more distressed than is my mind,*                             134
my fear outstrips my pain, I find;
How can I then, with this heart, find                            135
joy; and how think with such a mind?'
He spoke; for a few moments grieved;                             136
then a few bitter sighs he heaved.
That sight brought tears; he saw the mat,                        137
the head, the basin, and the blade.
He hid his passion in his heart;                                 138
his secret musings would impart
To none. Each dawn, when he with great                           139
desire, passed by the city gate,
He saw that novelty portrayed:                                   140
a Shîrîn's castle, Farhâd's grave.*
He tried that lock with hundred keys,                            141
but the thread's end escaped his eyes.
It bore a hundred thousand heads,                                142
but none could tell him of its end.
Although to every side he sped,                                  143
he could not loose that tangled thread.
In every realm a way he sought                                   144
to smoothe the strands of that tight knot.
In this he put aside his pride,                                  145
and sought a cure; until he heard
News of a learned man, who bound                                 146
foul demons, joined with fairies; tamed
Each science's rebellious steed,                                 147
and mastered every art; outstripped

148     His fellows; opened every door
        to others closed. When that youth heard,

149     From travellers worldly-wise, about
        this world of knowledge, he set out

150     Towards that glorious Sîmurgh;
        from mount to mount flew like a bird.

151     He found him, like a garden fair
        and blooming, in a ruined cave,

152     And lily-like before him bowed;
        prepared to serve him like the rose.

153     His smiling fortune then ordained
        that from that Khizr he obtained

154     Much knowledge. When he'd drunken well
        from that spring, he his secret told:

155     Of that fair one, her fortress, and
        the harm she'd done to many men;

156     That talisman fixed on her road;
        that cutting of a thousand heads.

157     He told all to the sage; nothing
        concealed. From secret reckoning,

158     The sage revealed to him all that
        might be of use. When he who sought

159     Had found the answer from that sage,
        with thousand thanks, he went away

160     Back to the city; rested there
        some days, and thought on that affair.

161     The means to try that narrow road,
        all he required, he found; then sought

162     A spiritual connection* that
        would render easy what was hard.

163     Thus reckoning, he made a plan
        to deal with every talisman.

164     First, for that quest, he sought the help
        of men of staunchness and resolve.

165     Since this was bloody work (he said),
        the cruel sphere's game, he dressed in red,

166     And entered in that sea of blood,
        with (like his tears) a blood-red robe.

167     He thought not of himself; but men

set up a cry, reproaching him.
'I strive not for myself,' he said, 168
'but to avenge a thousand heads.
I'll lift this deadly yoke from them, 169
or lose my head in the attempt.'
When he had dipped his robe in blood, 170
he pitched his tent, and grasped his sword.
Whoever heard of his intent— 171
that lion-heart on vengeance bent—
To that endeavour added his 172
resolve, that he might soon succeed.
Their firm resolve, his shining will, 173
protected him like iron mail.
He then, apologizing, sought 174
the king's permission to depart;
The road to the high fortress took, 175
and set about his well-planned work.
When he came near each talisman, 176
he breathed a spell which was its doom.
He shattered all its magic dire; 177
deprived it of its baneful power.
With force, each talisman he met 178
he cast down to the earth; and left
The mountain top free from their doom; 179
no talisman remained thereon.
He neared the gate, and with a thong 180
of leather, beat upon a drum.
All round the walls he sought its sound; 181
heard it and dug; a tunnel found;
And when his echoing drum disclosed 182
a breach, a door appeared above.
On learning this, that tented moon 183
dispatched a slave, who said to him,
'You who close tunnels, open ways, 184
whom Fortune's guided to this place:
When you first loosed the talismans 185
you found the treasure's door. Now turn
Towards the city, like the stream; 186
be patient two days, if you can,

187  Till I come to my father there
    and test your skill. I'll ask you four

188  Deep mysteries; if you reply
    correctly to these secrets, I

189  In love for you will be complete,
    and nought our marriage will impede.'

190  That hero, seeing his success,
    turned back, but forward still advanced.

191  When from the fort he came to town,
    he took that silken banner down,

192  Folded it, gave it to a slave;
    affliction perished, praise revived.

193  By force he cut down all the heads
    atop the gate; unbound them; gave

194  Them to the people; praising him,
    with those slain forms they buried them.

195  Much praised, he then went to his home,
    a minstrel summoned, brought forth song.

196  On him the citizens rained coins;
    his house with finest silks adorned.

197  Each swore an oath; said, 'If the king
    does not approve this marriage, then

198  We'll overthrow him swiftly; make
    you prince and king; for he did take

199  Our heads, and was cold to our plight;
    you saved us, with your manly might.'

200  Meanwhile, that lovely bride was pleased
    with her mate's suit. When night released

201  Black musk, and rubbed it o'er the moon's
    pavilion, she, within her own,

202  Rejoiced. Anon the moon's bright rays
    then drew her litter by strait ways

203  Unto the palace; when she came,
    the palace radiant splendour gained.

204  Her father's face bloomed at her sight;
    his daughter did not hide her state,

205  But of events, both good and ill,
    that had befallen, told him all:

206  Those horsemen she'd unhorsed; that pit

they'd dug, and fallen into it;
Those lions who spoke her name, and died,                  207
helpless, before her; till the day
That princely scion lost his heart                          208
to her in but a moment; sought
To gain her; like a mountain firm                           209
stood fast, and shattered one by one
The talismans; the fortress breached,                       210
and shrank from no condition set.
'Now that he's passed three of my tests,                    211
how will he meet the fourth?' she asked.
'What is the fourth?' the king replied;                     212
'Conditions for brave men are made
But one, not twenty.' 'I shall set                          213
four knotty problems as a test.
Should he solve them (Fortune his guide),                   214
I'll place a crown upon his head;
But if his ass should lamely go                             215
along this path, there where he knows
He'll pitch his tent. Tomorrow at dawn                      216
the king must sit upon his throne,
And summon him to be his guest;                             217
I, by the curtain veiled, will ask
Of him the secret mysteries,                                218
that, after thought, he may reply.'
'I'll do so,' said the king; 'your deed                     219
is mine as well; I give my leave.'
They spoke no more, but went away                           220
and sought their rest. On the next day,
When o'er the rocks the turquoise sphere                    221
blew ruby dust, and lit the earth,
The king, to Fortune's service girt,                        222
arrayed a stately royal court;
Assembled many famous men,                                  223
right–speaking and right–acting; then
Summoned the prince to be his guest,                        224
and scattered jewels upon his head.
A golden tray was brought, which filled                     225
the palace with its groaning load.

226    It bore so many wondrous dishes,
        it seemed a very hoard of wishes.

227    Of that fine fare on every side,
        each man ate all that he desired.

228    When all had eaten of that hoard,
        their natures were once more restored.

229    The king commanded then that they,
        in private, that pure gold assay.

230    He went and sat in his own place
        (the guest in his), so that he faced

231    His daughter, as he wished to see
        what game she'd with her suitor play.

232    She (who'd put Taraz maids to shame)
        behind the curtain played her game;

233    Two tiny pearls loosed from her ear,
        and gave them to a treasurer:

234    'Go, quickly take these to our guest,
        and swiftly bring his answer back.'

235    The messenger made haste; bowed low,
        and to the guest those fair pearls showed.

236    He weighed the tiny pearls with care
        and to their measure added more:

237    Of pearls which equalled them in worth
        he added three; then gave them to

238    The messenger, who sped with them
        back to that noble lady. When

239    That stony-hearted maid looked on
        the five pearls, she took up a stone

240    And weighed them; found them equal; then
        crushed them like dust with that same stone.

241    She added sugar to them; ground
        the whole together; then returned

242    Them to the guest, who once again
        perceived the secret they contained.

243    He asked the servant for a cup
        of milk; scattered both into it.

244    'Take it,' said he; the servant sped;
        that gift before her mistress laid.

245    The lady quaffed the milk, and then

she made a paste of what remained.

She weighed it to the former weight;     246
it differed from it not a whit.

She took a ring from off her hand     247
and sent it to him. That wise man

Took it; on his own finger wore     248
that precious ring, and held it dear.

A single world–illuming pearl,     249
night's lamp, day-bright, he gave the girl;

That hourî–maid returned, and brought     250
the single pearl to the ruby bright.

The lady placed it in her palm;     251
unstrung her necklace, till she found

A matching pearl, of lustre bright,     252
just like it, which lit up the night.

She strung together both the pearls,     253
each like, no more nor less. The girl

Those pearls then to the sea returned—     254
nay, gave the Pleiads to the sun.

The wise man looked on them, and found     255
no difference in those two pearls joined.

Except for being two, they gleamed     256
with the same light and lustrous sheen.

He asked the servants for a bead     257
of blue;* for there could be no third

To those two pearls. The bead he joined     258
to them, and sent them back again.

When his love saw both bead and pearls,     259
she sealed her lips and sweetly smiled.

Sagely, she took them back, and bound     260
pearls in her ears, the bead upon

Her hand. She told her father, 'Rise;     261
prepare; for I am satisfied.

See how my fortune is my friend,     262
that such a mate should come to hand.

I've gained a mate whose peer's not found     263
in his own realm. Although I am

Learned, and learning love, less wise     264
am I than he.' Then, at the grace

265  Of that sweet tale, her father said,
     'Those mysteries, O angelic maid,
266  Those questions and replies I've heard,
     were all beneath a veil obscured.
267  The secrets of that colloquy
     you must reveal in full to me.'
268  With thousand charms that fine-reared maid
     the symbols' secret sense* displayed.
269  'When I first set my mind to work,
     I loosed the pearls from my ears.
270  By their exemplar I did say,
     "Know that this life is but two days."
271  He, adding three to two, replied,
     "It passes quick, though it were five."
272  I, adding to the pearls some sugar,
     and grinding them to dust together,
273  Said, "This life with desire is mixed,
     like pearls and sugar mingled thus;
274  Who, by spells or by alchemy,
     can separate the two?" Then he,
275  Who poured the milk therein, so one
     dissolved, the other one remained,
276  Said, "Sugar mixed with pearls will melt,
     and vanish with a drop of milk."
277  In drinking sugar from his cup,
     I signed to him that I was but
278  A nursling to him; sent the ring,
     consenting to be wed to him.
279  He gave me back that pearl to say,
     "Like this, you'll find no mate for me."
280  Joining my pearl to his, I showed
     that I in truth his equal was.
281  When he, examining those pearls,
     saw no third like them in the world,
282  He found a blue bead; put it by
     those two, against the Evil Eye.
283  When I put on that bead, I meant
     thereby, the seal of my consent:
284  Upon my breast his seal of love

is that which guards my treasure-hoard.
Because of those five mysteries,                    285
I bowed before his mastery.'
When the king saw that wild colt tamed              286
by wisdom's whip, he then arranged
(According to the marriage rites)                   287
what was required, in finest wise.
Then, at her bridal feast, he joined                288
Venus and Canopus* in bond;
Arrayed a Paradisal feast,                          289
perfumed with musk and aloes sweet;
Adorned the marriage feast; the rose                290
and cypress seated, then arose.
The happy pair he did entrust                       291
to love; departed from their midst.
The ruby-miner gained the mine,                     292
and from his love assistance found:
Now kissed her cheeks and now her lips;             293
now tasted pomegranates, now dates;
The pearl by diamond pierced at last,               294
the hawk lit on the pheasant's breast.
Upon her hand he saw his bead;                      295
her languorous eyes her love betrayed.
He did not leave her jewel's seal,                  295a
but from her treasure took the pearl.
In love and joy they lived; he made                 296
his garment, like her bright cheeks, red;
Since, that first day, for luck, he'd ta'en         297
red robes as an auspicious sign,
And by that red from black escaped,                 298
he always dressed himself in red.
Since red had brought to him his fame,              299
the King of Red became his name.

❧

Red—wondrous, novel hue!—bestows                    300
upon red gems their value. Gold,
Which some do call red sulphur,* boasts             301
of red, its attribute foremost.
Blood, with the vital spirit* mixed,                302

is red because it has life's grace.

303    In those in whom you'd beauty find,
a ruddy hue is beauty's sign.

304    The rose would not the garden rule
if it were not bright red in hue.

❦

305    When this fine tale was ended, and
the air was filled with roses' scent,

306    From scattered roses, King Bahrâm
glowed ruddy as the fragrant wine.

307    He gave his hand to that red rose;
embraced her; slept in sweet repose.

## 36

## How Bahrâm Sat on a Wednesday in the Turquoise Dome: The Tale of the Princess of the Fifth Clime

1      One Wednesday when the blooming sun
suffused with blue the sphere's black dome,

2      The king, victorious as the sun,
bright sky-like robes of turquoise* donned,

3      Went to the turquoise dome for sport;
the tale was long, the day was short.

4      When night put on its veil of musk,
the king dismissed his watchmen; asked

5      That story-telling lady to
perform her duties as was due,

6      And tell him, lovingly, a tale
to please him. Thus that cypress tall

7      Opened her rosy lips, and poured
on rose-petals her sugared words.

8      She said, 'O you whom Heaven obeys,
fortunate Jupiter sings your praise.

9      I, and a thousand better, are
ennobled through your service. 'Twere,

10     Before the source of honey, base
to sell sour vinegar; but since

11     None can escape the king's command,
I'll speak, if he can bear the pain.'

## The Story of Mâhân and What Befell Him

In Egypt dwelt a man, Mâhân,*  12
more beautiful than the full moon.

Like Egypt's Joseph, fair of face;  13
a thousand Turks his Hindu slaves.*

His friends, companions of his age,  14
took pleasure at his sight. Some days,

beneath the azure sphere, with song  15
and pleasant games, they sported long.

Each, for that bright lamp's happy sake,  16
in house and garden held a feast.

A noble man, not small but great,  17
once in his garden made him guest;

A beautiful and pleasant bower,  18
the friends a hundred times more fair.

Till nightfall they rejoiced therein,  19
now savouring fruits, now drinking wine;

Each moment some new sport enjoyed;  20
each moment relished some new food.

When night its musky banner raised,  21
drew pitch-black lines on silver, they

Took pleasure in that garden, wine  22
in hand, and in their stories, song.

They to that garden pledged their hearts;  23
tasted new pleasures, fresh delights.

The moon's bright glow lit up the sky;  24
truly the night was bright as day.

When Mâhân's brain grew hot with wine,  25
he saw the brilliant moon, and round

That garden like a drunkard ran;  26
from verdure to a date-grove went.

He saw from quite some distance loom  27
a figure who seemed known to him.

It was indeed a friend, in trade  28
and wealth his partner. 'Why', he said,

'Have you come at this hour, without  29
companion, even slave, about?'

'From far away I've come this night,  30
my heart impatient for your sight.

31   I've brought immeasurable gain,
     such profit as your thanks will earn.

32   'Twas late when I arrived in town;
     the gates were closed; I'd no way home.

33   But when I heard you feasted here,
     I came; 'tis simple to return.

34   You'd better come to town; therein
     a village chief his welfare finds.

35   Then too, perhaps, in dark of night,
     we'll hide one half our gain from sight.'

36   Mâhân, gladdened by thoughts of wealth,
     followed his friend. With cunning stealth

37   They opened the garden gate; since none
     saw them, no one said anything.

38   They ran, swift as the wind in flight,
     through several watches of the night.

39   The fleeter partner went ahead;
     Mâhân behind like his dust sped.

40   When they had gone beyond the place
     the house should be, thought's arrow missed

41   Its mark. 'From our home to the Nile',
     thought Mâhân, 'it is but a mile;

42   But we more than four leagues have gone,
     and passed the encircling walls of town.'

43   Again he thought, 'Perhaps I've formed
     a false impression, being drunk;

44   He who assists by guiding me
     is sober, and must know the way.'

45   So they ran on; the one who led
     went swiftly, while the other lagged.

46   Though he who followed fell behind,
     the leader often called to him.

47   Nor did the two cease their swift flight
     till cock-crow marked the end of night.

48   When dawn's bird spread its wings, night's brain
     was emptied of its fancies vain.

49   The eyes of that deluded man
     were freed from fancy's falsehoods then.

50   Mâhân's friend vanished from his sight;

Mâhân, now lost, became distraught.
Exhausted, drunken, brain besot,    51
he laid him down upon the spot;
Like half-burnt candles showered down    52
hot tears, and lay there until noon.
When, from the sun's hot blaze, his head    53
grew hotter than his burning dread,
He opened his eyes to see the road,    54
and looked around himself. He sought
A rose garden; no flower found,    55
only a heart with a thousand brands.
Cave upon cave his stopping-place;    56
greater than dragons were their snakes.
Although his legs were failing, yet    57
he thought that to go on was best.
With no strength in his legs, he ran;    58
without a guide he travelled on.
Until the king of night displayed    59
his whipping post,* he was afraid
Of his own shadow. When night drew    60
its black design, and whiteness flew
From day, he swooned before a cave,    61
each plant a serpent to his gaze.
Senseless, he lay in that abode    62
of demons; suddenly voices heard,
Opened his eyes, and saw two forms,    63
one of a woman, one a man,
Each with a bundle on his back,    64
travelling slowly 'neath their weight.
When the man saw him on the road,    65
he stopped the woman, advanced, and said,
'Hey, who are you? With whom (like the wind)*    66
are you related? Who your kin?'
'I am a stranger, gone astray;    67
my name, Mâhân the clever.'* 'Say,
How did you come upon this place,    68
this ruin without human trace?
These lands are demons' country; lions    69
roar at their clamour.' 'Worthy man,

70  For God's sake, I entreat you, deal
    with manliness; hear my appeal.

71  This place myself I did not find.
    Demon? Leave off! I'm human kind!

72  Last night I was free of all care,
    a guest in Iram's garden fair.

73  A man appeared; said, "I'm your friend,
    your partner in great wealth and gain."

74  He cast me from that Paradise
    into this ruin, and left my sight.

75  I know not if that empty friend
    but made an error, or has sinned.

76  Act manfully with me, I pray;
    for God's sake, show me my lost way.'

77  The man replied, 'O handsome youth,
    you've escaped grief by a hair's breadth.

78  A demon he, that you call man:
    "Hâyil* of desert wastes," his name.

79  He who feigned partnership: his goal
    was your destruction, not your weal.

80  Hundreds like you he's led astray;
    each perished in some narrow way.

81  I and this woman are your friends;
    tonight we'll keep you safe from harm.

82  Make your heart strong, and walk with us;
    swerve not from every step and pace.'

83  Mâhân set off between those guides,
    mile after mile, with lengthy strides.

84  They spoke no word till break of day,
    trod only in each other's way.

85  When cock-crow beat its tabor, and dawn
    tied on its camel a golden drum,*

86  Those two—now locks without a key—
    vanished from sight quite utterly.

87  Again Mâhân collapsed and lay,
    exhausted, where he fell. When day

88  Reflected back the sun's hot light,
    and earth affirmed the death of night,

89  He wandered through those strait defiles,

the lair of leopards, hill on hill.

From lack of food his strength soon failed,  90
his nurture nought but sore travail.

He sought for roots or seeds, and ate  91
them bit by bit, instead of bread.

He dared not leave the road; and when  92
there was no road, he still went on.

Till night he walked from hill to hill,  93
sick of the world and sick of soul.

When the white world had turned to black,  94
the weary traveller ceased to walk.

Hiding from beasts, he quickly crept  95
into a cave, and fitful slept.

Suddenly he heard hoofbeats; spied  96
a horseman hurtling down the road,

Whose mount, all lathered, hotly sped;  97
another by the rein he led.

The rider, nearing Mâhân, saw  98
a figure crouching in the rocks.

He spurred his mount ahead; it seemed  99
the flesh was bitten by its reins.

He said, 'O skulking wanderer, who  100
are you; what place is this for you?

Tell me your secret, lest instead  101
I separate you from your head.'

Mâhân fell trembling in his fright,  102
and cast his seed, as farmers might:

'O stately traveller,' said he,  103
'hear out your servant's tale, I pray.'

All that he knew, both hid and clear,  104
he poured into that listening ear.

The horseman, when that tale he'd heard,  105
in wonder bit his hand, then said,

'Recite *Lâ hawl*;* for you've escaped  106
destruction by two demons. They,

Woman and man, are clever ghouls,*  107
who lead men from their path, and hurl

Them into pits, then shed their blood,  108
and flee at cock-crow. She is named

109 Haylâ, he Ghaylâ;* and they seek
    but evil and great harm to wreak.

110 Give thanks that you've escaped their harm;
    be quick, if you're a worthy man:

111 Ride my spare mount; come, seize its reins,
    and from all speech your tongue restrain,

112 But ride behind me like the wind;
    entreat God in your heart.' Alone

113 And helpless, Mâhân left the cave,
    and, mounted on that fleet-foot steed,

114 Spurred it so swiftly that the wind
    was left behind. When they had gone

115 A little way, and had traversed
    the dangerous mountains, there appeared

116 At the hills' base a level plain,
    as flat as what? the palm of a hand.

117 From every side came sweet lute-tones,
    the barbut's wail, the moan of strings,

118 One side cajoling, 'Come this way,'
    the other, 'Here; drink wine today!'

119 In place of grass and flowers, the plain
    held ghoul-filled pandemonium:

120 Demons whose clamour laid to waste
    the mountain, raised a mount of dust.

121 Thousands of demons milled about
    and filled the plain with cries and shouts;

122 They seemed dust-scattering dust-devils; nay,
    like leeches, black and long were they.

123 At last, on every side, their cry
    raised a great uproar to the sky.

124 They clapped and danced: a fierce turmoil
    that set brains in their skulls aboil.

125 Louder and louder grew their shrieks,
    each moment reaching some new peak.

126 A while thus passed; then, from afar,
    a thousand brilliant torches neared,

127 And several giant forms drew nigh,
    monstrous and fearsome, looming high;

128 All of them thick-lipped like blacks,

with pitchy robes and tarry caps,
With trunks and horns, so that they seemed　129
both elephant and ox conjoined.

Gruesome and ugly, each one held　130
a flame, drunk like the guards of Hell.*

Flames shot forth from their throats like tongues;　131
they clattered horns and blades,* and sang.

The whole world fell to dancing from　132
the bells they brought to noisy sound.

Then Mâhân's horse began to dance　133
coquettishly, with skittish prance.

Mâhân looked at it, marvelling:　134
why had his horse's hoofs grown wings?

Beneath himself a trial he spied,　135
for on a dragon he did ride:

A four-legged dragon, with two wings,　136
and seven heads—a wondrous thing!

Who's seen a four-winged quadruped—　137
nay, worse—a dragon with seven heads?

The sphere, a belt which binds us tight,　138
a seven-headed dragon's hight!*

Astride that Hellish dragon's back,　139
he gripped his legs tight round its neck.

And that cruel, playful demon each　140
moment would play him some new trick.

It stamped and twisted, writhed and roiled,　141
more twisting than a lasso's coils.

Like debris from a tree brought down　142
by floods from mountain slopes, Mâhân
Was tossed and borne from side to side,　143
exhausted by that shattering ride.

Drunken, it bore him up and down,　144
now high, now low; tossed him one time
Up like a ball, then bounced him back　145
to ride, affrighted, on its neck.

It played a thousand tricks upon　146
Mâhân, till the cock crowed at dawn.

When dawn exhaled its lion's breath,　147
it cast Mâhân down to the earth,

148    Then sped away; the world grew still;
       that blackened pot had ceased to boil.

149    The demon-rider fell to earth
       and swooned like one who's demon-struck.

150    He lay there senseless in the road,
       like one exhausted—nay, one dead;

151    Knew not himself, nor yet the world,
       till the sun set his head aboil.

152    His brain afire from heat intense,
       his body found its scattered sense.

153    He rubbed his eyes and struggled up,
       looking with care both left and right.

154    All round him stretched a desert plain
       to whose expanse there seemed no end.

155    Its coloured sands like carpets spread,
       as hot as Hell, than blood more red.

156    When the blade hangs above a head,
       sand is poured out, a mat is spread.

157    That desert showed its bloody threat;
       thus scattered sand, and spread a mat.

158    He, sorely tried the night before,
       his strength and wits somewhat restored,

159    Found, from that trap those beasts had laid,
       a narrow path towards broad dismay.

160    Away he ran, like smoke, in fear
       and terror from that poisoned air.

161    He sped so fast the flying barb,
       though swift, could not have matched his speed.

162    When night's black made the evening dark,
       he'd travelled all that desert parched.

163    He saw green fields and flowing streams;
       his aged heart grew young again.

164    He drank some water, washed, then sought
       a place to sleep. 'At night', he thought,

165    ''Tis better that I rest, for night
       confuses; puts my wits to flight.

166    My humour's melancholy; with
       this dry air, and a lonely road:

167    How should I not gross fancies form?

such fancy-playing has slain my mind.
Tonight, for solace, I'll seek ease, 168
that I may not night's fancies see.'
Then, in each sheltered spot and way, 169
he sought a safe retreat to lie,
Until a hollow place he spied, 170
and saw a shaft sunk deep inside:
A pit, a thousand steps therein, 171
where nought but shadows entered in.
Into that pit he tumbled, like 172
some Joseph, legs like ropes grown slack,
And at its bottom came to rest, 173
like to a bird that's reached its nest.
Once safe, he hid within that veil, 174
laid down his head, and slept a while.
Waking from that sweet sleep, he tried, 175
with twigs and thorns, to make a bed;
He groped about the pit, so dark 176
it seemed designed of blackest silk.
He saw a white light, dirham-shaped, 177
like jasmine 'neath a willow's shade.
Seeking its source, around that light 178
he searched, and looked to left and right.
He found a breach through which the sky 179
let in the moonlight's shining rays.
When he saw that that fount of light 180
came from the moon, and it remote,
With fingers and with nails he clawed, 181
to make that narrow opening wide
By force; till it so spacious grew 182
his head and neck could wriggle through.
He put his head out and saw there 183
a garden radiant and fair.
He dug still more; with skill and strain, 184
he got his body through, and found
A garden—nay, a Paradise, 185
besting Iram's in every wise,
Filled, as with myriad idols fair, 186
with box and cypress clustered there.

187  Its many fruit-trees, laden down,
     bowed low, in worship, to the ground.

188  Fruits without number, which refreshed
     the soul, themselves as fresh as life.

189  Like ruby goblets filled with wine
     its apples; pure carnelian

190  Caskets its pomegranates; balls
     bursting with musk its quinces; smiles

191  Rained from pistachios; nectarines,
     suspended from their branches, gleamed

192  Like red and yellow rubies; sweet
     as *halvâ*, its bananas kissed

193  Its dates; its pears their smiles bestowed,
     and clustered grapes like bright gems glowed.

194  With honeyed figs and almonds white
     it seemed a bowl of sweet delights.

195  Its grape-vines, with hats set awry,
     held white and black beneath their sway.

196  Grape juice and pomegranates red
     and fiery, took revenge for blood.

197  Orange-tree branches, citron leaves,
     formed in each space their canopies.

198  The garden, with a juggler's spells,
     played tricks with bright-hued melon balls.

199  When Mâhân found this Paradise,
     he turned his heart from that last night's

200  Tormenting Hell; then ate a few
     of those refreshing, luscious fruits.

201  Their sweetness such delights conferred,
     his smacking lips could loud be heard.

202  He marvelled at those fruits; ate some,
     cast some away; when all at once

203  From somewhere a loud cry arose:
     'Seize the thief, where'er he goes!'

204  An old man came, aboil with rage,
     a club upon his shoulder; said,

205  'Who are you, demon who steals fruit?
     Why come you to this place by night?

206  For years I've kept this garden safe,

and not been troubled by a thief.
What sort of man are you? what line?     207
what are you? who? what is your name?'

His questions thus to Mâhân put,     208
the poor man nearly died of fright.

'I am a stranger, far from home,     209
in a strange place,' he said; 'be kind

To strangers who have seen great pain,     210
that Heaven may call you welcoming.'

The old man, hearing his excuse,     211
towards him felt more well disposed.

He quickly laid his stick aside,     212
put him at ease, sat down beside

Mâhân, and said, 'Tell me your tale;     213
what have you seen? What ills befell

You, at the hands of ignorant men?     214
what evils have the evil done?'

Hearing these comforting words, Mâhân     215
saw sympathy in the old man;

He told his story—all the pains     216
and woes that had befallen him:

Of falling in plight after plight;     217
of suffering torments every night;

Now black with grief, now white with joy,     218
and, in the end, all hopes destroyed;

Till that pit and that blessed light     219
had brought him from the dark of night

Into the garden. Thus he told     220
his tale; his secrets all revealed.

The old man, at these wondrous words,     221
became amazed at what he'd heard.

'We must give grateful thanks', he said,     222
'that you've escaped torment and dread.'

Seeing his friendly attitude,     223
Mâhân expressed his gratitude,

Then asked, 'What was that dreadful place?     224
What land? What country is it which

Last night appeared like Judgement Day,     225
and not a soul heeded my cry.

226　Its fire made smoke rise from my brain;
　　one spark set all that stir aflame.

227　Demons I saw, and lost myself;
　　so is it with the demon-struck.

228　Against me came a thousand troops
　　of countless demons and wild beasts.

229　They pulled me, beat me, threw me down;
　　demons, wild beasts, bane piled on bane.

230　In darkness is the key to light;
　　only in black can one see white.

231　But I've seen so much black on black
　　I feared I would go blind from fright.

232　So great was my bewilderment—
　　my mouth was dry, my eyes were wet—

233　At what I saw I sometimes screamed,
　　or rubbed my eyes as in a dream.

234　I went ahead, and travelled on,
　　with "*There's no power*"* and "*In God's name*",

235　Till God delivered me from pain;
　　from dark the Water of Life I gained.

236　I found a garden fairer than
　　Iram; a fairer gardener. How then

237　Was last night's fear relieved; tonight
　　where do my ease and safety lie?'

238　'You have escaped from sorrow's bonds,
　　and come into salvation's shrine:

239　That desert which these lands surrounds
　　is frightful, bare, the demons' home;

240　And those black forms that filled the plain
　　were demons who devour men;

241　First they deceive and lead astray,
　　and then torment men utterly.

242　They feign right, but play crooked; take
　　one's hand to cast him in the pit.

243　Their love was but of hate the sign;
　　such are the demon's ways. The man

244　Who practises lies and deceit
　　is like the demons of that pit.

245　Many such demons has this world,

who, fools themselves, make mock of fools;
Sometimes conceal their lies with truth,      246
sometimes poison with honey brew.

False fancies are of no avail;      247
'tis truth that God has made prevail.

Truth is survival's key; thereby      248
are miracles known from magic's lies.

You are of simple heart, it's plain;      249
thus fancies could assail your brain.

The tricks those base ones played on you      250
they only to the simple show.

Your terror made a Turkish raid      251
on you; wove fancies in your head.

Those violent deeds, that dreadful play,      252
were meant to make you lose your way.

But had your heart been bold, your mind      253
would not have all those fancies shown.

Since you've escaped that demons' den,      254
how long drink dregs? now taste pure wine;

Think that tonight you're newly born,      255
and to us, from that world, God-given.

This precious garden, like to Heaven,      256
that you have with your heart's blood gained,

Belongs to me, without dispute;      257
no flower but affirms this truth.

Nourished with love its pleasant fruits,      258
each tree from some fair garden brought.

Although its income's meagre, yet      259
it would make any city great.

I have a palace; stores as well;      260
great heaps of gold, and precious jewels.

I have all this, but have no son,      261
on whom to fix my heart. Thus, when

I saw you, who've such virtue shown,      262
I set my heart on you as son.

If you're content (your slave I am),      263
I will put all this in your name,

That you may roam this garden fresh,      264
enjoy its blessings, boast of it.

265    If you desire, for you I'll seek
       a fresh and lovely bride; I'll fix

266    My heart on you, rejoice, provide
       all that you and your bride may need,

267    If you will honour my command,
       and swear to keep my covenant.'

268    'What are these words?' replied Mâhân;
       'the cypress far excels the thorn;

269    But since as son you welcome me,
       I bow to your authority.

270    May you rejoice, who've given me this
       great joy and fortune.' Then he kissed

271    The old man's hands with joy; and both
       then joined their hands to bind their oath.

272    The old man tightly gripped his hand,
       pronounced his oaths, and sealed their bond.

273    'Arise,' he said; the guest rose up;
       he led him to another spot,

274    And showed to him a lofty court,
       all spread with carpets of rich silk.

275    Its vaulted arches reached the sky;
       its dome above a pool rose high.

276    Its walls and court of marble were,
       that shone as bright as silver pure.

277    A broad façade made narrow by
       cypress, willow, and poplar trees

278    That girt it; such a lofty place
       the sky could barely kiss its waist.

279    Before that kingly portico
       a lofty, broad sandal-tree* grew,

280    Its branches heavily adorned
       with leaves, so that it kissed the ground.

281    Upon it was a seat, firm fixed,
       of solid boards and branches mixed.

282    Carpets were spread upon that seat,
       like the tree's leaves both soft and sweet.

283    'Ascend this tree,' the old man said;
       'and if you food and water need,

284    A wallet's there, a pitcher too,

with fresh white bread, and water blue.

I'll go and make all ready; make     285
my house for you a pleasant place.

Until I come, wait patiently,     286
but don't come down from this tall tree.

Whoever questions you, heed not;     286*a*
let silence be your sole response.

Let no one's courtesy deceive,     287
and to no one attention give.

If I come, seek from me the truth,     288
that it is I, and then admit

Me to you. Since our pact has formed,     289
like milk and honey, a new bond

Of friendship, house and garden both     290
are yours; my dwelling your abode.

Tonight beware the Evil Eye,     291
and rest at ease all other nights.'

When the old man added his oath     292
to this detailed advice, he showed

Mâhân a leather ladder, placed     293
for climbing to that lofty couch.

He said, 'Come, mount this leather; grip     294
it firmly as you climb; pull up

The leather from the ground, so that     295
no one may trick you. Thus tonight

Gird yourself 'gainst the serpent sly;     296
tomorrow with the treasure play.

Although my *halvâ* comes by night,     297
its saffron must be seen by light.

Though this night's pear be bitter, dawn     298
will bring sweet pomegranates' gain.'

He said this; towards his palace went,     299
to make all ready for Mâhân.

Mâhân climbed up that lofty tree;     300
rolled up the leather ladder. He

Then settled on that soaring seat,     301
all high ones low beneath his feet.

There, in that amber-shaded room,     302
he amber spread, like the north wind.

303 He opened up the pouch and ate
    some thin white and thick yellow bread,

304 And from that jar, cooled by the hand
    of the north wind, clear water drank.

305 When he found ease upon that fair
    Greek couch with Chinese carpets rare;

306 The camphor-scented sandalwood
    assuaged his melancholy mood.

307 He leaned back and surveyed the place;
    from far off twenty candles blazed

308 Held by fresh brides; the new-throned king
    bowed down in worship. Seventeen

309 Princesses to the garden came,
    with seventeen aspects of the moon.*

310 Each one in different mode adorned,
    white linen o'er sugared roses drawn.

311 When they the garden-palace approached—
    candles in hand, each maid a torch—

312 They decked a royal feasting-place;
    spread carpets as the foremost seat.

313 Candle on candle shone thereon,
    and all was joy and pleasure keen.

314 That perî-face who was their queen—
    in their jewelled necklace rarest gem—

315 Took her own place, and sat her maids
    beside her. Then they, like to birds,

316 Began to sing; their tuneful songs
    the true birds from the skies brought down.

317 Their sweet song, their seductive tones,
    stole peace from Mâhân and the moon.

318 Their feet beat wildly in the dance;
    their stirring rhythm did all entrance.

319 A breeze arose; played clever tricks,
    uncovering their citron breasts.

320 The darkened night poured sugar white;
    mixed sandal with their citrons bright.

321 In suffering for those citrons fair,
    Mâhân rubbed sandal from afar.

322 He tried a hundred remedies

to cast himself down from that tree:
Amongst those hourî forms to fall, 323
to Paradise, without the call
Of Judgement. Then he called to mind 324
the old man's warning; strove to bind
The demons of his nature, while 325
those beauties showed their conjuror's wiles.
When they had sported for a bit, 326
they laid a feast and set to eat;
A ruby tray with pearls adorned 327
(themselves bright pearls to rubies joined);
Foods that had seen nor fire nor water, 328
scented with aloes, musk, rose-water;
Soups made with saffron and with sugar, 329
and pomegranate soup still sweeter;
Lambs fattened on Bulgarian milk; 330
fresh fish and plumpest fowl, and disks
Of bread white as camphor, slim 331
and tender as the hourîs' forms;
Fine sweets preserved with sugar; more 332
varieties than can be told;
A myriad strange cakes, all formed 333
and dressed with oil and sweet perfume.
When they this sumptuous feast had laid— 334
a feast? nay, say, a very world—
Then sweetly spoke those beauties' queen: 335
'My odd will change to even soon.
From sandal pure comes aloes' scent; 336
go towards that scent; surely you'll find
One redolent of aloes, mixed 337
with sandalwood, by darkness hid.
Like aloes black and sandal gold, 338
night's wrought my lute of sandalwood.
A share of perfume has my brain; 339
how good are fragrance and pure wine.
A friendly soul, it seems to me, 340
who holds some wish, is in that tree;
Summon him down to be our mate, 341
that he may with my fancy sport.

342  If he'll not come, tell him the feast
     is laid; and that my love's too great

343  That I lay hand to it, till he,
     the guest, arrives. Then to him say,

344  "Arise; enjoy a friendly mate;
     the feast is laid; don't make her wait."'

345  That beauty, narrow-mouthed, approached
     the sandal-tree; cajoled and coaxed;

346  Like nightingale saluted him,
     and brought the fair youth, rose-like, down.

347  The guest, with beauty of his own,
     was pleased to dance unto that tune.

348  He who had sought a go-between
     went quickly after that new friend.

349  From that assault of youthfulness
     he quite forgot the man's advice.

350  When youth makes nature boil, how shall
     old men's wise counsel be recalled?

351  When passion had removed all shame,
     Mâhân that bright moon's guest became.

352  Seeing Mâhân's fair face, that moon
     bowed low to him, as to a king.

353  She sat him on her carpet; showered
     sweet sugar; he rose-water poured.*

354  With him she shared a tray of food
     (such is the custom of a host);

355  And every moment on him pressed,
     with tender love, some special dish.

356  The feast done (all had eaten well),
     the ruby winecup fed the soul.

357  When they had drunk some cups of wine,
     then from their path they banished shame.

358  When drink had rent shame's veil, Mâhân
     felt longing for that moon grow warm.

358a  He saw a spring-like beauty, fresh,
      an idol in her charm and grace;

358b  Like curds and whey all soft and white,
      more sweet than sugared milk her breast.

358c  With honey and rose-water filled,

her apple cheeks the heart enthralled.
Her form like quicksilver that slips     358*d*
quick through the fingers, in its grace.

Her bosom like the garden rose;     358*e*
her narrow waist a taper showed.

The moon spread over her its veil;     358*f*
Mâhân's desire grew greater still.

He'd bite her healing lips so sweet,     358*g*
or suck her honey like the bee.

But when he would that moon embrace,     359
from shame she turned away her face.

He clasped that Chinese beauty fast,     360
that hundred-petalled rose, cypress

Of silver; kissed that fount of wine;     361
with ruby sealed cornelian.

When on that eyes' light, sugared fount,     362
his own approving eyes he bent,

He saw a foul afreet,* from mouth     363
to foot created from God's wrath:

A buffalo with boarish tusks—     364
no one had ever dreamed of such

A dragon!—nay, a devil she,     365
with jaws that gaped from earth to sky.

A humped back—God forbid!—bent like     366
a bow that's bound with coarse *tûz* bark.*

Her back a bow, her face a crab;     367
a stench that reached a thousand leagues.

Her nose a kiln for baking bricks;     368
her mouth like a cloth-dyer's vat.

All grinning like a crocodile,     369
and holding fast her guest the while.

Upon his face and head she rained     370
wild kisses, and then to him said:

'O you whose head has fallen to     371
my grasp; whose breast my sharp teeth chew:

You laid both hand and tooth on me     372
to kiss both my mouth and chin. Now see

My claws and teeth, like spears and swords;     373
true claws and teeth are these, not those.

373ª   When you so hot at first did seek
       my love, why now is your lust weak?

374    These lips the same; seek kisses then;
       this face the same; don't shun this moon.'

375    (Don't take wine from a sâqî who
       will pour deceit-filled cups for you;

376    Don't hire a house within a street
       where the policeman is a thief.)

377    'Such acts as mine are fit and true;
       as should be done, I'll do with you.

378    If I do not as you deserve,
       then I am as you saw me first.'

379    Each moment she dealt such torments,
       her fiery acts of violence.

380    When, rendered helpless, poor Mâhân
       saw that fair moon to dragon turned—

381    Those silver limbs now hoofs of boar;
       cow's tail where cow-eyes were before—

382    Beneath that dragon black as pitch
       he lost control; in terror wet

383    Himself; screamed like a child in fright,
       or like a woman giving birth.

384    And, like the White Dîv,* that black bear
       with kisses set his willow afire.

385    Until, when the dawn's light appeared,
       the crowing of dawn's bird was heard;

386    The veil of dark was lifted from
       the world, and all those fancies gone.

387    Those forms of clay, who'd rubies seemed,
       all vanished; not a one remained.

388    Before the palace Mâhân lay,
       until there showed the light of day.

389    When bright day's healing fragrance brought
       back to Mâhân his vanished wits,

390    A hideous place assailed his eyes:
       a Hell in place of Paradise.

391    The music gone, laments remained;
       dust made the eyes of fancy blind.

392    That building high, by fancy formed,

now proved a rare, fantastic thing.
The garden was a thorn-filled place;   393
that portico all full of mists.

All weeds and thorns, cypress and box;   394
the fruits all ants, the trees all snakes.

Those chickens' breasts, kids' backs, were nought   395
but rotten carrion; the flutes,

The lutes and rebecs, turned to bones   396
of onagers—beasts of all kinds.

Those stuffs adorned with jewels were skins   397
of leather, with the tanners' stench.

Those pools that seemed like brilliant tears   398
trenches of stinking water were.

The remnants of his sumptuous feast,   399
the dregs left when the sâqî passed,

Were trash, where once fine things were found;   400
nay, reeking, suppurating wounds.

And where sweet wine and basil showed,   401
now stinking privies overflowed.

Once more Mâhân became dismayed   402
at his state; God's forgiveness prayed;

No power to set out again,   403
nor yet the courage to remain.

He thought, 'What an amazing thing;   404
what compass has this juncture drawn?

Last night to see a garden all   405
abloom; today a place of trials.

Why show to me both rose and thorn?   406
What harvest does life's garden bring?'

And he knew not that all we prize   407
is but a dragon in moon's guise.

See—if the curtain he'd but raise—   408
for what the fool his love displays.

Those forms so fair, Chinese and Greek,   409
are ugly blacks when you but look.

Blood hidden by a veil of skin;   410
like wine without, a privy within.

If from this bathhouse they'd but strip   411
the skin—none loves a rubbish-heap!*

412 Many a prudent man who thought
  to buy a snake-stone, snakes has bought;

413 Many a careless man has rued
  of buying musk; found it dry wood.

414 When Mâhân, from those who wished him ill,
  escaped—like I from Mâhân's tale—

415 He made intention to do good,
  repented, and made vows to God.

416 With a pure heart, to God he fled;
  set off, while weeping tears of blood,

417 Until he reached pure water bright,
  and washed; then on the ground he knelt,

418 Bowed low, abased himself, and moaned
  to Him Who aids those without friend:

419 'O Thou Who loosest knots, untie
  my tangle; Guide, show me the way.*

420 You only can these knots unloose;
  You guide my way, and no one else.

421 Yet You are not my guide alone:
  whom else the way have You not shown?'

422 A while he wailed unto his God,
  and rubbed his face upon the ground;

423 Then raised his head; and lo! there came
  before him, one in his own form,*

424 Like April's season, dressed in green,
  and ruddy as the radiant dawn.

425 He said, 'In truth, who are you, lord?
  Oh what a precious essence is yours.'

426 'I am Khizr, o pious man;
  and I have come to take your hand.

427 By your new, pure intention formed,
  I'll take you back to your own home.

428 Give me your hand, there, as you stand;
  then close your eyes, and open them.'

429 When Mâhân heard Khizr greet him thus,
  thirsting, he found the Water of Life.

430 Quickly he gave the saint his hand
  and closed his eyes; then opened them,

431 And found him in that refuge, from

which that foul dîv had led him wrong;
Opened the garden gate; made haste 432
to Cairo from that land of waste.

He found his friends, all silent, there; 433
each one blue mourning garb did wear.

All that had passed, from start to end, 434
he told in full to all his friends.

Since, in their love of him, his friends 435
had for his sake blue garments donned,

And, testing them, their colour stayed; 436
their blue would not be washed away;

He strove to harmonize with them; 437
brought robes of blue and put them on.

Blue settled on him firmly then; 438
sky-like, he took the hue of Time.*

❧

The lofty sky has found no hue 439
nobler for its silk robes than blue.

Who wears the colour of the sky, 440
the sun's but bread upon his tray.

That flower blue which is so prized 441
a disk from the sun's disk receives.

Whichever way the sun inclines 442
the flower regards it. Indians,

Because of this, call every flower 443
that's blue in hue, 'sun-worshipper'.*

❧

When she had told her tale, the king 444
embraced with love that lovely moon.

# 37

## How Bahrâm Sat on a Thursday in the Sandal Dome: The Tale of the Princess of the Sixth Clime

On Thursday—that auspicious day 1
owes Jupiter felicity—
When morning's breath its musk unloosed, 2
the sandal earth burnt aloes-wood.

3    On its exemplar, Bahrâm made
     of sandal hue his cup and robe;

4    Departed from the dome of blue,
     and went towards that of sandal hue.

5    That Chinese beauty gave him wine:
     a Kawsar from a hourî's hand.

6    He drank, intent on joy, till night,
     and in the wine took great delight.

7    When the kohl-coloured sea's pearl-shell
     filled up the whale-sky's maw with pearls,

8    The king besought that maid of Chîn
     with slanting eyes, to clear his mind.

9    The Chinese princess smoothed her brow;
     from date-like lips made honey flow:

10   'O you who life to this world brings;
     loftiest king among all kings:

11   May you, more than the desert sands,
     the mountains' rocks, the waters in

12   The seas, live long, Fortune your friend;
     know life and fortune without end.

13   O lord who, like the sun, light brings;
     not merely king, but making kings:

14   I am continually undone
     by my own halting, stammering tongue;

15   But now, the fragrant wine before,
     some pearls of discourse I must pour.

16   Yet since the king desires ease;
     wishes that saffron may him please,

17   My rag-bag tongue I'll open wide,
     and laughter add to his delight.'

18   That sun-adoring moon bowed down
     before that sun, and kissed his hand.

### The Tale of Good and Bad

19   Once, from my city, two young men
     went journeying towards another town.

20   Each in his travelling pouch had made
     his own provision for the way.

21   One was named Good, the other Bad;

each one was like his name in deed.
They spent some days upon the road; 22
from those provisions which they had,
Good ate of his, while Bad his kept; 23
one sowed his corn, the other reaped.
Then, travelling side by side, at last 24
they reached a boiling desert waste:
A fiery furnace, whose fierce heat 25
would make the hardest iron grow soft.
It was a hot and arid land 26
which turned the north wind to simoom.
Bad knew well that that blasted waste 27
was vast, of water there no trace.
Slyly his waterskin he filled, 28
and hid it in his bag, like pearls.
'There's water on the way,' Good thought, 29
not worrying, and knowing not
There was none, but a pit.* So they 30
sped through that desert hot and dry.
When seven days they'd travelled on, 31
Bad still had water; Good's was gone.
Bad, who from Good his water hid, 32
said nothing either good or bad.
When Good found that that evil man, 33
ill-natured, had some water hidden,
And secretly from time to time 34
drank of it, as of scented wine,
Although he burned with thirst, Good sealed 35
his lips from any vain appeal;
Thirsting, he saw that water, shed 36
bitter salt tears; his pain endured,
Until he grew so parched and dry 37
he could no longer close his eyes.
Before and after prayer each day, 38
his thirst drained all his strength away.
He had with him two flame-hued gems, 39
two lustrous rubies, like water in stone.
Those hidden gems brought water forth 40
from viewers' eyes (not for the mouth).*

41 Now he took out those lustrous gems
and placed them on those waterless sands.

42 'I die of thirst; help me,' he said;
'my fire with some water quench.

43 A drink of water sweet and clear:
grant it to me, or sell it dear.

44 Into your water cast these gems;
my essence with your water bless.'

45 Bad—may God's wrath fall on him—then
opened the pages of his name.

46 'Don't hew a well from stone,' he said;
'I care not; so leave off this fraud.

47 You'd give me jewels in this waste land
to take them from me in the town.

48 I am no fool, to be deceived!
I trick more humans than a dîv.

49 And when I play my game, your piece
can't match my tricks. Of such deceits

50 And spells, a hundred I've performed;
don't try to gamble; for I scorn

51 To let you drink my water; then,
when you reach town, my honour ruin.

52 How should I take from you that gem,
when you will take it back again?

53 I'll have a jewel you can't take back
in any way.' 'What jewel is that?'

54 Good said; 'tell me, that I may give
it to the jewel-seeker, and live.'

55 Bad said, 'The two jewels of your sight,
each one more precious than its mate.

56 Sell me your eyes for water; or,
if not, of water think no more.'

57 Good said, 'Have you no shame before
your God? cold water for hot fire?

58 I find a source of water sweet:
what work is this, my eyes to take?

59 How should I bid my eyes farewell?
what use were then a hundred wells?

60 To give my eyes for water—how

can I? sell it to me for gold,
Then take the gems; take all I own;    61
I'll write a deed for everything.

I swear that I will be content    62
(by the world's Lord) with this judgement.

O upright man, spare me my eyes;    63
let not cold water turn to ice

Your heart.'—'This is but talk; for he    64
who thirsts', said Bad, 'makes empty pleas.

I want those eyes; these gems will bring    64a
no gain; those eyes outvalue gems.'

Good was perplexed; shed bitter tears    65
for that spring's water; truly feared

He'd die of thirst, and could not save    66
his life; and so he did deceive

His warm heart with cold water; where    67
is one who thirsts, who'll water forswear?

He said, 'Rise; sword and dagger bring;    68
but give the thirsting man a drink.

Take out my burning eyes; and then    69
my fire with cold water quench.'

He thought that, by surrendering, he'd    70
once more find hope, after great dread.

When Bad saw this he drew his knife;    71
like wind drew near that thirsting earth.

The lamps of his two eyes he pierced,    72
and quenched their light without remorse.

His blade made the narcissus* stained    73
rose-red; took from the crown that gem.

The thirsting man's eyes thus destroyed,    74
Bad gave no water, but set off.

He took Good's jewels, and his effects,    75
and left the blind man destitute.

When Bad departed, Good knew nought    76
of good or ill. He rolled about,

All bloodied, in the dust; 'twas well    77
he had no eyes to see himself.

Had he had eyes to see his state,    78
he would have surely died from fright.

79   —There was a Kurd, a noble chief,
     who kept his flock safe from the wolf.

80   He had fine herds of beasts as well,
     like no one e'er possessed; there dwelled

81   Seven, eight tents of kinsmen there,
     he wealthy, while the rest were poor.

82   The Kurd, who wandered hill and plain
     like desert-roaming nomads, came

83   For pasture to the desert; grazed
     his flock from plain to plain some days;

84   Where grass and water might be found,
     some two weeks made his camping-ground;

85   The grass devoured, that place forsook,
     and elsewhere drove his hungry flock.

86   By chance, those two days, that bold man
     had loosed his claws there like a lion.

87   The Kurd a lovely daughter had,
     a beauty Hindu-moled, Turk-eyed;

88   A cypress watered by the heart;
     tender, and raised by loving art.

89   Her rope-like curls fell past her waist,
     and yoked the bright moon to her face;

90   Like garden violets they streamed,
     locks blacker than the raven's wing.

91   Her magic glances, drunk with charm,
     held power o'er the false world's harm.

92   Her Babylonian charms* made all
     yearn to be captured by her spell.

93   Her mole gave blackness to the night;
     her radiance made the moon shine bright.

94   Her narrow, sugar-biting lips
     made strait the way to loving kiss.

95   That tented moon, so full of grace,
     came seeking water like a fish.

96   Far from the road a cool spring lay,
     from which that tribe its water drew.

97   She filled her pitcher there, then went
     to bear it, hidden, to her tent;

98   When suddenly she heard a moan

from that poor desperate wounded man.
She followed it, until she found       99
a youth, stretched on the bloody ground.

He jerked his limbs in pain, and called      100
in supplication to his God.

The charmer thought no more of charm;      101
she went straight to the wounded man.

'Alas!' she cried; 'Say, who are you,      102
abased and bloody? Tell me, who

Against your youth has done this crime?      103
who brought you such a grievous wrong?'

'O heavenly angel, if you be      104
angel or perî-born,' said he,

'I've suffered many wondrous things;      105
the tale thereof is very long.

I thirst; I die from water's lack;      105a
help, if you can, my thirst to slake.

If you've no water, go; I'm dead;      106
but if there is a drop, I'm saved.'

That sweet-lipped sâqî, key to life,      107
gave water pure as the Water of Life.

The suffering, thirsty man drank deep,      108
much as he could, of that cold draught.

His parched soul was revived again,      109
and that bright lamp rejoiced in him.

His eyes, that from their place were torn,      110
she put back, and invoked God's name.

Though the white membrane had been scratched,      111
the pupils still remained intact.

She saw his legs had strength enough      112
that from his place he might be moved.

She put his eyes in place, and bound      113
them tight, then nobly took his hand.

She laboured; brought him to his feet,      114
and guided him by the right path.

The blind man went with her, until      115
they reached the place wherein she dwelled.

To a familiar servant she      116
entrusted him: 'Gently, that he

117  May not be made to suffer more,
     carry him slowly to my door.'

118  She quickly to her mother sped
     and told the tale. Her mother said,

119  'Why did you leave him when you came,
     not bring him with you? We might find

120  Some remedy to ease his pain,
     and make him comfortable again.'

121  She said, 'I've brought him; if he live,
     at any moment he'll arrive.'

122  The servant who had brought him led
     the weary man to a soft bed.

123  They settled him, and brought him food,
     gave him some roasted meat and broth.

124  The heat-struck man, with cold sighs, ate,
     then in great pain laid down his head.

125  When in the evening from the plain,
     the Kurd came, ate, and ease regained,

126  He saw an unfamiliar scene
     which but unsettled him again:

127  He saw one lying senseless there,
     like one hurt who of life despairs.

128  'Whence came this helpless man?' said he,
     'and why so weary and so weak?'

129  None could explain what first befell
     the youth; and they could only tell

130  How his dear eyes were from him rent:
     bright onyx pierced by adamant.

131  When the Kurd saw that suffering man
     was sightless, his eyes tightly bound,

132  He said, 'From that tall tree there must
     some leaves be gathered, then be crushed,

133  Their juice obtained, rubbed on the wound,
     to take away its burning pain.

134  Were such a remedy obtained,
     his eyes their brightness would regain.

135  A wound to the eyes, though it be grave,
     will by those leaves' juice be assuaged.'

136  He told them where the tree was: 'Close

by that well-spring of ours, there grows
A rare and ancient tree, whose scent,                137
perfumed, relieves the brain. Its trunk
Has, from its root, formed branches twain,           138
set far apart. The leaves of one,
Like hourî's robes all fair and bright,              139
bring brightness to departed sight;
The other's, like the Water of Life,                 140
cure epileptics of their fits.'
When the Kurd's daughter heard these words,          141
she set her mind to make that cure.
She begged her father to restore                     142
that poor man's health; and when the Kurd
Heard her entreaties, he set out                     143
to seek the tree. He took from it
A handful of those precious leaves,                  144
a sovereign remedy from death.
He brought them; that maid took them then            145
and pounded them; their juice obtained,
She strained it till no dregs remained,              146
and poured it in those blind eyes; bound
Them with that remedy. The man,                      147
weary, sat up a while from pain;
Then fixed his eyes upon success,                    148
and laid his head again to rest.
For five days, with those salves upon                149
his eyes, his head was tightly bound.
They loosed the bandage the fifth day;               150
wiped from his eyes the remedy.
His ruined eyes were sound once more;                151
he was as he had been before.
The sightless man opened his eyes                    152
like twin narcissi at sunrise;
Then Good gave thanks for that good deed:            153
from blindness by that blindfold freed.
All in that house, their worry healed,               154
opened their hearts, their faces veiled.
The Kurdish maid had taken such pains                155
that lo! she fell in love with him.

156   That cypress, his narcissi bright
      (unlocked, the pearl-casket of sight),

157   That perî-maid more loving grew
      towards that fair and noble youth.

158   Good also loved her, for her deeds
      of kindness, and the love she showed.

159   Although he had not seen her face,
      he saw her move, observed her grace.

160   Often her sweet discourse he'd heard;
      been tended by her gentle hands.

161   He'd fixed his heart on her; that fair
      had done the same—oh blessed pair!

162   Each day at morning Good would gird
      himself in service to the Kurd.

163   He guarded camels, kept the flocks;
      gentle and vigilant, he watched.

164   He kept the plague of wolf from all
      the flock; protected great and small.

165   When the nomadic Kurd had gained
      much ease of body due to him,

166   He honoured him with friendship; put
      him over both his house and goods.

167   When Good became one of the house,
      that question once again was broached:

168   They sought the tale of his wounded eyes;
      who had abused him in this wise?

169   Good did not hide the tale of Bad;
      he told them all that had occurred:

170   The jewels' tale; the water bought
      when scorched by fires of thirst so hot;

171   How these gems from his eyes were torn,
      and how those other jewels were stolen:

172   How Bad pierced these and took the others,
      and left him thirsting without water.

173   When the Kurd heard Good's tale, he laid
      his face upon the ground and prayed;

174   Gave thanks that that relentless storm
      had done no damage to this bloom.

175   When they heard that angelic man

had from that demon seen such harm,
Good grew more famous than his name,                     176
more precious than their lives to them.

They treated him as he deserved;                         177
that beauty would let no one serve

Him but herself; so, veiled, she'd give                  178
him water, and her own fire hid.

At once Good gave his heart to her;                      179
pledged her that life she had restored.

Grateful to that rare pearl, he served                   180
the cows, the sheep and camel herds.

'Could such a lovely one', thought he,                   181
'be wed to a poor man like me?

For such a lovely, perfect maid                          182
without great wealth cannot be gained.

I, who from need their bread consume:                    183
how should I hope for such a bond.

'Tis best to flee this peril; make                       184
a shrewd pretext; a journey take.'

A week passed in this woeful state;                      185
one evening he went home, his heart,

Afflicted by that beauty, sore:                          186
a beggar by a treasure's door.

Facing pure water, more athirst                          187
than ever he had been at first.

That night, from his heart's grievous wound,             188
his sad tears made his clay to bloom.

He told the Kurd, 'O kindly man,                         189
who treats a stranger as a friend:

You gave me back my eyes' bright light;                  190
restored to me both heart and life.

Your table's crumbs have nourished me;                   191
I've countless blessings from your tray.

Your brand is nobler than my brow;                       192
I can't express the thanks I owe.

But search me, both inside and out:                      193
my blood gives off your table's scent.

I can't repay your care; my head                         194
I place upon your tray instead.

195 I can no longer be a guest;
    rub salt upon my wounded breast.

196 For all the blessings given by you,
    I can't give thanks in measure due,

197 Unless God in His grace will grant
    me that which will discharge my debt.

198 Though leaving you will bring me grief,
    I ask permission for relief

199 From service to you; for I've long
    been far from my affairs and home.

200 I am resolved, tomorrow at dawn,
    to set out homewards. If in form

201 I'll be apart, your threshold's dust
    my mind holds ever uppermost.

202 I hope that you, a fount of light,
    when I am far, won't think my heart

203 Far from you, but will spread the wings
    of my resolve; make what I've consumed

204 Lawful to me.' He ceased his words;
    great grief arose among the Kurds.

205 Loud Kurdish weeping could be heard,
    and cries from left and right. The Kurd

206 Was sobbing, that fair maid more so;
    their brains were parched, their eyes aflow.

207 When they had wept they bowed their heads,
    like water turned to ice. The Kurd,

208 So wise and sage, then raised his head,
    and bade the servants leave. He said

209 To Good, 'Wise youth, who clever art,
    and virtuous, loving and quiet:

210 What if, returning to your town,
    you're injured by another friend?

211 Here you have ease, success, and love;
    you govern all. Men who are good

212 Do not to evil men give rein;
    deliver to their foes their friends.

213 Only one precious daughter do
    I have (and I own great wealth too):

214 A loving and obedient maid——

to say she was not would be bad.
Though musk within its sac is hid,   215
its scent is plain throughout the world.
If you will set your heart on me,   216
and on my daughter, you will be
Dearer than life; for such a maid,   217
I freely choose you as a mate;
All that I own, camels and sheep,   218
I'll give to you, that you may be
A wealthy man; with love, among   219
you twain live, till departure come.'
When Good this happy news had heard,   220
he did due homage to the Kurd.
Their joyous words thus said, they went   221
to sleep, both loving and content.
When dawn's bright Aaron girt its belt,   222
the cock crowed forth like golden bells.*
The Eastern sultan's fortune shone   223
full regal as he took his throne.
The joyful Kurd rose from his bed   224
and readied all, that they might wed.
(Strong are the seeds of progeny   225
from marriage, which true union be.)
He gave to Good his daughter; joined   226
Venus and Mercury* in one bond.
The thirsting man found the Water of Life;   227
upon the bloom shone the sun's light.
To him who thirsted, that sâqî bore   228
a draught far sweeter than Kawsar.
If first she gave him water plain,   229
the Water of Life 'twas in the end.
Together happily they lived,   230
and lacked for nothing they might need;
They called those former times to mind,   231
and joyed in what they had content.
What substance that he had, the Kurd   232
bestowed on those he held most dear,
Till all his wealth, his flocks and land,   233
belonged to Good. When they moved on

234    From that well-watered pasture fair,
tree-girt, towards the desert sere,

235    Good passed that sandal-scented tree
from which his life found remedy.

236    Not from one branch: from both of those
tall trunks, he plucked many broad leaves.

237    The one was epilepsy's cure;
the other wounded sight restored.

238    Two sacks with those rare leaves he filled,
and placed them in the camels' load;

239    To no one else the leaves revealed,
but kept those remedies concealed,

240    Until they reached a town, in which
the king's fair daughter suffered fits.

241    Though they'd tried many remedies,
she was not cured, and all did grieve.

242    Each doctor who some knowledge claimed
came to that town in hope of fame,

243    That, with a cure, they might dispel,
from that fair perî, the dîv's ill.*

244    The king made a condition first:
'Whoever finds a proper cure,

245    On him my daughter I'll bestow,
and honour him as son-in-law.

246    But he who sees this maiden fair,
and does not make a fitting cure:

247    I shall attack him with the blade,
and from his body cut his head.'

248    When that incurable obtained
no cure, those doctors were then slain.

249    A thousand lost their heads, of them
some strangers and some citizens.

250    This story spread throughout the land;
yet everyone, in hope of gain,

251    Lost his head in return for nought;
the shedding of his own blood sought.

252    When Good heard of this he was sure
he could himself provide the cure.

253    He sent a message to the king:

'I can remove this painful thorn.
By God's grace, I will cure her ill,                    254
and your condition will fulfil.

But my condition—by your leave                          255
(your servant's far removed from greed)—
Is, that the cure I shall effect                         256
shall be done only for God's sake,

That God to me success may grant,                        257
and thus the means unto that end.'

His message reached the king, who gave                   258
permission to pay homage. Good

Went there; made his obeisance;                          259
the king then asked, 'O virtuous man,

What is your name?' ''Tis Good,' said he;                260
'my star foretold felicity.'

The king in this good omen saw;                          261
said, 'Man of Good, who maketh cures:

May, in this task of good intent,                        262
the outcome be good like your name.'

He bade a trusted servant bear                           263
Good to his daughter's chamber, where

He saw a sun-like, cypress form,                         264
turned willow by the fever's wind;

A restless lion, that cow-eyed maid:                     265
no ease by night, no sleep by day.

He had with him a few leaves from                        266
that blessed tree, all tightly bound.

He ground them; from their powder made,                  267
a cool, sweet drink that would assuage

The thirsting; gave it to the maid,                      268
and her affliction quickly fled.

She drank; and, from that tumult freed,                  269
she slept at once. When Good could see

That that fair spring was fast asleep,                   270
and from all fear of anguish safe,

Out of that heavenly palace he went,                     271
and set out for his home, content.

That perî-faced maid slept three days;                   272
the king knew nothing of her state.

273 On the third day she raised her head,
and ate whatever she desired.

274 Hearing this news, the king, with joy,
ran barefoot to her chambers; saw

275 His daughter well, her wits restored,
seated upon a couch. He bowed

276 Before her; said (his joy intense),
'O maid who has no mate but sense,

277 How is your grievous illness now
(may trial's wind blow far from you)?'

278 She, awed by his magnificence,
addressed the king with loving thanks.

279 He left the harem, with his grief
now lessened, and his joy increased.

280 His daughter bade an intimate
to tell that king of good repute,

281 'Since (I have heard) 'tis writ that kings
must keep their oaths; and since, that time

282 When sharp blades severed heads, the king
fulfilled his oath; now that there's come

283 A head that's earned a crown, he must
again fulfil his oath, so that,

284 Firm with the sword as it has been,
it will not fail him with the crown.

285 So many heads by sword undone:
let one be honoured by the crown.

286 He who my remedy obtained,
who loosed the bonds of bitter pain:

287 I will not leave him to his fate;
for none but he shall be my mate.

288 'Tis best that we not break our troth,
but fittingly discharge our oath.'

289 The king too judged it best he should
fulfil his pact. Thus noble Good

290 Was summoned to the king, and sought,
found in the road, and quickly brought

291 Before the king. They treated him
like a found pearl. Then said the king,

292 'O great man, why do you conceal

your face from Fortune's happy weal?'
From his own body he took off                          293
a robe more than a kingdom's worth;
Gave other ornaments of wealth:                        294
a jewelled baldrick, golden belt.
The citizens bedecked the town                         295
with fair pavilions all around;
The girl came from her vaulted room,                   296
and saw a bridegroom like the moon:
Quick, of tall stature, wondrous fair,                 297
with musky down and musk-black hair.
With willing father, yielding bride,                   298
Good married her, in spite of Bad.
O'er treasure-door the king prevailed;                 299
broke the unviolated seal;
Thenceforth enjoyed life fully; read                   300
designs which were both fair and glad.
—That king had a vizier of might,                      301
the populace's great support,
Who had a daughter, wondrous fair,                     302
her face like snow with crow's blood smeared.
That moon had suffered smallpox's blight;              303
it had destroyed her brilliant sight.
That minister asked the king's leave                   304
that Good might light to her eyes give.
On that condition as before,                           305
Good's remedy made good the cure,
And she became his wife as well:                       306
see how that gem pierced several pearls!
From those three lovely brides, Good found             307
Kaykâvûs' throne and Kisrâ's crown.
Now he would sit with the vizier's                     308
fair daughter, and gain his desires;
Now with the princess his eyes shone                   309
(for he was sun, and she the moon);
Now with the daughter of the Kurd                      310
he joyed; thus won three games of *nard*.
At last one day his fortune kind                       311
raised him to kingship and the throne.

312    He took to him that city's reign,
       and was established as its king.

313    One day he to the garden strayed,
       to sport there with a lovely maid.

314    Bad (his companion on the road)
       was by his secret heart betrayed.

315    He stood there, haggling with a Jew;
       Good saw him (Jewish too) and knew

316    Him then. He said, 'When I am free,
       bring him to the garden after me.'

317    He sought the garden, sat therein;
       the Kurd stood present, sword in hand.

318    Bad came, all innocent, and kissed
       the ground, not knowing Good, who asked,

319    'Tell me your name, O you whose head
       will soon lament for him.' Bad said,

320    'I am the traveller who's called
       Mubashshir,* in all rare arts skilled.'

321    'Tell me your proper name,' said Good,
       'and wash your face in your own blood.'

322    'I have no other name,' said he;
       'now sword or winecup show to me.'

323    Said Good, 'You bastard, base and vile,
       your blood is lawful blood to all.

324    Your nature's bad; you're called the same,
       your deeds more evil than your name.

325    Are you not he who water prized;
       whose cruel hand tore out that man's eyes?

326    And even worse, in burning heat,
       you carried water, gave him nought.

327    You took the jewels both from his belt
       and from his eyes, and caused him hurt.

328    *I* am that thirsting man you robbed;
       my fortune lives, but you are dead.

329    You slew me, but God willed it not;
       happy is he whom God supports.

330    Since God my fortune guarded, see:
       both throne and crown He's given me.

331    Woe to your life, O evil one;
       you took mine; you'll not save your own.'

Bad looked at Good, who knew him well;      332
quickly upon the ground he fell.

He cried, 'Have mercy; if I've wronged,      333
o'erlook it; 'tis myself I've harmed.

Think rather that the turning sphere      334
named me Bad and you Good. Before,

If I did do you such a wrong      335
as is entailed by my name,

In such a grave affair, perform      336
that which is ordered by your own.'

Good, when he grasped that point, then spared      337
the man from execution. Bad,

Freed from the blade, leapt up in joy      338
at that reprieve, and ran away.

The Kurd, athirst for blood, pursued,      339
struck with the sword, cut off his head.

'If Good has kindly thoughts,' he said,      340
'you're Bad, and merit nought but bad.'

He searched his body, found those gems,      341
wrapped them inside his belt, and then

He swiftly brought them back to Good;      342
'Gem has returned to gem,' he said.

Good kissed the gems and gave them to      343
the Kurd; thus honoured jewel with jewel.

He touched his eyes, and then declared,      344
''Tis thanks to you these jewels were spared.

Those jewels I give to you by right,      345
because these once again have light.'

When Good's affairs thus prospered, men      346
saw only good from him. And when

Felicity gave him its throne,      347
his sackcloth turned to silk, his iron

To silver. Where Fortune guides, the thorn      348
is turned to dates, to gold the stone.

He settled justice firm in place,      349
and gave his rule a stable base.

Since that tree's wondrous, healing leaves      350
to harshest pain brought precious ease,

From time to time, to ward off pain,      351
he'd haste to that tall tree again,

352    Dismount beneath it, give his praise
       and greetings to that land. Because

353    Of his deep love and gratitude,
       he dyed his robes in sandalwood.

354    With nought else would he have to do,
       and dressed in nothing but its hue.

                    ❦

355    In sandalwood lies the soul's ease;
       its odour doth the spirit please.

356    Rubbed sandalwood cures headache; treats
       the fevered heart, the liver's heat.

357    That sandal is earth's colour is
       no wonder; it earth's colour gives.

                    ❦

358    After that Chinese Turk had told
       this clever tale, with broken words,

359    The king did place her in his soul,
       there from the Evil Eye concealed.


# 38

## How Bahrâm Sat on a Friday in the White Dome:
## The Tale of the Princess of the Seventh Clime

1      On Friday when this willow vault*
       with sunlight turned its black house white,

2      The king, in robes of white adorned,
       went joyfully to the white dome.

3      Venus o'er the fifth kingdom* shone;
       played for him fealty's five tunes.

4      Till night's black Ethiops rushed day's Turks,
       the king ceased not his joyful sport.

5      When, with the heavens' collyrium, night
       made eyes of moon and stars shine bright,

6      He bade that maiden (loving, kind;
       a night companion, born of dawn)

7      To make her sweetest music sound,
       and through the echoing dome resound.

8      When she had worthy praise intoned

upon his crown and lofty throne,
And prayers which make prosperity    9
increase, befitting sovereignty,
She said, 'Since the king asks a tale    10
that pleases, I'll say what I can tell.'

### The Tale of the Man who Wished to Sport in the Garden with his Beloved, and was Prevented each Time

My mother said (a worthy dame;    11
all men are wolves, but she a lamb):
A friend of my own age—may she    12
and her house thrive—invited me
One day. She brought a tray, well-filled    13
with foods, much more than I can tell:
Lamb, fowl, and cumin-flavoured stew;    14
round cakes, oil cakes, and thin cakes too;
Rare sweets which have no name, made with    15
pistachios, or almond pith;
Delicate fruits which tempt the tongue:    16
Rayy's grapes, apples from Isfahan;
To say nought of the drinker's sweet,    17
the pomegranate; for those breasts
With pomegranates filled the house.    18
When we'd enjoyed those luscious foods,
We turned to wine, and laughing, we,    19
all story-tellers, mingled free.
Each told a story: one about    20
herself, another of her mate.
The turn came to one silver-limbed,    21
like milk in sugar, honeyed milk;
A charmer, whose enchanting words    22
did lull to rest both fish and birds.
From her carnelian lips she loosed    23
fresh founts; began a tale of love.

### The Young Master's Tale

There was a youth (she sweetly said),    24
as eloquent as sugar-reed;
A Jesus at his studies, and    25

|     | a Joseph who the feast illumed. |
|-----|---------------------------------|
| 26  | A wise, accomplished man was he;<br>of all things best, his chastity. |
| 27  | He had a garden like Iram,<br>that gardens circled, like a shrine.* |
| 28  | Its fragrant earth with amber mixed;<br>its fruits like those of Paradise; |
| 29  | Like pomegranates filled with hearts;<br>all roses, with no thorns about. |
| 30  | (Rose gardens sport sharp thorns to guard<br>the garden from the wounding Eye.) |
| 31  | Beneath young cypresses fresh streams<br>flowed, girt about by verdure green. |
| 32  | Bird upon bird raised song on high,<br>as if an organ filled the sky. |
| 32a | An emerald palace the cypress seemed,<br>a dove on every branch enthroned; |
| 33  | Beneath its clay-bound feet they moved<br>to song all those with hearts to love. |
| 34  | Its four walls, carefully designed,<br>were smooth and solid all around. |
| 35  | Its buildings to the moon rose high;<br>no way therein for Evil Eye. |
| 36  | The wish for such a bower would brand<br>the heart of any wealthy man. |
| 37  | Each week that man, in his free time,<br>went to enjoy his garden; ranged |
| 38  | Tall cypresses, and jasmine sowed;<br>rubbed musk, mixed amber moist, renewed |
| 39  | The cup in the narcissus' grasp;<br>gave violets' promise to the grass. |
| 40  | Around that garden he would roam<br>a while, and then return to home. |
| 41  | Once, at the time of noonday prayer,<br>he went into that garden fair. |
| 42  | He found it shut up like a stone,<br>the gardener lulled by the harp's strains. |
| 43  | The garden reeled from that sweet song, |

and from the beauties that there thronged.
Each tree had joined them in the dance; 44
the leaves refreshed, the fruits entranced.

The master, hearing these love-songs, 45
tore at his robe; no cup in hand,
No self-control to turn away, 46
no key to open up the gate.

He pounded loud, but no one answered; 47
roses asleep, cypresses dancing.

He ranged the garden's walls and sought 48
a way to enter; finding that
There was no entrance through his door, 49
he breached one through the wall's support.

He entered, so that he might watch, 50
and dance among them, Sufi-like;*
That he might to this music listen 51
(pretending to inspect the garden),

See who was making this uproar, 52
how fared the garden and gardener.

Among the roses that he saw 53
making his garden bright that day,
He spied two jasmine-breasted maids— 54
nay, silver-limbed—who at the gate
Kept watch, that on those hourî forms 55
like moons, no stranger's eye might come.

When he had entered through that hole, 56
the maidens found him rude and bold.

They thrashed him till they wore him out; 57
called him a thief, and bound him tight.

The master suffered their abuse, 58
fearing that he might be accused
Of wrong. With nails and fists they hit 59
and wounded him; then loud did shout:

'You garden-violater! There's 60
no one to guard the garden here!
For when one's garden's breached by thieves, 61
the gardener a good beating gives.
We, who beset you with our clubs, 62

were right to bind you hand and foot,
63    Since you have entered through a hole,
ignored the gate, and breached the wall.'

64    He said, 'Indeed, this garden's mine;
but for my act I bear the brand:

65    With gates that gape like lion's jaws,
why should I creep in like a fox?

66    Who enters his own land this way
will see its ruin one fine day.'

67    They sought from him some signs of proof,
and recognized him then in truth;

68    Seeing his evidence was true,
abuse was ceased, affection grew.

69    The garden's owner known to them,
their hearts were filled with love for him.

70    He comely, eloquent, and young:
all women lost who see these things.

71    They thought it fitting to make peace,
for with his nature they were pleased.

72    They loosed his hands and feet, and kissed
them lovingly, and sweetly asked

73    His pardon many times; became
his staunch supporters, loyal friends.

74    Then (for when foe becomes a friend,
a once-breached wall's made sound again),

75    With brambles they closed up the breach,
and freed themselves from robbers' reach.

76    They sat in friendship with the lord;
to him their lengthy story told:

77    'Within this garden, like the spring
in bloom—the lord rejoice therein!—

78    There is a feast of moon-faced maids,
loving heart-ravishers, arrayed.

79    Each lovely woman in the town
whose beauty cheers the sight, is found

80    Ingathered here, like candles with no
smoke; fair pictures without flaw.

81    To make amends for all our ills,
for throwing dust in our own well,

Rise, stroll with us a while; fulfil      82
your heart's desire with whom you will.

Hide in some secret corner; there      83
observe these scattered roses fair.

Whichever idol your heart moves,      84
you give your love to, and approve,

We'll bring her to your hiding-place,      85
to serve you there with love and grace.'

When the lord heard this, in his heart      86
sleeping desire awoke, cried out.

Although by nature continent,      87
he was with passion well acquaint.

Manhood humanity beguiled;*      88
a man, he bent to woman's wiles.

So, full of hope, he went with them      89
of jasmine breasts and silver limbs,

Until they came unto a place      90
which set the anxious heart at ease.

There rose before those heavenly maids      91
a chamber high,* of dried bricks made.

He went inside and closed the door;      92
his guides then left. He saw a hole

In the front centre of the room,      93
through which a beam of bright light shone.

Through this hole's fount the master spied      94
rosy-faced maids with narrow eyes.

On every side were roses strewn:      95
sweet pomegranate-breasts, and limbs

Of silver had those maids, who lit      96
the eyes' lamps; sweeter than ripe fruit.

Each fair, as at her wedding feast,      97
made sweet song to excite the heart.

Dragon-like locks on treasures rested;      98
not tangerine- but orange-breasted.

Pomegranate breasts, and chins like sweet      99
cleft apples which were out of reach.

Gardens, indeed, lack not for such,      100
when gardeners are not unjust.

Amid that garden's verdure was      101

a grassy mead by a cypress grove.

102     There was a pool of marble there
to which Kawsar could not compare,

103     With water clear as tears therein,
and fishes who had ne'er known harm.

104     Around that purest fountain grew
lilies, narcissus, jasmine too.

105     Those idols came, and saw their moons
among the fishes in the pond.

106     Warmed by the sun's heat, they had found
water as brilliant as the sun.

107     Gracefully to the pool they came,
and loosed their flowered wrappers' bands.

108     They doffed their robes, removed their veils,
entered the water, fair as pearls;

109     Splashed water on their silvery forms;
in black concealed their silver. Moons

110     And fish played in the pool; enflamed
the world with ardent passion. When

111     The moon its coins on water casts,
where is the fish that will not rise?

112     Their moons, with such heart-grasping grace,
coin-casting, stirred the master's fish.

113     A while they played, their hands clasped tight,
mocking the jasmine with their white;

114     A while they scattered pearls about,
and launched fair rounded fruits like boats.*

115     Aping a serpent, one bold girl
cried out, 'A snake!' and tossed her curls.

116     Fair as white columns in Bîsitûn
(their Farhâd with a sharp axe slain),

117     They filled the pool with milky streams
like those in Shîrîn's castle.* When

118     The lord saw this, his patience fled.
What help? he had no friend or aid.

119     Like one who thirsts and, drunken, sees
water but cannot grasp it, he;

120     Or one with fits who sees the new moon,

sometimes leaps up, sometimes sits down.

He gazed at every cypress form                        121
and saw there Resurrection's dawn.*

His blood, aboil in every vein,                        122
made all his limbs cry out in pain.

He stood there, hidden like a thief,                   123
with what you know as you might think,

Wishing to leap among them, bold,                      124
bird through the nook, snake through the hole:

Alas! his snake could not be bold;                     125
why? from the narrowness of that hole.

Their rosy faces washed, those fair                    126
like jasmine over bright silk flowered;

Then sky-blue silken robes put on,                     127
and put to shame the sky's own moon.

Amongst them one fair harpist made                     128
all blacks before her Rûmî face.

A sun, her chin a crescent moon;                       129
her lips a date tasted by none.

Each glance more swift and sharp than that             130
before; each smile more sugar-sweet.

Her burdened cypress put to shame                      131
the pomegranate; *hers* lustre gained.

Her charms a thousand hearts had lured;                132
whoever saw her quick expired.

Whenever to her harp she sang,                         133
love grew awake, and reason drunk.

The master, from afar, was more                        134
bewitched than Hindus by light's glow.

Although each maiden was a moon,                        135
among them she was like a queen.

The eremite strayed from his path.                     136
Such unbelief! alas for faith!

Anon those two gazelle-eyed maids,                     137
whose fur flashed bright with lightning's blaze,

Roused the musk-deer in that Cathay                    138
and showed the cheetah swift his prey,

That slim gazelle. They came to speak                  139

sweet words, and ply matchmaking tricks.

140    They found the master hidden there,
       and, like door-keepers, questions fired:

141    'Amongst these idols, hourî-born,
       to which of them do you incline?'

142    The master then described his love
       to those two fair designers. Up

143    They leapt—his words were scarcely done—
       like twin gazelles—nay, furious lions.

144    With magic spells they brought to him
       that perî-maid, to the harp's strains.

145    By hidden ways, that none might see,
       or, seeing, might those watchers flee,

146    They brought that wondrous maiden there,
       and—yet more wondrous—locked the door!

147    The master knew not that his love
       was willing, his task simply done;

148    That harpist who had hastened there
       amenable to his affair.

149    Those two fair ones to her had told
       the tale of that maid-loving lord;

150    And she, approving, had, unseen,
       fastened her heart on him in turn,

151    Seeing him finer than they'd told;
       his iron pure silver, his silver gold.

152    Impatient with desire, the lord
       reproached that supple cypress; said,

153    'What is your name?' 'Bakht,'* said she.
       'The Evil Eye?'—''Tis far from me.'

153a   'What is your source?'—''Tis purest light.'
       'And what your place?'—'The throne of might.'

154    'What is your veil?' ''Tis song,' said she.
       'What is your mode?'*—''Tis coquetry.'

155    'A kiss?' he begged; 'Sixty,' she said.
       'Come, is it time?'—'It is, indeed.'

156    'Will I attain you?'—'Soon,' she said.
       'Gain my desire?'— 'You shall.' At this

157    The master burned in every limb;
       all grace and shame abandoned him.

He grasped the maid's hair like her harp;            158
embraced her tightly like his heart.

Upon her sugared lips he rained                      159
kisses and bites, ten score times ten.

Those heated kisses stirred his heart;               160
the heat gave keenness to his dart.

He longed to taste her sweet spring; break           161
the seal from off the Fount of Life.

When the black lion seized the wild ass;             162
drew her with force beneath his claws:

Their place was weak; beneath the strain             163
its bricks were breached. The ancient room

Came tumbling down; but righteous men's              164
affairs do not come to bad ends.

They 'scaped by but a hair, a tear;                  165
one leapt one way, and one, in fear,

The other; so that none might spy                    166
them on the path, they far did fly.

The lord, in pain and grief, retired;                167
crept in a corner, wept and sighed.

Among her friends the maiden sat,                    168
her brows bound tight by sorrow's knots.

She called to mind her past distress,                169
and took the harp in her embrace.

When she brought forth her harp's lament,            170
lovers were maddened by her plaints.

She sang: 'My harp, with plaintive strings,          171
greetings to weary lovers brings.

A lover he who brooks fatigue,                       172
bears weariness, endures defeat.

How long must I conceal my love?'                    173
she loudly sang; 'I love, I love.

My passionate love has made me lose                  174
control; the ardent lover knows

No patience; but though love demeans,                175
repentance is a greater sin.

Love cannot sing repentance's tune;                  176
regret and true love cannot join.

The lover's he who gives his life;                   177

what need he fear from sword or shaft?'

178 That Turkish harpist, scattering pearls
from rubies, thus her plight did tell;

179 And those two pearls who pulled the string,
to her sweet love-plaint listening,

180 Thought, 'From the garden a strong wind
has blown upon those bright lamps twain.'

181 They sought that lost Joseph to find,
and like Zulaykhâ to him clung.

182 They asked the truth of the affair;
the tale he told brought forth their tears.

183 At this affair they were dismayed,
and made new plans. 'Tonight,' they said,

184 'We'll make this place a home, nor shirk
what we owe you with others' work.

185 We'll make excuses; not allow
any to her own home to go,

186 That you may grasp within your arms,
quite firmly, your beloved moon.

187 Daylight exposes all; dark night
will guard the curtain, hinder light.'

188 Saying these words, they went and made
some pretext to the other maids.

189 When night 'neath its black furs concealed
the day's bright Russian cloth-of-gold,

190 The nail's breadth of the sun effaced,
night's breastplate sprouted myriad rays;

191 Those maidens came and kept their word;
gave up that idol to the lord.

192 The thirsting cypress gained the stream;
bright sunlight joined with pale moonbeam.

193 An empty place, and such a love:
what man could then restrain himself?

194 The master, with his blood afire
in every vein, sought his desire.

195 Of that which from all should be hid,
I've told this; no more—God forbid!

196 But when the ruby sought to pierce

the pearl, and join them each to each:
A wild cat, crouching on a branch,                        197
espied a bird, and quickly pounced
On it; and, crashing to the ground,                       198
disturbed the lovers; in alarm
Each one sprang up, a fiery heat                           199
within their hearts; with hastening feet
They parted, unfulfilled: observe                         200
that raw dish, neither cooked nor served.
The sweet-lipped maid fled to her mates,                  201
and played her harp throughout the night.
She plucked her harp and sweetly sang:                    202
'The Judas-tree has flowered;* 'tis spring.
The cypress risen to lofty stature;                       203
the smiling rose its sugar scattered.
A nightingale perched on the bough;                       204
love's commerce seemed broad day to show.
The gardener perfumed the bower;                          205
a king came to observe it; saw
A beaker there, and took it up;                           206
a falling stone shattered the cup.
You, who have left me all bereft,                         207
'tis only you can make things right.
Although my actions bring me shame,                       208
my heart won't hear of severing.'
Her mode of music made her friends                        209
discern her secret. Once again
They went, lamenting, all about,                          210
and finally sought the master out.
The master, like a thieving slave,                        211
had found a secret hiding-place.
Beneath a narrow stream he crept,                         212
'neath willow, poplar, cypress, box,
Bewildered at his unripe plans:                           213
yellow wallflower from white jasmine* sprung.
They sought from him what he concealed;                   214
to them his story he revealed.
Those plotters took it on themselves                      215

|       | to reunite the two in love. |
|-------|-----------------------------|
| 216   | The maids returned, the path disclosed, and sent the essence to the rose. |
| 217   | That loving songstress came and showed renewed affection for her love. |
| 218   | He took her hand and went ahead, until he found a likely bed. |
| 219   | The thick-spread branches of the trees upon their heights formed many seats. |
| 220   | He hastened 'neath that kingly throne, and made a place to sit upon. |
| 221   | With love that ravisher he pressed, close as his own heart, to his breast. |
| 222   | That graceful cypress form, which might, like jasmine, royal carpets deck. |
| 223   | He clasped her joyfully; thus rose and cypress joined in passion close. |
| 224   | The master thus embraced his moon; his hand was busy, unrestrained. |
| 225   | The master's piece a house had seized; his partner had the stakes agreed. |
| 226   | But when he was about to take the castle; fire with water slake— |
| 227   | A field mouse, from the branches high, some hanging gourds did then espy, |
| 228   | Flew at the string, bird-like, and cut the gourds' string with a single bite. |
| 229   | The gourds all crashed upon the ground, each empty as a drum, and round. |
| 230   | Their sound was heard for miles; what drums! that signal when departure comes. |
| 231   | The gourds kept up their clatter; thus the deer escaped the lion's claws. |
| 232   | The master thought the bailiff come to war with stones, the guard* with drums. |
| 233   | He left his shoes, and ran pell-mell; once more thought only of himself. |
| 234   | That idol fled, with thousand fears, back to her music-loving peers. |

When some time passed, the veil she rent     235
to sing a song of love's lament:
'Once on a time (so lovers say),     236
a lover went his love to see.
He sought to find (in great desire)     237
a happy union, joined with her;
As passion wills, to hold her close     238
(beside the cypress grows the rose);
The apples of her chin to eat;     239
taste pomegranates from her breast;
Extend his hand to her pearl-store,     240
and open up the treasure's door;
With sugar-loaf mix sugar; shed     241
the tulip's blood with willow red.
Disturbance brought a mighty clash     242
and clamour; thus their hopes were dashed:
The moth still yearning for the light,*     243
the thirsting far from the Water of Life.
O you whose moves are all unfair,     244
now make your moves with proper care.
You give me but discords; 'tis wrong;     245
but true to you will be my song.'
When she had sung this song, her mates,     246
true confidants, perceived her state.
Seeking to make amends, they found     247
the master, stretched out on the ground;
Ashamed, his heart distraught, he lay     248
exhausted, on the earth. When they,
With sympathy and kindness great,     249
had raised him from his fallen state,
They asked, 'What's wrong?' He told a tale     250
that would produce cold sighs in Hell.
Those plotters, by their strategies,     251
set his bad thoughts once more at ease.
The bonds that bound his heart they loosed;     252
encouraged him with promises.
'Be wiser henceforth, if you will;     253
you love; but be more loving still.
When the time comes, a nest prepare     254

|     |     |
|-----|-----|
|     | where no calamity will dare. |
| 255 | We, from afar, will keep our watch; |
|     | like sentinels we'll guard your path.' |
| 256 | Then to his lover they returned |
|     | (that rosy-cheeked, fair cypress form); |
| 257 | Once more, Turk-like, she sallied forth, |
|     | the master found, and soothed his heart. |
| 258 | She came to him, his grief assuaged; |
|     | he put all mastery aside, |
| 259 | Clung to her curls like one who's drunk, |
|     | and sought within the garden some |
| 260 | Retreat. He found a place, remote, |
|     | where jasmine made a dome of light, |
| 261 | Against a wall its banner raised; |
|     | above, a wood; below, a cave. |
| 262 | The master found no better place; |
|     | he made his workshop in its midst. |
| 263 | He brushed the jasmine branch aside, |
|     | and drew the maiden safe inside. |
| 264 | He loosed her shirt, and all shame fled |
|     | (what other bands, cannot be said). |
| 265 | He clasped a heap of roses; held |
|     | almonds in sugar. Yet the rod |
| 266 | Had not yet in collyrium dipped, |
|     | when the bent sphere played one more trick. |
| 267 | Some foxes, deep inside the cave, |
|     | together went in search of prey. |
| 268 | A wolf had closed the way behind, |
|     | to separate them from their kin. |
| 269 | The foxes, from that ravening wolf |
|     | (an evil dreadful to behold!), |
| 270 | The wolf behind them, quickly fled— |
|     | their path, over the master's bed. |
| 271 | Over those schemers two they ran, |
|     | foxes before and wolf behind. |
| 272 | The master's court had crumbled down; |
|     | he saw an army; with a bound |
| 273 | Leapt up; not knowing what was what, |

covered with dirt, he ran about,
His heart disturbed, his mind aflame,    274
seeking to leave that bower soon.

Those cypress-forms appeared, who'd given    275
so many fruits and flowers to him.

They grasped his lover by her skirt    276
(a precious pearl between two sharks),

And screamed at her: 'What are these tricks?    277
What demon is it that afflicts

Your nature? How long try this youth?    278
Your treachery has killed his love!

No one who for him friendship feigns    279
would play a stranger such a game.

How many times tonight you've fled!    280
How many tricks and spells you've played!'

She made excuses, swore them true;    281
they would not hear the tale from her,

Until the master came and found    282
his candle 'twixt two snuffers, shamed

By their reproofs, and taking slaps    283
from this one, and sharp blows from that.

He said, 'Beware! take off your hands!    284
Don't torment an unhappy friend!

No wrong's been done me by this moon;    285
you must play her a better tune.

If in this treachery there was sin,    286
against the guilty raise your hands.

Her nature from all sin is free;    287
what sin there was came from *this* clay.

In this world, those who clever are    288
and quick, are slaves before the pure.

God's grace, eternal and divine,    289
save us from being harmed by sin.

And my defective reason: those    290
calamities removed its flaws.

Since Fortune gave me continence,    291
it guarded me from such a sin.

He who's not mastered by a devil    292

is good; and no good man does evil;

293  But he who for the unlawful yearns—
saving your presence—is baseborn.

294  With such a perî-visaged bride
no true man could her love avoid;

295  Especially a man who's young,
manly, and passionate. But when

296  Chastity bars the way to him,
no man can keep pursuing sin.

297  No one can eat fruit from the tree
that's gazed on by the Evil Eye.

298  The eyes of hundred beasts* were on
us two; thus we became undone.

299  Let's say no more; what's done is done;
and let's not ruin what we've won.

300  Public and private, I repent,
and am with God's decree content:

301  That if my Hour* be delayed,
and if I still may hunt this prey,

302  I'll make of her my lawful wife,
and serve her ever through my life.'

303  Seeing things thus the plotters, awed
by his God-fearing, quickly bowed

304  Their heads before him in the dust:
'May such pure faith in one be praised

305  In whom are sown the seeds of good;
who from bad nature is preserved.

306  How many trials which brought great grief
were seen as trials, but bore relief.

307  How many pains men sorely try
in which is the soul's remedy.'

308  The beauties ceased their coquetry,
amazed at the sphere's puppetry.

309  When light's fount from the hills sprang high,
it drove away the Evil Eye;

310  And, like the astrolabe's spider, dawn
o'er the earth's pole its fine web spun.

311  A breeze arose with lamp in hand,
and bore the gardener to the town.

He raised his flag in mastery,  
released from bonds and slavery.     312

His mind had boiled from the flame  
of last night's passion. When he came     313

To town, he loyally contrived  
to seek his goal. He brought his bride,     314

That last night's moon, unto his bed;  
fulfilled the vows of those who wed;     315

With coral pierced the pearl unbored;  
his fish slept; wakeful grew dawn's bird.     316

Where'er you look, from fish to bird,  
all are by lawful passion stirred.     317

What fortune! he clear water gained,  
and when it was made lawful, drank.     318

He found a fountain clear as the sun,  
as silver white, pure as jasmine.     319

❧

From white does the day's brilliance come;  
from white the world-illuming moon.     320

All hues with artifice are stained,  
except for white, which pure remains.     321

He who despairs when stained will be,  
when pure, called 'white' by all who see.     321*a*

In worship, when men strive for right,  
it is the custom to wear white.     322

❧

The jasmine-scented maid now done,  
the king embraced her as his own.     323

Many such nights he went and stayed  
within each dome, in joy and ease.     324

Before him this dome-building sky  
the Seven Domes' doors threw open wide.     325

# 39

## Description of Spring

When—Jupiter and Saturn in trine—  
the planets' king left Fish for Ram,*     1

2    The Khizr-like verdure sprouted fresh,
and the springs found the Stream of Life:

3    Each well-spring gushed a heavenly Nile;
each path led to a Salsabîl.*

4    The sandal earth was garbed in musk;
the wind's trade in that scent grew brisk.

5    The New Year's temperate air went straight;
suffused the world with brilliant light.

6    For the sweet herbs the New Year's breeze
had pledged its life, by a new lease.

7    From the earth's heart the green shoots thrust
their heads; sun's disk was cleansed of rust.

8    The air's skirt freshest dew unfurled;
warmth bathed the limbs of bitter cold.

9    The camphor snow from passes high
shed brilliant tears o'er rivers dry.

10    The plants, to eyes like brilliant jewels,
gave fertile verdure to the world.

11    The fresh narcissus' languorous eyes
stole sleep from any who could see.

12    The morning breezes' musky breaths
perfumed the violet's dark dress.

13    The cypress shade formed canopies,
and combed the locks of the box-trees.

14    The lotus, which the sun made sleep,
fled for its life to water's keep.

15    Fresh buds on branches high unfurled,
like tulip-petals, scattered pearls.

16    Lilies, for the narcissus' crown,
held golden ingots in their palms.

17    The fragrant ox-eyes scattered stars
without the Resurrection.* Tears

18    Assailed the fenugreek, which ate
of saffron,* laughed again. A writ

19    The rose, with the Water of Life, inscribed
(like Scripture)* to shed poppies' blood.

20    The white-rose petals strung their pearls;
the lily stems applied their kohl.

The mouse-ear, like a Daylamite,                    21
cast curl on curl upon its back.

Both leaves and grass contented were,               22
one carpet and the other shears.

With musky blooms, the hyacinth                      23
loosed its sharp fragrance o'er the pink.

The wallflower had made a pact                       24
that jasmine be its heir. The scent

Of wild mint, heady, melted down                     25
the sting of heaven's Scorpion.

Rose-buds romanced ox-eyes; dawn's bird              26
breathed secrets in the elephant-ear.

The camphor-scented musk-rose wore                   27
silver and gold like lovers' ears.

Like aloes-wood, the tamarisk                        28
spread sometimes camphor, sometimes musk.

Judas and jasmine raised their flags                 29
before the willow, white and red.

Stricken by autumn wind's cruel barbs,               30
the willow trees put out fresh buds.

The rose put on a sovereign's belt;                  31
both earth and wind in fealty knelt.

The nightingale sang like a drum                     32
throughout the night, till cock-crow came.

On fields of green the rose's red                    33
the fivefold royal fanfare played.

On cypress trees the ring-doves' plaint,             34
like lute-song, soothed the tender heart;

The turtle-doves with morning wail,                  35
like flutes, stole laughter from the quail.

About the fields, the francolin                      36
cried like a Paradisal poem.

The reader of the heavenly Zand                      37
at night its holy words intoned;

From its shrill cries that nightingale               38
had grown, like harp-strings, slim and frail.

The garden like a picture limned,                    39
both bird and fish rejoiced therein.

## 40

## How Bahrâm Learned of the Chinese Ruler's Second Invasion and of the Army's Revolt

| | |
|---|---|
| 1 | On such a day did King Bahrâm<br>in royal style a feast illume, |
| 2 | And, like his seven pavilions, raise<br>another higher than the sky. |
| 3 | A burdened messenger arrived<br>and sought that tent, which had six sides;* |
| 4 | On entering that heavenly place,<br>his heart swelled vast as Paradise. |
| 5 | He praised the prince; and, having done,<br>bowed low before the royal throne |
| 6 | And said, 'Once more, from templed Chîn,<br>an army's tumult has arisen. |
| 7 | Faghfûr has set at nought his oath;<br>once more departed from good faith. |
| 8 | The Chinese keep no pact; within<br>they're poison, though they honey seem. |
| 9 | Their troops, with swords to Heaven raised,<br>have reached the Oxus, wave on wave. |
| 10 | A flood has overwhelmed the plain,<br>each monster like a sea therein. |
| 11 | If the king be not watchful, they'll<br>soon drink our blood in brimming bowls.' |
| 12 | The king, learning of this sedition,<br>sought for a way to heal affliction. |
| 13 | Before the trap could close on him,<br>he left the cup, abstained from wine. |
| 14 | He plotted how he could destroy,<br>with judgement sure, the enemy. |
| 15 | He needed troops and treasury,<br>for both are tools of victory. |
| 16 | An empty treasury he found,<br>and troops and weapons scattered round; |
| 17 | He, helpless as a toothless lion,<br>his realm a gaol, his collar* a chain. |
| 18 | I've heard the king had a vizier* |

who, far from God, did not Him fear.
He called himself (in wishful thought)     19
Râst-Rawshan; was not straight nor bright.
Both light and straightness did he lack:     20
his straightness bent, his brightness dark.
He tricked the king with his good name,     21
while he himself earned evil fame.
His office, when in Narsî's hands,     22
was filled with fear of God; but when
Râst-Rawshan seized the vizierate,     23
rightness and brightness perished straight.
While the king drank and sported, he     24
oppressed; aroused disloyalty;
Destroyed the public welfare; strained     25
to gather wealth, amass much land.
The king's vicegerent he seduced     26
by alchemy of gold and jewels.
'The people', he said, 'are filled with greed;     27
they've grown bold, mannerless, and rude.
Those comforts, given to make them full,     28
they've used against us; if we will
Not punish them with wit and sense,     29
the Evil Eye will punish us.
Bad men, of evil nature, all:     30
false Josephs worse than dogs and wolves.
Wolves must be trapped and tightly bound;     31
how long shall they, like foxes, dance?
Although they're earthlings, of earth born,     32
they're wild beasts in the forms of men.
Wild beasts for faith have no regard;     33
they'll not submit, save by the sword.
You've read, in books, what Siyâvash     34
had suffered from such savage beasts;
How they Jam's glory overthrew,     35
and how the great Darius slew.
Their wealth's a pool, and they are full;     36
so water standing in a pool
Stagnates; but murky water, when     37
earth filters it, grows sweet again.

38  Sober the foe, if the king's drunk;
    though the watch sleep, the thief's awake.

39  For when the king forgets the rod,
    his kingship will be ruined; but

40  From one who punishment decrees
    both enemies and demons flee.

41  Bold subjects are like demons; let
    them be, their bounds they'll overstep.

42  Be sure, with your chastisement, you
    harm not the brilliance of your rule.

43  Don't trust the friendly acts of men;
    know only your own sword as friend.

44  The king, who trusts us, worships wine;
    you hold the sword, and I the pen.

45  From you force, from me strategy;
    now seize whomever I may say.

46  Punish the rich man through his wealth;
    deal with the poor by blood; for both

47  Good men and bad are lawful;* take
    the good man's wealth, the bad man's life.

48  Abase all men with wealth and place,
    and grow exalted in their eyes.

49  With subjects lowly and abased,
    dominion will be firmly based.'

50  The deputy, drunk at these words,
    joined with him in his cruel deeds.

51  In harsh oppression shown the way,
    he harassed the king's subjects; preyed

52  Upon them, till he went beyond
    all bounds; held no man anyone.

53  In their oppression they stood fast,
    seized men and stole all they possessed.

54  Village and town heard nought but cries:
    this man arrested, that wealth seized;

55  Till, by a year's time, in that realm,
    no one retained his land or wealth.

56  Râst-Rawshan, from both small and great,
    unjustly stole both right and bright.

57  Slaves male and female, gold, and gems
    were left to no one in the realm.

Thus lack of money—not its use—                     58
rich men to poverty reduced.

Householders, from those burglars' wrongs,           59
found their own homes in others' hands.

Citizens, soldiers, outcasts all,                    60
roamed, tired and worn, from hill to hill.

Throughout the land no cow nor field                 61
remained; none could record a yield.

The realm in grievous ruin lay,                      62
and empty the king's treasury.

Save the vizier, with house and wealth,              63
no one reaped ought but toil and grief.

When, readying for war, the king,                    64
lacked wealth and troops, he felt great pain.

From his informers, one by one,                      65
he sought this ruin's cause; but none,

Dreading the world-burning vizier's might,           66
would tell by day what passed at night.

Each one advanced some false pretext:                67
'This one grew poor; another fled;

The land gives no return; no grain                   68
is there; therefore no wealth remains.

From lack of work and ready cash,                    69
there's no one left to pay his tax.

If the king show mercy, they'll return               70
and go about their work again.'

Though this did not convince the king,               71
he did not haste to beard the lion

With ill-timed war, but pondered on                  72
the evil of the cruel dome.

He found no way to mend his state;                   73
left off his struggle against Fate.

# 41

## How Bahrâm Came to the Hut of the Old Shepherd

Unhappy at these straits, the king                    1
would go out hunting, all alone.

He'd hunt, and grow more cheerful; then,              2

|    | with lighter heart, he'd turn towards home. |
|----|---------------------------------------------|
| 3  | When, on that day, grief gripped his reins, |
|    | he longed to seek the prey; he went |
| 4  | Alone to hunt, to wash the blood |
|    | from out his heart, with crimson flood. |
| 5  | Whatever quarry he desired |
|    | he took; bound grief and care; then, tired |
| 6  | From hunting leopard, lion, and boar, |
|    | he turned back towards his home once more. |
| 7  | His brain was all afire with thirst |
|    | From his quick rushes in the hunt. |
| 8  | He ranged that region all around; |
|    | the more he sought, the less he found. |
| 9  | Some smoke he spied, like dragon black, |
|    | head raised, the full moon to attack, |
| 10 | Writhing in coils and billowing high, |
|    | preparing to assault the sky. |
| 11 | He thought, 'If smoke from fire doth wind, |
|    | from its kindler I must water find.' |
| 12 | When towards that smoke the king drew nigh, |
|    | he saw a humble tent raised high; |
| 13 | A flock of sheep, from hoof to ear |
|    | stewing like meat in the sun's glare; |
| 14 | And from a tree's tall branch there hung |
|    | a dog, his limbs all tightly bound. |
| 15 | Towards the tent he urged his mount; |
|    | saw an old man like kindly dawn. |
| 16 | The old man rose, seeing his guest; |
|    | prepared to serve him as was best. |
| 17 | Like humble earth he waited on |
|    | his guest, and held the reins of Heaven.* |
| 18 | He offered him great praises first, |
|    | then helped him dismount from his horse. |
| 19 | Whatever food he had prepared |
|    | he brought for him, and gently said: |
| 20 | 'Without a doubt, this poor repast |
|    | does not befit a noble guest; |
| 21 | But we are far from humans here; |
|    | excuse it, if the meal is poor.' |

When the king saw his bits of bread,          22
he asked for water, left the food.

He said, 'I'll only eat when you          23
answer my question right and true:

Why has this dog (the house's lion)          24
helplessly, like a wolf, been bound?'

The old man said, 'O handsome youth,          25
I'll tell you what has passed, in truth:

This dog was my flock's guardian;          26
I trusted my affairs to him.

Loyal and trustworthy was he;          27
I, happy in his company;

For through the years he kept all safe          28
from wolf's sharp claws and grasping thief.

I made him watchdog of my home;          29
called him not dog, but guardian.

He, day and night, was my iron arm,          30
with teeth and claws that all foes burned.

If I went from the plain to town,          31
I knew my flock was safe with him;

And if my work in town dragged on,          32
'twas he who'd bring the flock back home.

For several years he was my guard,          33
played straight, and acted as he should;

Till one day, in my reckoning,          34
I counted up the flock; I found

That seven sheep were missing; gone;          35
I feared an error in my sums;

Next week I counted up again,          36
again fell short; I told no one.

I watched with care and caution, but          37
I found no one that I could fault.

Though for some nights I kept a watch,          38
I never could the culprit catch;

But that dog knew much more than I,          39
and kept a far more watchful eye.

When yet again I counted up,          40
like the first day, it still came short.

All night my mind felt great distress,          41

because my flock kept growing less.

42  They disappeared by fives and tens,
    like ice that's melted by the sun,

43  Until the alms-collector* came
    and took as alms those that remained.

44  I, desert-dwelling, now became
    a shepherd, after having owned

45  Great flocks. That suffering humbled me,
    and caused me heartfelt misery.

46  I thought, "If this breach issues from
    the Evil Eye, what beast has done

47  The deed? With such a lion-like dog,
    who'd brave a guardian so bold?"

48  Until one day, beside a stream,
    I dozed; and, waking from my dream,

49  Just as I was, with my head bowed
    over my staff, I silent stood.

50  I saw a wolf bitch from afar
    approach; the dog grew weak before

51  That wolf. She called, in dog-like tongue;
    the dog ran to her like a friend.

52  He ran around her, raising dust;
    now wagged his tail, and now his mace.

53  At last he mounted her, and took
    his pleasure; the affair was lost:

54  He went and slept, and rested well;
    his mouth by secrecy was sealed.

55  The wolf, who'd given her bribe, now sought
    the due reward her service bought.

56  A strong ram, leader of the flock,
    whose fat tail weighed it down, she took

57  And carried off; devoured it quick;
    she'd eaten many bribes like that.

58  The cursed dog, by his lust driven,
    to the wolf's care the flock had given;

59  The flock in payment gave away,
    to settle up for lustful play.

60  For several times I pardoned him;
    left him alone, although he'd sinned;

I caught him with the wolf at last, 61
and tied him up for that trespass;
Punished him with imprisonment, 62
that he might grow obedient.
My dog a wolf in ambush deep 63
became—nay, butcher of my sheep.
He trust with treason did repay: 64
to traitor sold his charge away.
'Tis fitting that, until he die, 65
he never from his bonds go free.
Whoso with wrongdoers in like ways 66
deals not, let no one give him praise.'
King Bahrâm, when these words he heard, 67
perceived in them a lesson hid.
When he had grasped those symbols, then 68
he ate, and hastened to the town.
'From this old shepherd I have learned 69
(he thought) true kingship; clever plan!
My human exemplar* is thus: 70
I'm shepherd, and my subjects flock.
If the foundation is not sound, 71
in one of trust the breach is found.
My sharp-sighted vizier, he that 72
I trusted to protect my flock:
Let him tell me what caused this ruin, 73
from whom did this destruction come.'
Returning to the town, he asked 74
the officials for the prisoners' list;
And when he close examined it, 75
the day grew blacker than the writ.
Amazed, he found a world of pain, 76
each victim's name there written plain.
He thought, 'In mourning and in feasts, 77
the king kills, the vizier forgives.*
His tyranny brings me ill fame; 78
puts good repute in his own name.'
The king knew well the plot: the thief 79
within the house, who'd bear it off;
Just like that dog who gave the flock 80

|    | to wolf; distressed that shepherd Kurd. |
|----|------|
| 81 | (Dogs are by nature never fair; |
|    | they make an outcry as they tear.) |
| 82 | He deemed it best to have him seized, |
|    | and let him languish some ten days. |
| 83 | He thought, 'If I should leave him in |
|    | his high post, none will bring forth pen |
| 84 | 'Gainst him; but, strip him of his might: |
|    | bright light shows best in darkest night.' |

## 42

### How Bahrâm Tried his Vizier

| 1 | At dawn, when shining day grew light, |
|---|------|
|   | dark night rolled up its carpet tight. |
| 2 | Dawn, with one stroke of its two swords,* |
|   | sated the moon with its dark blood. |
| 3 | Bahrâm set up his court against |
|   | the sky, thrown open to all men. |
| 4 | From all the land the nobles came, |
|   | drawn up according to their rank. |
| 5 | Râst-Rawshan entered through the gate, |
|   | and boldly went to his high seat. |
| 6 | The king regarded him with wrath; |
|   | shouted (it nearly caused his death!): |
| 7 | 'You, who have ruined my domain; |
|   | destroyed the kingdom's honoured name; |
| 8 | Who've stuffed your store with jewels rare, |
|   | and scattered my wealth everywhere; |
| 9 | Deprived my army of its needs, |
|   | so that both wealth and glory fled; |
| 10 | My subjects' homes unjustly robbed; |
|   | planted your feet in each man's blood; |
| 11 | Instead of lawful taxes, took |
|   | from men now riches and now rank: |
| 12 | You have forgotten gratitude; |
|   | have you no shame before your lord? |
| 13 | Ingratitude is worse in faith |

than irreligion. To requite
The favours that a man receives,    14
to him still greater blessings gives.

What light, what truth, have you displayed?    15
brightness has vanished, truth has fled.

You've ruined treasury and men;    16
now neither wealth nor troops remain.

What did you think? that, drinking, I    17
would sleep, and in a stupor lie?

That you'd disarm the drunkard's hand,    18
cripple my subjects? If Bahrâm,

Grasping the cup, forgets the sword,    19
may dust upon his head be poured.

If wine and music bring me cheer,    20
I'll not forget the azure sphere.'

Of such words he made myriad yokes,    21
and laid them on the vizier's neck.

He ordered that a guardsman fell*    22
drive him from Paradise to Hell.

With his own turban tightly bound,    23
they dragged him off and fettered him.

His legs in fetters, arms in chains:    24
no vizier this, but one who's sinned.

When might against that mighty one    25
was brought, the king a crier sent

To town: 'Let the oppressed complain,'    26
he cried; 'seek justice from the king.'

When citizens and soldiers heard,    27
they made their way to the king's court;

Of that base wretch's evil told;    28
with serpent's bane that dragon slew.

The king gave the command: that those    29
imprisoned should make known their woes;

Reveal the crimes of which accused,    30
to forge a key their chains to loose.

The prisoners, freed from their bonds,    31
approached, more than a thousand strong.

The king chose seven men from them,    32
and asked of each, 'What is your crime?

33    Of what are you accused? From whence
      have you come here? what your descent?'

# 43

## The First Victim's Tale

1     The first addressed said to Bahrâm,
      'May your foes perish!—Râst-Rawshan,

2     With great abuse, by torture killed
      my brother; seized and plundered all

3     He had—belongings, mounts, and goods
      he took; his life and wealth destroyed.

4     All grieved the loss of life of one
      who was so handsome and so young.

5     When I cried out in protest, he
      for the same crime arrested me;

6     Said, "He gave comfort to our foe;
      a traitor he, and so are you."

7     He signalled to a savage Ghûr,*
      his slave, who plundered my house too;

8     Bound me with fetters forcibly,
      and made my house a grave for me.

9     He wrongly took that brother's life;
      condemned this one to living death.

10    I've been imprisoned for a year;
      my sovereign's face now brings me cheer.'

11    When Bahrâm, from that victim's words,
      learned of his vizier's evil deeds,

12    All that he'd stolen was returned;
      his brother's blood-wit paid to him.

13    He freed him, put him at his ease;
      restored him to his former place.

# 44

## The Second Victim's Tale

1     The second man his homage gave
      unto the gentle king; then said,

'My garden overflowed with plants,      2
whose sight brought brightness to the heart.
A Paradisal carpet, green      3
and broad; fruits from its branches hung.
It gave me spring in autumn drear;      4
a memory of my father dear.
One day that tyrant, all aflame      5
with greed, unto my garden came.
I treated him to fruit and wine,      6
and suitably did entertain
The man; all in both bower and house      7
in gratitude before him placed.
He slept and rested, ate and laughed,      8
and drank as much wine as he wished.
He strolled around the garden; waxed      9
quite wild with longing to possess.
"Sell me your garden," he said then;      10
"prosperity to you I'll bring."
"How can I sell this garden? Nay,      11
it is as dear as life to me.
Each man has some great passion; mine,      12
poor wretch, this garden, fair and fine.
Consider it as yours always,      13
and I your gardener—nay, your slave.
Hasten to it when you're inclined;      14
eat fruit; beside its stream drink wine.
Whatever my poor kitchen has,      15
a lovely slave will to you serve."
"Leave off! don't make pretexts," said he;      16
"sell it, and take your things away."
We argued bitterly a while;      17
I would not sell for force or gold.
At last, inflamed with rage, he made      18
false charges; for that crime, he seized
My garden, through his treachery,      19
and left me in deep poverty;
And then, so that I might not bring      20
this wrong to trial before the king,
Imprisoned me in great distress,      21
and kept things hidden for two years.'

22    The king gave him a garden, fields,
      and house as beauteous as Baghdad.


# 45

## The Third Victim's Tale

1    The third man spoke: 'O king, who have
     whatever you desire; your slave

2    Was once a merchant on the sea;
     I earned my livelihood that way.

3    Sometimes I sought the coast, and found
     great profits there. When I grew known

4    For knowledge of the good and bad
     of sea-pearls, finally I acquired

5    Some pearls, lustrous and radiant,
     as brilliant as the morning's lamp.

6    I came to town well satisfied,
     my eyes by that pearl-string made bright.

7    I sought to sell that pearl-string; buy
     my food and clothing with its price.

8    When the vizier heard that I owned
     a necklace of fine pearls, he sent

9    For me and bought them, feigning shame,
     so that I lowered the price for him.

10   But when it came the time to pay,
     he made excuses, sought delay;

11   I sought my money, sore distressed;
     he gave me nought but cold pretexts.

12   For a few days, with guile and fraud,
     he played with me, while I still hoped;

13   Till he, in secret, summoned me,
     with murderers imprisoned me.

14   He made a pretext of my crime,
     and kept his money; in exchange

15   For my rare necklace, which he stole,
     he bound my limbs with irons cold.

16   He seized my gems; while I became,
     from his vile tortures, like a stone.

He pearls within his turban hid;                 17
I, shell-like,* dwelt within a pit
Three years in chains; but now content,          17*a*
since my eyes the king's face have seen.'
The king, from that base vizier's hoard,         18
returned the pearls, and added gold.


# 46

## The Fourth Victim's Tale

The fourth man, trembling greatly, said,          1
'O king, who merits countless praise:
I am a minstrel, young, in love;                  2
as sweet as flowing streams my lute.
I had a love, of beauty rare;                     3
a Chinese maid, my comforter.
Her sunny love stole the moon's light;            4
the envy she of day and night.
Her tiny mouth gave name to "nought";*            5
her smile broke sugar-cones to bits.
Beauty she stole from fair-faced spring,          6
which faded by comparison.
Though bought for money in my land,               7
her blessing caused my eyes to shine.
From me she'd learned to sing and play;           8
charming and pleasing were her lays.
We dwelt together, warm in love,                  9
like candle flame and fluttering moth.
She lit my heart like night the lamp;            10
she, in my bower, like grass, content.
So bright and light, a candle she                11
that Râst-Rawshan took far from me,
And kindled in his palace; burned               12
with flames of grief the moth's sore heart.
Distressed at separation's night,               13
I sought a path towards her light.
He, mocking, had me bound; implied              14
that I was mad; he, with the bride

15   He'd taken from me, dwelt at ease,
     and I in prison, with dire need.

16   For four years, wrongfully, he kept
     me, innocent, in abject state.'

17   The king returned the maid to him
     at once, with many other things.

18   He gave his wedding-price, and freed
     him from his bonds, with his fair bride.

## 47

## The Fifth Victim's Tale

1   The fifth man spoke: 'O mighty king,
     to whose high tent the sphere is joined:

2   I head a certain custom-house,*
     and serve the king's good fortune. Once,

3   My work was to adorn the land
     and serve the king, obedient.

4   By the king's fortune, God did grant,
     through wealth and state, magnificence

5   And ease; that the king live prosperous,
     I drowned the world in happiness.

6   I made provision for the road
     from prayers; for the king's sake did good.

7   I made new every town and street;
     all men of wisdom sought me out.

8   Seeking to make the kingdom thrive,
     each man his daily bread I gave.

9   Through me the straitened gained great wealth;
     widows, their children too, were filled.

10   To all who sought, I granted gold;
     I grasped the hand of all who fell.

11   No helpless one remained in bonds,
     without my freeing him from harm.

12   Whatever income I received
     from the *dihqâns*, I spent on guests.

13   Income, expense, both as they should:
     well pleased with me both men and God.

But when the vizier heard my tale,  14
injustice's pot began to boil.

He took my stewardship from me,  15
and seized my wealth and property.

"You have not earned this wealth (he said)  16
by toil; your largesse far exceeds

Your wealth; you've practised alchemy,  17
or gained great treasure in some way.

Give me my portion, as is due;  18
deliver, or I'll ruin you."

All of the means which I possessed  19
he seized upon this crude pretext,

And then abased me, who had been  20
my own man, binding me in chains.

Five years, within this jail, I've been  21
far from my children and my home.'

The king commanded he return,  22
in wealth and ease, to his domain.

# 48
# The Sixth Victim's Tale

When the count reached the sixth, the wine  1
of justice healed his fortune's pain.

He blessed the king; 'O lord,' he said,  2
'whose virtue gives men's daily bread:

I am a soldier and a Kurd,  3
through my forebears of noble birth.

I am the sovereign's soldier brave;  4
my father too was the king's slave.

I serve the king, loyal and true,  5
as did my father; I pursue

My sovereign's foes unceasingly,  6
with life and sword in hand. To me,

By his great grace the king did grant,  7
from his domains, a bit of land;

I worked it for my livelihood  8
in happiness, and loyal served.

9   That cruel vizier seized it from me;
    no one can withstand tyranny.

10   I had a family, but no wealth
    or property, except that field.

11   Time and again I begged him loud,
    "Assist me, for the sake of God,"

12   That he might render justice, and
    be merciful to me and mine,

13   Or, like retired soldiers, give
    a pension from the treasury.

14   He cried at me, "Be silent! Scrub
    the rust from your own arrowheads!

15   The king with no one knows discord,
    that he might worry or make war;

16   No enemy is at his gates,
    that he might call his troops to fight.

17   Do not sit idle; you are strong
    and healthy; go and labour then.

18   If you have nought, don't strive for more,
    but sell your saddle, horse, and gear."

19   "Beware the demon's ways," I said;
    "see my misfortune, and fear God.

20   Do not, through loss and poverty,
    give pain to a poor wretch like me.

21   You've slept in comfort every night,
    while I have drawn my sword to fight.

22   You rule the kingdom by the pen;
    I with the sword the realm defend.

23   You dip your pen in the army's blood;
    'gainst the king's foes I draw the sword.

24   Don't take that which the king has given,
    or I'll soon take my suit to him."

25   These words inflamed him; at me then
    he threw his inkwell (I'd no pen).*

26   "You stupid fool, who make me threats
    with justice's water.—Me, a clod?*

27   Now you call me a hypocrite,
    Now threaten me with the king's might.

28   *I* placed the king upon his throne;

without *my* writ no deed is done.
The heads of sovereigns lie beneath     29
*my* feet; all live but for *my* sake.
Did they not treat me as a friend,     30
vultures would feast upon their brains."
He said this; threw the inkwell; seized     31
my horse, effects, and weapons; me
Dispatched with murderers to dwell,     32
imprisoned in his own stout gaol.
For nigh six years—nay, more—my mind     33
is anxious, and my soul in pain.'
The king gave to him robes and gear—     34
may gracious rulers long endure!—
And, having made the man rejoice,     35
his land's return twofold increased.

# 49

## The Seventh Victim's Tale

The seventh victim came; he bowed     1
before the king, thanked him, and said,
'I have renounced the world; I tread     2
the ascetic's path, and worship God.
Though poor, my vision's broad, just like     3
a candle; I consume myself
Before mankind; and since I've learned     4
the end is death, forsake this world.
Of food nor sleep I have no share;     5
I watch by night, and fast by day.
No food by day, for I have none;     6
no sleep by night, since I've no home.
I dwell within a holy place;     7
in nought but worship spend my days.
I seek to please all whom I find,     8
and pray for all I call to mind.
The vizier summoned me; I went;     9
he sat me at a distance; said,
"I am suspicious of you; if     10

I make you suffer, it is fit."

11 "O lord, what do you doubt in me,
that I may live as you decree?"

12 "I fear your evil prayers," he said,
"and I will seek your death from God,

13 Lest, out of rancour and despite,
you call down curses on my might.

14 From those night vigils, I do fear,
your shaft will find this target. Ere

15 Your hatred's fire shall bring to me
the fell spark of your curse, I'll tie

16 Your hands, that you may nought beseech
in prayer; nay, more, I'll bind your neck."

17 Without remorse he bound me tight,
and grieved not at my soul's sad plight;

18 For seven years of torment, cast
me in the stocks, my feet bound fast;

19 My hands as well so tightly bound
I could not lift them up to Heaven.

20 He bound the prayers of my hands;
but I against him bound the realm.

21 He prisoned me by devious trick;
but I have broken down his keep.

22 Now God has brought me to the king;
his mercy to me joy will bring.'

23 The king embraced the holy man,
that infidel-destroying lion.

24 'Save for that fear of prayer,' he said,
'Râst-Rawshan never spoke the truth.

25 But prayers are not prevented thus,
nor pious men dealt with like thieves.

26 Whate'er that evil man has wrought,
he curses on himself has brought,

27 Until those curses, in the end,
stole both his turban and his head.'

28 All the vizier possessed, the king
bestowed upon the holy man;

29 But he renounced those worldly goods,
like the unburdened sky, and said,

'I need no worldly wealth; bestow          30
better than this, as I have you.'

Then, dancing to no music's score,          31
he disappeared; none saw him more.

Thus were the Travellers on the Path:          32
their heads have rubbed the sky from earth.

But *those* base men, though Adam's kin,          33
are demons all, and not true men.

To find mature wine in the cup          34
you must see many unripe grapes.

The river's waves which raging swell          35
with water from small streams grow full.

He is mature who will withdraw          36
both sleeve and skirt from those so raw.


# 50

# How Bahrâm Killed the Unjust Vizier

When the earth shook clay's shadow from          1
its dusty carpet on the sun,

The king, in this brick-kiln, from care          2
was like damp bricks.* To mend affairs,

He sought a method to remove          3
the thorn's sharp harshness from the rose.

He pondered the world's tyranny,          4
and sought, through justice, remedy.

When that vizier he called to mind,          5
thoughtful, he laid his head on hand.

He did not sleep till dawn from shame,          6
nor did he close his eyes from pain.

When, in this earthen pot, the sun's          7
bright fount had basil sown, the king,

Like basil that's refreshed with rain,          8
strewed justice's flowers on thirsting men.

He ordered that his throne be raised;          9
set up a scaffold by the gate.

Enthroned, he gave his audience;          10
his nobles stood by, sword in hand.

11      His kingdom's nobles he did seat;
        spurred justice's camel to the heights.

12      A mighty mass he gathered there
        of men, his justice to observe.

13      That tyrant vizier, tightly bound
        from head to foot in chains, he hung

14      Alive upon the gibbet; showed
        no mercy, so that, like a thief,

15      He died in shame. 'Who lifts his head
        thus, Fate will cast him down,' he said.

16      'From treachery comes a bad name,
        from evil-doing a bad end.

17      A tyrant who does so much hurt:
        just men will bury him. Say not

18      That justice lacks support; both earth
        and Heaven are about this work.

19      He who brings nails and boards will find
        he's nailed himself to his own plank.'

19a     This show of justice done, Bahrâm
        recalled the shepherd, wolf, and dog;

19b     Summoned that shepherd; gave him rule;
        good fortune and success bestowed.

19c     He took all harshness from his reign;
        allowed no tyranny; this plan

19d     Within a little while did turn
        to silk his sackcloth, gold his iron.

19e     His troops and treasure passed all count;
        surpassed the sea, o'ertopped the mount.

# 51

## How the Chinese Ruler Sent his Apologies to Bahrâm

1       When news of this reached the Khâqân,
        he soon withdrew, and caused no harm;

2       An envoy came with his excuse;
        his words were nought that would not please:

3       'He who deserved death, whom the king
        killed, was a rebel, bent upon

4       Sedition. Summoning us, he wrote

a letter which bewitched the heart,
Till, with deceptive wiles, he stole     5
all prudence from our simple soul.
He said, "The mine is full of gold;     6
the way is empty; haste, be bold.
The king's so drunk he lacks the wits     7
to throw cold water on his face.
In friendship I'm prepared to serve;     8
homage from me, from you the sword."
But when I heard of the king's deeds,     9
I knew I must act opposite.
In peace and war alike, the king     10
does ever that which should be done.
I'm still his humble slave; of Chîn     11
at home, but Ethiop to him.
My daughter's handmaid of your house;     12
my crown, before your threshold, dust.'
All that the traitor, seeking ruin,     13
had writ, complaining, of the king:
Those scrolls, rolled up, he then sent on,     14
by messenger, unto the king.
Reading those letters, King Bahrâm     15
grew sharper than a scribe's sharp pen;
Thanked God that the vizier was slain,     16
and kept good order from then on.
When Justice's face, in the king's eyes,     17
made him aware of black and white,
He made, before her beauteous face,     18
his seven beauties sacrifice.
He rooted up all fancies; bent     19
his heart on her, and was content.

# 52

## The End of Bahrâm's Affair;
## How He Disappeared into the Cave

He who joins rubies to these pearls;     1
who's loaded the world's ears with jewels,
Said: When the Seven Domes, with wine     2

and cup, resounded for Bahrâm,

3    Reason, within his dome-like brain,
gave knowledge of *this* moving dome:

4    'Avoid the temples of earth's dome,
that ruin avoid you.' The high dome

5    Of the king's brain began to boil,
that he'd been charmed by idle tales.

6    He saw that this dome rolls all up
at last; turns mortal domes to dust.

7    He left the Seven Domes to the sky,
and towards another took his way:

8    A dome which death won't tumble; where
the enraptured rest till Judgement Day.

9    He summoned seven priests, the sons
of priests, and charged to each a dome.

10    In each, at once, a fire he kindled;
that is, made each a fire-temple.

11    That cypress tall, to sixty come,
saw jasmine on his violets* bloom.

12    He turned, sincere, to worship God,
and worship of himself left off.

13    One day he set aside his crown
and throne; went with his lords to hunt.

14    All others bent on worldly prey;
but hunting for himself was he.

15    The army, scattered wide, gazelles
brought down, and wild asses felled.

16    *They* sought the wild ass of the plain,
but *he*, the lonely grave to gain.

17    He sought a grave in which to dwell:
gazelles, but from himself, did fell.

18    From this salt plain gazelle, wild ass,
seek not: one tomb, the other vice.*

19    At last, from desert side appeared
a wild ass, towards the Ass-King veered.

20    That angel beast, the king knew then,
would set him on the path to Heaven.

21    He urged his horse towards the beast,
spurring to action his swift steed.

After his prey he sped in haste,     22
through ruined spots and desert waste.

His swift-paced steed had taken wing;     23
but one or two slaves followed him.

That waste land held a cave, more sweet     24
than an ice well in summer's heat.

In it a deep chasm, like a well;     25
the way therein no man could tell.

Into that cave the wild ass ran;     26
the king pursued her like a lion.

He spurred his horse within, and gave     27
his kingly treasure to the cave.

Under its veil the king embraced     28
the One Companion of the Cave.*

Those pages guarding him stopped short     29
before the cave's mysterious door.

They found no way to enter in,     30
nor would they to the hunt return.

They watched the road, with bitter sighs,     31
to see the army's dust arise.

A long time passed; the troops arrived,     32
seeking Bahrâm, from every side.

They sought the king; they saw the cave,     33
the stone within the serpent's head.*

About the king those pages told     34
the story that had been concealed:

How, when the king pursued his prey,     35
he urged his horse into that way.

No one would credit what they heard,     36
and no one would believe their words.

All said, 'This is a dreadful dream     37
told by some childish fools. The king—

By God!—an elephant, robust,     38
could not fit in this narrow place!'

(Not knowing that that elephant     39
had dreamed, and gone to Hindustan.)*

Time held in check the mighty king;*     40
how should one loose the bonds of Time?

They beat those slaves without remorse,     41

to learn the lost king's whereabouts.

42    At the sighs of those suffering youths,
dust issued from the cave like smoke.

43    'The king is in the cave,' there cried
a voice; 'go back; he's occupied.'

44    Those courtiers, men of action, went
into the cave, seeking the king.

45    Its bottom sealed, no one they spied;
there, many spiders, but no flies.*

46    A hundred times they sought him there;
a hundred times washed it with tears.

47    But when they could not find the king,
snake-like,* outside they formed a line,

48    And, eyes abrim with tears, sent to
King Bahrâm's mother the dire news.

49    His mother came, like one in pain
and grief, at losing such a son.

50    She sought the king (not like the rest:
she with her soul, they with their eyes);

51    She sought the rose, but found a thorn;
the more she sought, the less she found.

52    She poured out gold in mountainous heaps,
that they might dig there, group by group.

53    She dug a pit; no treasure found,
no Joseph in that pit. The ground

54    Which the old woman dug away
remains in fissures to this day.

55    The region's experts all concur;
call it 'the Cave of Bahrâm Gûr'.

56    For forty days they dug that ground:
in grave-diggers the world abounds!

57    They dug until they reached the stream;
found not that treasure, even in dream.

58    He who's moved on to Heaven above,
to seek him in the ground is hard.

59    Body and bones lie in the ground;
what's heavenly's in Heaven found.

60    Each body 'neath the sphere's bestowed
a mother of earth, and one of blood.*

The one with love will nourish him,                61
the other take him back again.

Though Bahrâm had two mothers, she                62
of earth behaved more lovingly:

She took him, and returned him not,               63
and gave no cure to those who sought.

So cruel was she, the mother of blood             64
with pain and grief destroyed herself.

When fever boiled within her brain,               65
she heard a hidden voice proclaim:

'O you who're heedless, like the beasts;          66
the birds' milk* of the Unseen seek:

God placed a charge within your hands,            67
and took it back when the time came.

In giving up that charge, beware,                 68
lest you, like fools, yourself impair.

Return, and tend to your affairs;                 69
leave off this suffering.' When she heard

This message from the voice, she then             70
detached her love from King Bahrâm.

She left; that heart, once pledged to him,        71
gave to the interests of his son.

Crown and throne to his heirs she gave            72
(for all of Bahrâm's heirs survived).

O you who tell of Bahrâm Gûr:                      73
seek Bahrâm's grave, and say no more.

King Bahrâm Gûr's no more among                    74
mankind; nor can his grave be found.

You saw that once, by force, he named             75
the onager 'the branded one':

Think not of that first mighty brand,             76
but of the marked grave at the end.

He who'd a thousand asses slain                    77
at last was trampled by the tomb.

Two doors has this abode of dung;                  78
it takes one and another brings.

Three ells of earth (one ell in breadth)          79
are you; four jars in the dyer's shop.*

All nourishment your stomach takes                 80

is mixed with the four elements.

81  From head to foot you clothing wear
that's borrowed from these humours four.

82  Why fix your heart on borrowed hues,
since you must give them back? Those who

83  Are gone, their faces veiled by earth,
are from these scents and colours freed.

84  Until the dawn of Judgement Day,
the veil will not be torn away.

85  A fearsome path, a perilous night;
the guard asleep, the thief in flight:

86  The earth-born will by earth be filled;
the lowly bow to lower still.

87  Since you're above all these indeed,
why under every hand then bleed?

88  If you'd subdue the sky, then rise:
tread on the heights, the earth despise.

89  Proceed; do not look back at all,
lest you from sky to earth should fall.

90  The lofty sky's bright stars are jewels
in your sword-belt; they're all your tools.

91  Throughout their narrow sphere you roam;
these fancies' Teukros* you alone.

92  Each one from you its image takes;
why then from each an omen seek?

93  That which they do, you are that light;
but from their worship be remote.

94  Save One Line, Point of origin,*
those other letters are your own.

95  You are the angel who defends
God's praise; knows the Creator's signs.

96  Contemplate goodness; be not bad;
observe the beasts; be not a beast.

97  Both good and evil you can weigh;
aspire to Reason's sovereignty.

98  Or seek that door where bread abounds,
or like no other man become.

99  When the eye falls on the veil of light,*
of Heaven and angels it loses sight.

Earth's the exemplar of the sky,                                    100
and man invites the angels nigh.

Turn from grief's market-place;* how long                          101
for earth, air, fire, and water long?

A room, four smokey chimneys: why                                  102
should it not straiten heart and eye?

A two-doored house—a robbers' street—                              103
a traveller's four-banded bag.*

Before from out this town you're cast,                             104
load up your goods on ox and ass.

Travel by soul; the body's slow;                                   105
the horse is restive; therefore throw

Away your load. The dying man,                                     106
despairing, for the body yearns;

But he who knows his soul's true source,                           107
can live without his body coarse.

Think not, who fabricate pretexts,                                 108
that nought but these two worlds* exists.

Existence's length and breadth are great;                          109
but all *we* know of is this cave.*

Far from all this are beings who                                   110
nothing of light and darkess know.

Creation's multiple, 'tis known;                                   111
but its Creator is but One.

These seven four-sided tablets'* plan                              112
was drawn by but a single Pen.

Were they four hundred, not seven or four,                         113
they serve One governance, no more.

The First Point, Final Circle, part                                114
not from the One. Do not regard

Dualities, and how they join;                                      115
see but the single Source, the One.

Though every two has come from One,                                116
the One remains when two is gone.

Who comes into this transient sphere,                              117
retracing his steps, he must return.

Traverse it gently; keen its skills:                               118
it slowly takes, but quickly kills.

Though just, the humble slaying not,                               119 none's by its reckoning forgot.

120    A hundred clever tricks won't gain
you more than what's to you ordained.

121    The heavens an ice-bound pool possess;
how long seek profit from this ice?*

121a    In air in which you'll frozen be,
strive to find life before you die.

122    He who, sphere-like, the broad world spans,
departs and leaves all in the end.

123    The world, no person, kills for nought;
the turning sphere will roll him up

124    And slay him. Thus, the goals you have
within this world, enjoy in life,

125    That when the sword and shaft arrive,
for what they take you will not grieve.

126    From this world, ere you pass, cut off
your soul, that it be freed from death.

127    Make your house humble, your food small;
thus from the world you'll save your soul.

128    Salvation in these two things lies:
in giving much, consuming slight.

129    Whoever makes his way to fame
from those two things will gain his name.

130    No greedy man high rank obtains;
no niggard great position gains.

131    The bailiff wields his shaming scourge
'gainst villagers who give short curds.

132    He's favoured who, in such a place,
holds goodness better than high price.

133    This world with high and low is full;
for none high status in this world.

134    How can you fix your heart upon
that deed which carries your own doom?

135    Each building high beneath the sphere:
cast dust on it, for 'tis but earth.

136    Escape its snare; do not be slow;
your pulpit, scaffold;* be not bold.

137    You seek for life upon that cross;
but one Messiah* is enough.

If a mortal reached the highest sphere,            138
his clay would draw him back to earth.

One raises to the skies his crown;                 139
takes taxes from the Seven Climes:

See how one night he dies, head bowed              140
in pain. The earth is not without

Those fearsome spears that nothing reck;           141
its treasury no dragon lacks.

Where is the date without a thorn;                 142
without a snake, where the snake-stone?

Yea, all that's good and bad in time               143
is poisoned honey, honeyed bane.

Who is it not that honey drinks,                   144
that after does not feel the sting?

Honey and sting, before and aft,                   145
of the same bee is tail and breath.

Within the veil of dark and light,                 146
where Jesus' love, where donkey-bead?*

Who o'er the earth his throne's not raised         147
that earth's not tightly grasped at last?

O Lord, grant that which bringeth ease,            148
and will not, last, repentence cause.

Be generous to Nizâmî; make                        149
safe refuge for him near Your gate.

You gave him good repute at first;                 150
give a good outcome at the last.

# 53

## Prayer for the Ruler's Good Fortune; Conclusion

Since, by its assay and design,                    1
this coin of Ganja's treasure shines

Like Rûmî gold, the king's great name              2
I've bound to it, to gain me fame.

With Chinese robe and Grecian crown,               3
paid tribute by both Chîn and Rûm,

By the Law's root and branch he's gained           4
Bakhtîshû''s judgement, Jesus' fame.*

5    The heavens at his service stand;
     his grandeur all the world maintains.

6    In Heaven's order, the reward
     of service is two disks of bread.

7    *His* chivalry, which musk exhales,
     like dry earth scatters lustrous pearls:

8    From earth to ether, others foam
     and dregs; *his* essence pure alone.

9    In his largesse, Egyptian gold
     outnumbers Mecca's sands. His sword

10   Treats hardest rock as does hot fire
     dry poplar chips. His arrow's barb,

11   Its point hair-splitting, cleaves the mount
     in twain. From the resplendant dawn

12   His shining mail wrests light's bright lance;
     *his* lance from the moon's mail its rings.

13   The six directions' mail his robe;
     the seven spheres by his lasso caught.

14   O you in whom Nizâmî puts
     his hope; who shapes this age's fate:

15   You're viewed as Heaven by both the earth
     and Heaven itself, so great your worth.

16   Like sky in water, near and far;
     like sun in mirror, quick and slow.

17   Maintainer of the world; the one
     not yet arrived,* by you cast down.

18   Like angels, you all men excel;
     you the high sphere above them all.

19   'Tis fit that I address this poem
     to you; for thus will it gain fame.

20   Since rubies deck its crown, I have
     addressed it to you, fearing thieves.

21   And if it please your hearing, like
     your throne, it too will be raised high.

22   When men pour honey over thorns,
     as 'Persian manna'* it is known.

23   From my mind's garden I have brought
     to you a fruit as rich and sweet

24   As honeyed milk. Its seeds of figs

do taste; its centre almond-pith.
For lesser men its outside's fine;                    25
for those who see, the pith's within.
It has a casket full of pearls,                       26
locked tight; the key thereto its words.
The pearl glides easily on that string               27
whose key will loosen knots. All things
Are on its string; good, bad; and all                28
allusion, wisdom, and symbol.
Each story is a treasure-house,                       29
and no mere fable. Each one whose
Garment was shorter than its form,                   30
I've with my verses made it long;
While that which was too long, with art              31
I've shortened to a perfect fit.
A tale both fine and rare, my gift,                  32
with supple bones and sweetest pith.
That you may see its beauty clear,                   33
with every art I've decked it fair.
My grace comes easy, costs me slight;                34
it decks with precious gems each point:
Some untouched lovelies, virgins all,                35
like rose-buds 'neath a silken veil;
One line of gold, and one of pearl,                  36
empty of sham, of meaning full;
That men may know, from lofty thought,               37
I what I wish bring forth from nought .*
All that which, in these Seven Domes                 38
of mystery, I have adorned
With length and width, 'twas that the eyes,          39
from full adornment, might find ease.
All that you see, in this broad space,               40
that I've thrown wide to ears and eyes,
Are meaning's beauties, narrow-eyed,                 41
their faces veiled from narrow sight;
Each bride a treasury shut fast,                     42
the golden key beneath her locks.
He will find gold who opes this mine;                43
who finds the door fair pearls will gain.

44    I, who paint words with sugared pen,
      strew fresh dates from this shrine's high palm.

45    From fields of art my reed-pen brings
      to Mercury fresh ears of corn.*

46    These he has made his own; no matter
      that 'story-tellers love not each other'.*

47    Since, from the fort of my content,
      this treasure to the king I've sent,

48    In paying my reward of gold
      his brazen fort* in debt I hold.

49    This debt stems not from hunger; brass
      the fort which silver dirhams lacks.

50    Its stony peak's sharp iron blade
      has scattered for a hundred leagues

51    Both rubies, to the hands of friends,
      and, 'neath his foes' feet, diamonds.*

52    No fort, but Ka'ba: holy shrine,
      the pilgrims' blessed Jerusalem.

53    The golden nail,* the world's strong pole;
      Rû'în-Diz for its power called.

54    And he who would that fort assail,
      his fear finds armour no avail.

55    The Mount of Mercy is its gate;
      Bû Qubays* crowns it with its belt.

56    May ever live this circle's line
      by that high sun, its central point.

57    From forts besieged the people send
      their messages on pigeons bound,

58    So that the joyous bird may bear
      them to those who their cries will hear.

59    So I, in my own land confined,
      with all ways shut, before, behind,

60    Have tied a message to a bird;
      if it comes to the king, I'm freed.

61    O you to whom the sky bows low;
      who pardons sins; wears Cathay robes:*

62    Since that your fortune aided me,
      my nature's magic work now see.

63    In the year five hundred and ninety-three,

like poets famed, this book achieved
Have I, on fourteenth Ramazân,*      64
four hours past the break of dawn.
And may it augur well for you,      65
as long as you're enthroned. May you
Drink from its verses the Water of Life;      66
through it, like Khizr, ever live.
Lord—may you ever live in joy      67
and happiness; long life enjoy:
Forgive me should I cause offence,      68
and give me leave to make this point:
Although your banquets are unmatched,      69
yet *this* is an eternal feast.
Men reckon gems and treasures wealth:      70
*this* is true ease, the rest all trial.
That, should it last five hundred years—      71
may you live long!—will not endure;
*This* treasure, destined for your court,      72
will ever be your firm support.
These wisdom-nourished verses now      73
with prayer I will conclude. May you,
Where'er you be, be fortunate;      74
may the sky at your stirrup wait;
And, as your fortune waxes, may      75
your end be true felicity.

like poets famed, this book achieved
Have I, on fourteenth Ramazán,
four hours past the break of dawn.
And may it augur well for you,
as long as you're enthroned. May you
Drink from its verses the Water of Life;
through it, like Khizr, ever live,
Lord—may you ever live, in joy
and happiness, long life enjoy;
Forgive me should I cause offence,
and give me one leave to make this point,
Although your banquets are unmatched,
yet this is an eternal feast.
Men reckon on gems and treasures wealthy,
this is one case, the rest all real:
That, should it last five hundred years—
may you live long!—will not endure.
This treasure, destined for your court,
shall ever be your firm support.
These wisdom-nourished verses now
with prayer, I will conclude. May you,
Where'er you be, be fortunate;
may the sky of your stirrup wash
And, as your fortune waxes, may
your end be true felicity.

# EXPLANATORY NOTES

1: 2  *The Source . . . the End*: God is the soul's place of origin (*mabda'*) and of its return (*ma'âd*) on completion of its journey through life; cf. Koran 2: 157: 'Surely we belong to God, and to Him we will return.'

1: 6  *and have no like nor peer*: an allusion to Koran 42: 12, 'There is nothing which is His like'; God is utterly unlike His creation.

1: 16  *he who would not bow to man*: an allusion to Satan (Iblis), who refused to bow down before Adam on the day of creation; cf. Koran 2: 35, 7: 12–19.

1: 28  *The Universal Intellect*: the *'aql-i kull*, the first (male) principle created by God, which is with respect to Him passive, obedient, and the recipient of divine guidance. From it the second (female) principle, the Universal Soul (*nafs-i kulliyya*) receives virtues, forms, and qualities, which it transmits to the third principle, matter, to form the created universe.

1: 32  *the ruby's flame . . . fiery gem*: rubies were said to be formed by the penetration of the sun's rays into rock, which is 'cooked' over the ages to form the gem.

2: 1  *the Seal upon Creation's line*: Muhammad is considered the 'Seal of the Prophets' (cf. Koran 30: 41), after whom there will be no other, and the goal of creation.

2: 3  *most praised*: Ahmad (in Arabic 'most praised') is another form of the Prophet's name, by some considered its primordial or spiritual form (cf. Koran 61: 6, where Jesus gives 'glad tidings of a messenger who will come after me who will be most praised [named Ahmad]').

2: 4  *the Ascent his crown, the Law his sword*: the Ascent (Mi'râj) refers to the Prophet's ascent to Heaven (see §3), the *Law* to the Sharî'a (see the Glossary).

2: 5  *Unlettered . . . High Throne's shade*: the Prophet was said to have been illiterate (*ummî*; cf. Koran 7: 158, where he is called *al-nabî al-ummî*, 'the unlettered prophet', and 29: 49–50, 'Thou didst not recite any Book before the revelation of the Koran, nor didst thou write one with thy right hand'). *Carpet* is a metaphor for the earth; the *High Throne* (*'arsh*) is the throne of God (cf. Koran 9: 129, 'He is the Lord of the Mighty Throne'), in Islamic cosmology equated with the ninth sphere (the encompassing sphere), in esoteric thought with the Universal Intellect.

2: 6 *five turns . . . fourfold rule*: the *five turns* (*panj nawbat*) are a royal fanfare: drums placed before a ruler's palace were sounded five times a day (the custom was introduced by the Seljuk sultan Sanjar (d. 1157); previously the number had been three, then four). Here they herald the Law brought by the Prophet and signify the five daily prayers of Islam. *Fourfold rule* (literally, *chahâr bâlish*, the four cushions of a royal throne) refers to the four 'Orthodox' caliphs (Abû Bakr, 'Umar, 'Uthmân, and 'Alî) who succeeded the Prophet. Together, the *five turns* and *fourfold rule* signify the combination of spiritual and temporal rule.

2: 7 *Muhammad . . . praised*: *mahmûd*, 'praised' (also used as a name), is derived from the same root as Muhammad and Ahmad (cf. note to §2: 3 above).

2: 8 *Of that first clay that Adam pressed*: i.e. in coming into being. Adam, first man and first prophet, was created from earth (Koran 3: 66) or clay (Koran 38: 72); according to tradition, Muhammad was the pure essence of that clay, all other prophets inferior to him.

2: 11 *His boast, of poverty*: an allusion to the Prophet's saying *al-faqr fakhrî*, 'Poverty is my pride.'

2: 12 *what talk of shade*: according to legend, Muhammad did not cast a shadow.

2: 21 *Turned not aside*: an allusion to Koran 53: 9–19. The Prophet, on his Ascent, witnessed the Divine presence, 'near the farthest lote-tree, close to which is the Garden of Eternal Abode, at the time when the lote-tree was enveloped in Divine Glory. The Prophet's eye did not turn aside or wander [53: 17]. Thus did he witness one of the greatest Signs of his Lord.' On the 'farthest lote-tree', see note to §3: 51–2 below.

2: 22 *From seven hundred thousand years | seven thousand*: Dastgirdî (p. 8 n. 2) glosses this line as referring to the duration of the world, reckoned at 700,000 years, and to the Prophet's birth 7,000 years after creation (Wilson and Bausani omit the line). Astronomers reckoned a world-year at 360,000 years (the cycle was said to have been invented by the ancient Iranian king Jamshîd; the notion is supported by Koran 22: 7, 'A day in thy Lord's reckoning is as a thousand years in your counting'; a lunar year is 360 days). The Ismailis believed that a Grand Cycle, after which would come the final Resurrection of Resurrections, consists of 360,000 × 360,000 years (see David Pingree, *The Thousands of Abu Ma'shar* (London, 1968), 17, 23, 30–7.) Each planet was said to rule over one 7,000-year cycle, for the first 1,000 years alone and for the remaining 6,000 in conjunction with each of the other planets in turn; Muhammad was said to have been born in the seventh and last cycle, that of the moon.

2: 23 *the servants of the blue-robed sphere*: the planets.

2: 24 *His four true friends*: the four Orthodox caliphs (see note to §2: 6 above).

2: 26 *His soul . . . his body*: Wilson glosses, 'Muhammad, as Universal Spirit, the first creation of God, was the Universal Intellect and the Universal Soul, so that the whole universe was as his body' (ii. 6 n. 54). The Prophet is both macranthropos, the world's body, and the World Soul which gives life to all creation.

2: 30–1 *His nail . . . cataract*: an allusion to Koran 54: 1, 'The Hour has drawn nigh, and the moon has been split in twain,' and to an explanatory Tradition according to which the Prophet is said to have split the moon by drawing his fingernail down it, a miracle by which he demonstrated the truth of his mission. The poet puns on *nâkhun*, 'fingernail'/*nâkhuna*, 'cataract', comparing the moon, which obscures the light of the stars (the 'eyes of the sky'), to the white film which obscures the sight.

3: 1 *his Ladder*: the literal meaning of *mi'râj* is 'ladder' (cf. §3: 55); versions of the Mi'râj account describe the ladder on which the Prophet ascended to Heaven.

3: 2 *Burâq*: the magical mount brought by Gabriel to the Prophet, on which he made his ascent. Originally conceived of as something between a horse and an ass, this creature has acquired many different, often magical features, being depicted, for example, with wings and a human face.

3: 8–9 *seven roots . . . Fish*: the *seven roots* are the seven earths; the *six directions* are north, south, east, west, up, and down. The *nine spheres* are the seven spheres of the planets, that of the fixed stars and the empyrean or encompassing sphere; the *four nails*, glossed by Dastgirdî (p. 9 n. 10) as the four elements (the planets were also said to be fixed to their spheres by nails), are the 'four pivots' from which stem the four imaginary lines which divide the celestial vault into four quadrants; the position of the planets with respect to these pivots determines their influence. The *Fish* (*simâk*) refers to the two stars Arcturus and Spica Virginis, the fourteenth lunar station, whose auroral rising in Central Arabia in early October coincides with the date of the Prophet's Flight (Hijra) from Mecca to Medina in 622, which marks the commencement of the Islamic (Hijri) era; cf. note to §3: 37 below.

3: 11–12 *The Egyptian beauties . . . ecstasy*: in the Koranic story of Joseph and the Egyptian ruler's wife (later called Zulaykhâ), when the Egyptian women mocked Zulaykhâ for her love of Joseph she invited them to a banquet to observe him; they were so amazed at his beauty that they cut their hands with the knives with which they were peeling citrons (see Koran 12: 31–2).

3: 14 *Lamp-like*: the Prophet is described in Koran 33: 47 as a 'light-giving lamp' (*sirâjun munîr*, the term used in §3: 26).

3: 15 *This night is yours*: a variant has, 'This is the Night of Power,' alluding to the night that the Koran was revealed (cf. Koran 97); on this night the doors of Heaven are opened and all prayers are answered.

3: 16a *fold up the carpet*: the 'angels' carpet' is the heavens which veil God from man; as the Prophet draws closer to God, he rends these veils and folds them up as he travels further on towards God's Throne.

3: 18 *both worlds*: this world and the next, the created and the heavenly.

3: 30–1 *Like peacocks' wings . . . four eagles*: Dastgirdî glosses, 'The shape of the moon appears on peacocks' wings; the throne of Kâvûs had the emblem of a moon above it. That is, [Burâq] sped so swiftly that its hoofs went over its head. The peacock sometimes displays its tail like the shape of a moon above its head' (p. 11 n. 6; on Kâvûs (Kaykâvûs) see the Glossary). *The four eagles* (here the four elements): in the *Shâhnâma* Kaykâvûs attempted to ascend to Heaven by harnessing four eagles (or vultures) to his throne.

3: 37 *showed now as Lancer, now unarmed*: the *Lancer* (*simâk-i râmih*) is Arcturus, the *unarmed* (*simâk-i a'zal*) Spica Virginis (see note to §3: 8–9 above). The word for *stream* (*jadval*) also means an astronomical table.

3: 45 *like Caliph of the West*: the Prophet is clad in green, the sacred colour of Islam, the royal colour of the Umayyad caliphs (644–750), whose capital was Damascus in Syria (Shâm), and the colour of the moon. *Shâm* in Persian means 'evening'; *Caliph of the West* also refers to the setting sun, which gives a reddish light in a greenish sky.

3: 46 *rubbed sandalwood*: a preparation made by rubbing sandalwood with water on stone was used as a remedy for headache.

3: 47 *Saturn's crown*: its rings.

3: 51–2 *From Michael's couch ... the Lote*: i.e. he went beyond Michael's throne, the 'tower' (*rasadgâh*, 'observatory') of Isrâfîl's trumpet, whose blowing will announce the Day of Judgement, and the Sidrat al-Muntahâ, the 'furthest lote-tree', the abode of Gabriel. *Rafraf*, which occurs in Koran 55: 77, is variously interpreted as 'green cushions' or 'carpet'; in other Mi'râj accounts by Nizâmî (*Laylî and Majnûn*, the *Sharafnâma*) it means either a mount or a litter which carries Muhammad on the final stage of his Ascent and is abandoned at the Sidrat al-Muntahâ.

3: 56 *the mystery of 'Praise be Mine'*: literally, 'To the perilous place of the mystery, "Praise be to Me" [*subhânî*].' An allusion to Koran 17: 1, *Subhâna alladhî asrâ bi-'abdihi laylan*, 'Praise be to Him who made His servant ascend by night' (the Prophet's Night Journey, *Isrâ*, said to have taken place from the Sacred Mosque of Jerusalem, is often conflated with his Mi'râj); possibly also to the mystic Bâyazid Bistâmî (d. 874 or 877–8), who claimed to have experienced a mystical ascent like that of the Prophet, passing beyond the self to complete unity with God, and who expressed this state of union in the phrase, 'Praise be to Me! How great is my state!'

3: 58 *'two bowlengths' ... 'nearer yet'*: an allusion to Koran 53: 9–11: 'Then he [Muhammad] approached closer, and [God] leaned down towards him, so that it was (like) two bows with one string [or: twin bows], or closer still. Then He revealed to His servant that which He had willed to reveal.'

3: 59 *the veil of thousand lights*: the veils of light interposed between God and man are variously reckoned as 700, 7,000, 70,000, etc., figures expressive of inifinite numbers.

3: 60 *Beyond his being's bounds*: Wilson glosses this line as referring to the mystical concept of *fanâ*, annihilation of the self with respect to all else but God, which is the only means of seeing Him (ii. 15 n. 123); most commentators consider Muhammad's vision of God to have been in full consciousness, proving both his superiority and that of 'sober' over 'ecstatic' mysticism.

3: 74 *all he brought*: the Prophet's spiritual knowledge, embodied in the Koran and the Law; also referring to his role as intercessor for the Muslim community.

4: 1 *Solomon*: the ruler who commissioned the poem.

4: 3 *Make a new moon rise*: the major festival of Islam, 'Îd al-Fitr, which celebrates the end of the fasting month of Ramadan and is eagerly awaited, begins on the first of Shawwal and is announced by the sighting of the new moon, which marks the beginning of the Islamic lunar month.

4: 5 *your enchanted words*: on the basis of a Prophetic Tradition, poetry is often termed 'licit magic'.

4: 6 *Some pepper grains on fire pour*: pepper grains over which a charm has been recited are cast into the fire as a spell to make the beloved anxious to see the lover.

4: 8 *narrow road . . . lame mule*: the poet alludes to his previous romance, *Laylî and Majnûn*, in which he says, referring to the slightness of its subject, 'When the vestibule of story is narrow, discourse may go lame in passing through it.'

4: 16 *Raise the curtain*: an allusion to the shadow-play, whose figures are revealed when the curtain is raised; to the 'virgins' or 'brides' of the poet's thought (the meanings he creates and puts into verse); and to the seven princesses of the poem.

4: 19–21 *one book of lore . . . shards*: the source of Firdawsî's *Shâhnâma*, Nizâmî's chief source for the *Haft Paykar*, is said to have been the prose *Shâhnâma* of Abû Mansûr Mi'mârî (957); Firdawsî is the 'one of keenest mind' who put its materials into verse. The *shards* are the minor epics which derived from the *Shâhnâma*, such as Asadî Tûsî's *Garshâspnâma* (see note to §4: 48 below).

4: 28 *From Persia's speech . . . Tabarî's*: *Persia's speech* is Darî, the language of the *Shâhnâma*, which by the early eleventh century was already giving way to the more polished and Arabicized Fârsî; *Araby's* (*Tâzî*) is of course Arabic. *Bukhârî* (d. 870) was an exegete and a collector of Prophetic Traditions (Hadîth), Muhammad ibn Jarîr *Tabarî* (d. 923) a traditionist and historian whose great universal history was translated into Persian in 963. Wilson's gloss of 'Bukhârî' and 'Tabarî' as 'works (found) in Bukhara [in Transoxiana] and Tabaristan [Western Iran]', i.e. east and west (ii. 18 n. 160) is unlikely.

4: 33–4 *This written temple . . . sky-brides*: the poet describes the design and ornament of his work, compared to a temple and to scripture (I have preferred Dastgirdî's reading *dayr*, 'temple', to Ritter and Rypka's *naqsh*, 'design': 'This poem's design I have adorned . . .'). While the Zand (see Glossary) may have been adorned with paintings of the planets, Buddhist temples were decorated with images of the Buddha which became types of ideal beauty (see note to §15: 7 below), making this reading more probable. The *sky-brides* are the seven planets.

4: 36–40 *seven lines . . . fixed my gaze*: the *seven lines* are glossed by Dastgirdî (p. 17 n. 8) as an allusion to geomancy (*raml*), in which an arrangement of lines produces the 'point of prosperity'; but the passage seems also to describe procedures for generating geometrical patterns. See, further, Meisami, *Medieval Persian Court Poetry*, 299–304.

4: 43 *From but a droplet man is made*: the human embryo was believed to be formed from a drop of 'water' (sperm) deposited in the womb (cf. Koran 76: 9).

4: 44 *If, shell-like, I from raindrops make | a pearl*: pearls were (on the authority of Aristotle) said to be formed from drops of rain entering the oyster-shell. Pearls are a common metaphor for poetic verses.

4: 47 *Firdawsî's bounty . . . decreed*: Firdawsî's *Shâhnâma* (his 'bounty) was said to have been poorly rewarded by its dedicatee, Mahmûd of Ghazna (r. 999–1030); the blame is placed on the incompatibility of their (supposed?) ascendants, Sagittarius (watery) and Scorpio (fiery), which are inimical and, being next to each other, inconjunct.

4: 48 *Bû Dulaf . . . Asadî*: Asadî Tûsî (d. 1072–3), who composed the *Garshâspnâma* for Abû Dulaf, the Shaybanid ruler of Nakhjavan in Arran, in 1066, was (in contrast to Firdawsî) treated generously by his patron because of the agreement of their common ascendant signs (which are not indicated). Asadî also composed a dictionary, the *Lughat-i Furs* ('Language of the Persians'), to explain Persian (Darî; see note to §4: 28 above) to the people of Arran and Azerbaijan.

4: 53 *in garments new for New Year's time*: the 'newness' of the poet's enterprise is compared to new clothing, which it is the custom to put on at the Persian New Year (Nawrûz), celebrated at the vernal equinox.

4: 54 *demons' eyes . . . Solomon*: the ruler is again compared to Solomon, who exercised power over the demons with his seal-ring (cf. §4: 57), on which was engraved the Mightiest Name of God.

4: 71 *Jesus' breath . . . Mary's tree*: *Jesus' breath* restored the dead to life (see Koran 3: 50); he was said to have been supported by the Holy Spirit (*rûh al-quddus*; see Koran 5: 111), customarily equated with Gabriel. *Mary's tree*: Jesus was born under a withered date-palm which became green and brought forth dates for Mary (cf. Koran 19: 23–6).

5: 3–7 *fourfold . . . final chapter*: the passage involves a pun on *fasl*, 'season', 'chapter/section' of a book.

5: 11 *ʿAlâ al-Dîn*: the title means 'sublimity of the faith'. On Nizâmî's patron, see Introduction, pp. xiii–xiv.

5: 14 *a saviour sage*: the ruler is called *Mahdî*, the divinely guided leader whose rule, coming just before the end of the world, will restore religion and justice and lead all to the true faith (cf. note to §53: 17 below).

5: 16 *a lion in form as well as name*: Arslân, a Turkish word for 'lion', is part of the ruler's name (Körp Arslân, 'small lion').

5: 17–18 *one Essence . . . pearls without end*: pun on *jawhar*, which means both 'essence' and 'pearl' (or more generally 'jewel'). The *One Essence* which brought the world into being is the Universal Intellect.

5: 22 *the sphere's twin*: literally, 'the sphere's brother'; the title of the ruler's brother was Falak al-Dîn, 'sphere of the faith'.

5: 25 *His bright blade . . . the air perfumes*: âb, 'water', has also the sense of 'lustre' (and is used metaphorically to mean 'honour'); by virtue of this pun the line contains mention of all four elements, earth, air, fire, and water.

5: 28 *Armageddon*: literally, Resurrection (*Rastakhîz*; also *Qiyâmat*), when the dead rise from their graves and there is general confusion.

5: 38 *His lion-taking no drunken riot*: lion-taking (*shîr-gîrî*) is a state of intoxication or tipsiness.

5: 39 *Mount Sahand*: a mountain (elev. 3,710m.) north of Maragha in Azerbaijan.

5: 59 *two rules in two abodes*: this and the next line refer to the concept of the king as Perfect Man (see Introduction, p. xi), both temporal and spiritual ruler, mediator between God and man, between macrocosm and microcosm; the *two abodes* are this world and the next, the earthly and the heavenly.

5: 68 *He who follows me is praised*: the prince's name, Ahmad, means in Arabic, 'most praised'; the allusion is to Koran 61: 6 (see note to §2: 3 above). Both Ahmad and Muhammad are derived from the same Arabic root *h-m-d*, 'to praise'.

5: 78 *that veil*: the ruler's queen.

6: 6 *twe disks of bread*: the sun and the moon.

6: 8 *God's victory*: nusrat-i ilâhî, a pun on the title of the ruler's brother and predecessor Nusrat al-Dîn ('victory of the faith') ibn Âq Sonqor.

6: 22–3 *seven feats . . . towers*: the *seven feats* are the seven adventures of Rustam recounted in the *Shâhnâma* (seven feats were also performed by Isfandiyâr); the *twelve champions* refers to a famous battle between the Iranians and their Turanian (Turkish) enemies in which the Iranians, led by Rustam, were victorious. The ruler's *feats* (*khvân*, literally 'feast', as a feast followed each of Rustam's adventures, but also figuratively 'stage') are the seven spheres, the twelve *champions* the houses of the Zodiac.

6: 29 *a mirror of iron*: according to traditions deriving from the Alexander Romance, Alexander the Great constructed a great mirror which he set atop the lighthouse of Alexandria; in it he could see any place in the world. Nizâmî in his *Sharafnâma* presents Alexander as the inventor of the mirror; having tried various substances, only iron proved satisfactory, and of geometrical forms only the circle.

6: 33 *the Fifth Clime*: Azerbaijan.

6: 35 *Four kings, four royal jewels have owned*: the poet lists four famous kings and their advisers: *Aristotle*, the teacher of Alexander, said to have authored the letters on government known as the *Secretum Secretorum* (in the Islamic tradition, the *Sirr al-Asrâr*); *Buzurgmihr*, the vizier of Khusraw I Anûshîrvân (Nûshîrvân), whose wise sayings are recorded in the *Shâhnâma* and in Arabic collections of wisdom literature; *Bârbad*, the minstrel of Khusraw II Parvîz, known for his influence on that ruler and for inventing the Persian musical modes; and *Nizâm al-Mulk*, vizier of the Seljuk sultan Malikshâh, whose *Siyâsatnâma* (Book of Government) was one of Nizâmî's sources (see Introduction, p. xxiv).

6: 54 *this cycle of time*: literally, 'this seven-thousand-year cycle'; see note to §2: 22 above.

6: 57 *sphere-related*: a pun on the title of the ruler's brother Falak al-Dîn; see note to §5: 22 above.

6: 60 *at the king's feast*: i.e. as at a marriage feast, where it was the custom to scatter sugar; the poem is the 'bride'.

6: 70 *Venus-like song . . . moon*: Venus is the heavens' musician; the poet's 'song' is like Venus' heavenly music. On the (new) moon, see note to §4: 3 above.

7: 2 *The mother 'Be!'*: a reference to the divine fiat, *Kun*, 'Be!'; cf. note to §8: 1 below.

7: 7 *the worlds of mineral,|plant, animal, and rational*: the four realms of creation.

7: 13 *Doors cleaned of smoke . . . sun*: the meaning is that, although there is no obstacle obscuring the light of self-knowledge, people are content with themselves as they are, and ignore their own faults; thus the sun's light is wasted on them. Cf. the maxim attributed to various sages (including the Prophet's son-in-law ʿAlī): 'The sun is of no use where the eye's light is denied.'

7: 19 *guards it with gum*: the merchant protects his precious musk by storing it in ill-smelling gum (*anguzha*, asafoetida or gum in general) to conceal its scent.

7: 27 *That draught of pearls and rubies made*: a remedy (*mufarrih*) made of ground rubies and pearls was said to dispel melancholy; here, pearls and rubies signify grinding teeth and bloody tears, i.e. riches bring suffering rather than joy.

7: 32 *when Time began*: an allusion to Pre-Eternity (*azal*, from the Pahlavi *a-sar*, 'without head', i.e. beginning), when all that was to be was preordained.

7: 42 *lest they twist, snake-like*: dragons and snakes were said to guard hidden treasures.

7: 54 *life from the snake-stone*: the bezoar (Persian *pâ-zahr*) or snake-stone, the antidote against venom, is found in the snake's head.

7: 57 *a patched cloak*: an allusion to hypocritical ascetics or Sufis, who wear patched cloaks (*muraqqaʿ*) as a sign of renunciation of worldly things.

7: 60 *fourfold purse*: the 'four-banded' purse [*chahâr-bandî*] is a sort of knapsack carried by travellers, held by four ties, which can be opened and spread out like a tray; metaphorically it refers to the world, composed of the four elements and with four cardinal points.

7: 61 *the Josephs wolves*: when Joseph's brothers cast him into the pit they told his father Jacob that he had been killed by wolves; the meaning is that those who pretend to be pious are in reality vicious.

7: 64 *seek naphtha, and pour talc away*: naphtha (Greek fire) was used for incendiary purposes, *talc* to extinguish fire; the meaning is that those who should strive to set an example through piety instead foment disorder.

7: 68 *wormwood*: pun on *diramna*, 'wormwood,' which can be read as *diram-na*, 'without a dirham', 'penniless'.

7: 73 *two letters, unconnected*: in Persian orthography the word *zar*. 'gold', consists of two unjoined letters, *z-r*.

7: 75 *golden forms . . . blue mourning robes*: blue was the colour of mourning; here, the allusion is to the medical practice of treating jaundice ('golden forms') by the application of blue or black garments.

7: 76 *Each scale . . . doors*: *is stoned* refers to the stones put in the scales to weigh gold; the *doors* are those of the money-changers.

7: 84 *three porters' loads . . . the four porters' abode*: the three natures of creation (mineral, plant, animal) and the four elements of which creation is composed; meaning, you will gain nothing but the corruptible body, whose final abode is the grave.

7: 101 *seven-rooted branch . . . four-nailed horseshoes*: the sky, whose seven roots are the seven earths, and the earth, whose four nails are the four elements (or perhaps the four 'pivots' of the celestial vault (see note to §3: 8–9 above), the four cardinal points).

7: 110 *The Ethiop scorns my Turkish wares*: literally, 'The Ethiops (of this region) reject my Turkish delicacies,' that is, in this dark and savage region my fine words go unappreciated.

7: 112 *collyrium for the sight*: tûtiyâ, tutty (zinc oxide), was dissolved in sour grape juice and used as a remedy for the eyes; the meaning of this and the next line is, 'When I was young I was sought out; now that I have matured I suffer the stings of enemies.'

7: 119 *Sîm . . . reversed*: in Persian orthography sîm, 'silver', is written with the letters sîn-yâ-mîm; when the yâ is dropped and the letters sîn-mîm are reversed, they spell miss, 'brass'.

7: 148 *patched cloak*: the dalaq (also muraqqaʿ; cf. note to §7: 57 above) is the garb of the ascetic, or darvîsh, who has renounced the world; the poet hopes that his piety will extinguish the flames of envy.

8: 1 *Those students in the school of 'Kun'*: Kun, 'Be!', is the divine fiat (cf. note to §7: 2 above); its students are those who have studied the lessons of existence and who have become skilled in discourse.

8: 6 *the Prophet's name*: the name of Nizâmî's son was Muhammad.

8: 13 *who swallows gold*: pilgrims to Mecca would often swallow their gold in order to protect it; brigands who heard of this would attack the pilgrims' caravan and cut open the stomachs of many men in hopes of finding the gold.

8: 17 *Like a white falcon*: an allusion to Körp Arslân's father Âq Sonqor, whose name in Turkish means 'white falcon'.

8: 18 *the sky is armed with shaft and bow*: an allusion to the Arabic proverb, 'The sky's a bow, and calamities arrows.' The bow (kamân) is the Persian name of Sagittarius, the shaft (tîr) that of Mercury.

8: 35–6 *is lawful food . . . aright*: in Islamic law, the prey of the trained hunting dog is lawful food, while that of the untrained dog is forbidden. Wilson (ii. 59 n. 496) discerns an allusion in line 36 to the dog of the Seven Sleepers in the cave (cf. Koran 18: 10–23), which became purified through association with them (see Introduction, p. xxxiii).

8: 41 *Till from two you've not reached that One*: reason and soul combined lead to awareness of the divine Unicity; until you have reached that stage, do not pretend to have done so by telling others that they have not. Lines 40–6 develop the topic that all learning leads to knowledge of God's Unicity.

8: 43 *Ignore three . . . abandon two*: possible allusions to Christianity and Zoroastianism respectively.

9: 11 *the scales which Heaven weighed*: the astrolabe.

9: 14–17 *Pisces ascendant . . . the sun in Aries*: Bahrâm's natal horoscope (idealized rather than actual) predicts his good fortune and anticipates his career. Sun and moon, in exaltation in *Aries* and *Taurus*, represent kingship and love, as do their analogues *Jupiter* (in his nocturnal, feminine house) and *Venus*, in exaltation in the ascendant *Pisces*; a person born under the sign of these two planets will gain felicity in both this world and the next. Jupiter, Venus, and the moon are in sextile, denoting a friendly relationship. *Mercury*, representing intelligence, wisdom, and eloquence, is in its (nocturnal, feminine) house of *Gemini*, a sign both restless and intellectual, suggesting conflicting aspects of Bahrâm's nature, as does the fact that the ascendant planets are in quartile or unfriendly aspect to it; Mercury and Gemini are both signs of the interdependence of this world and the next. *Mars* (in apogee in *Leo*) and *Saturn* (in its diurnal, masculine house of *Aquarius*), boldness and caution, are in opposition, suggesting potential conflict; the *Dragon's Tail* (the moon's descending node), in sextile with Jupiter and Venus and turned towards *Saturn*, represents possible disaster that will ultimately be overcome. The outstanding aspects of Bahrâm's nature, represented by Aries/Sun and Leo/Mars, are in trine with each other and with Sagittarius, which has no planet in its house.

9: 26 *Fortune's on lands bestowed*: an Arabic proverb meaning that fortunes are bestowed on lands by their rulers; here, the intent is that Bahrâm should find his fortune in the region to which he is sent.

9: 28 *in Yemen's land*: the Lakhmid rulers Nuʿmân (d. 418) and his son Munzir (418–52?), vassals of the Sassanians, ruled from their capital at Hira (near present-day Najaf ) in Iraq; the founder of the dynasty and builder of Hira, ʿAmr ibn ʿAdî, originated from the Yemen. Nizâmî follows Firdawsî in placing these kings in Yemen. Nuʿmân, the builder of Khavarnaq, is known in the Arabic tradition for his killing of Simnâr (Sinimmâr; hence the proverb 'the reward of Sinimmâr') and for his renunciation of the world.

9: 30 *That his anemone might bloom*: a pun; *lâla-i Nuʿmânî*, 'Nuʿmân's tulip', is the anemone.

10: 6 *Of Sâm's race*: Sâm was the progenitor of the hero-kings of Sistan and the grandfather of Rustam.

10: 9 *The Greeks . . . in Chîn*: both the Greeks and the Chinese were famed for their artistic skills; Nizâmî's *Sharafnâma* features a competition between Greek and Chinese artists.

10: 12 *the spider of the astrolabe*: the centre of the plate of the astrolabe, which shows the sphere of the fixed stars around the earth (represented by the astrolabe's plate), is called the 'spider' because of its resemblance to a web; its central and most important part is the circle of the Zodiac.

10: 13 *Apollonius*: Apollonius of Tyana (Bâlînâs, Bâlînûs), the neo-Pythagorean astrologer and magician of the first century, known as *sâhib al-tilasmât*, 'lord of the talismans'. Talismans were images designed for magical purposes (see further note to §35: 57 below).

10: 27 *Teukros' work*: Tingalûshâ is glossed by both Wilson (ii. 68 n. 561) and Dastgirdî (p. 60 n. 7) as 'the Tang [sc. Artang, i.e. 'paintings'] of Lûshâ [Zeuxis]'. In fact the allusion is to the Babylonian astrologer Teukros, known in Arabic as Tinkalûshâ, whose work on the Paranatellonta ('The Book of Tinkalûshâ') was translated from Middle Persian into Arabic and was well known by Muslim writers, including Abû Maʿshar (Albomasar, d. 886) and Nizâmî's contemporary Fakhr al-Dîn Râzî (d. 1209), who used it as a source for his great compendium on astrology and magic the *Sirr al-maktûm fî mukhâtabat al-nujûm* ('The Hidden Secret of Dialogue with the Stars') (see C. Nallino, 'Trace di opere greche giunti agli arabi per trafila pehlevica', *A Volume of Oriental Studies Presented to E. G. Browne* (Cambridge, 1922), 356–63; M. Ullmann, *Die Natur- und Geheimwissenschaften im Islam* (Leiden, 1972), 278–9, 321, 329–30, 388–90).

10: 32 *both swift and slow*: referring to the swiftness of the sky's turning versus the slowness of the earth's.

10: 57 *The king's a vine*: the origin of this topos (that the ruler prefers those closest to him, i.e. relatives and sycophants) is the eighth-century Arabic translation of the book of fables known as *Kalîla wa-Dimna* (see J. Sadan, 'Vine, Women and Seas: Some Images of the Ruler in Medieval Arabic Literature', *J. of Semitic Studies*, 34 (1989), 133–52); Nizâmî amplifies the topos by associating it with the ruler's destructive power.

11: 9 *like the Ram*: the sun entering the Ram (Aries) signals the onset of spring; the house of Mars (Persian: Bahrâm) is in Aries.

11: 10 *and Venus bore his festive cup*: signifying the conjunction of Mars (Bahrâm) with Venus.

11: 16 *Sadîr, like Sidra*: Sadîr was another of the Lakhmid palaces on the Euphrates; Sidra is the Sidrat al-Muntahâ, the 'farthest lote-tree' (see note to §3: 51–2 above).

11: 26 *its seven forts*: the seven planets.

11: 47 *Mijistî-like*: like the *Almagest* (*al-Mijistî*), the Arabic name for Ptolomy's astronomical work the *Megale Syntaxis*.

11: 51 *slate and stylus*: an iron slate and stylus were used in the teaching of astronomical calculations.

11: 70 *Yemen's star*: Canopus (Suhayl).

12: 2 *Like Yemen's leather by its star*: Yemenite leather was said to gain its red colour from the brightening effect of Canopus.

12: 9 *the grave*: the line involves the recurrent pun on *gûr*, which means both 'onager' and 'grave'; see Introduction, pp. xvi, xxi–xxii.

14: 1 *he launched his ship upon the wine*: he began drinking. Drinking vessels were often formed in the shape of a boat.

14: 24 *Ass-King*: Gûr Khân, the Turkish form of Bahrâm's title, was historically the title borne by the non-Muslim rulers of Qarakhitay (Persian Khatâ, 'Cathay'), whose first king defeated the Seljuk sultan Sanjar in 1147. It is also a pun on *gûr* in its meaning of 'grave': 'Lord of the Grave'.

15: 7 *a hundred Chinese temples*: the Buddhist temples of Chîn (Turkestan) were adorned with decorated statues of the Buddha and with wall-paintings. The word 'Buddha' passed into Persian as *but* (sometimes translated 'idol'), used figuratively for the type of ideal beauty, male or female. On Iranian Buddhism and its literary survivals, see A. S. Melikian-Chirvani, 'L'Évocation littéraire du bouddhisme dans l'Iran musulman', in *Le Monde iranien et l'Islam: Sociétés et cultures* (Hautes Études islamiques et orientales d'histoire comparée, 6; Geneva, 1974), ii. 1–72.

15: 9 *Seven beauteous images*: the portraits are of the princesses of the Seven Climes: India, China (Chîn, Turkestan), Khwârazm, Russia (Siqlab, Slavonia), the Maghreb (North Africa), Rûm (Byzantium), and Iran. Nizâmî's adaptation of the division of the world into regions (*aqâlîm*, sing. *iqlîm*, from the Greek *klima*) owes less to Arabic geographical tradition (based on Ptolemaic geography) than to ancient Iranian cosmology, in which the seven *keshvars*, the seven great kingdoms of the world, India, China, the Turks, Rûm, Africa, and Arabia, were ranged around the central kingdom of Iran, the 'heart' of the world (cf. §6: 24–5); see further M. Pantke, *Das arabische Bahrām-Roman* (Berlin, 1974), 168–79. In Islamic cosmology the earth is placed in the centre of the seven planets, a spatial image echoed here.

15: 15 *noble in name and nature*: a pun on the princess's name, Humây, and *humâyûn*, 'noble', 'royal'.

15: 16 *Durr-Sitî named*: *Durr-Sitî*, 'lady of the pearl', is required by the scansion; orthographically it is identical with *durustî*, 'rightness, honesty, truth'. The pearl symbolizes wisdom.

16: 27 *An aged sage*: on this usurper, a distant descendant of the Kayânids, see Introduction, p. xx.

16: 29 *the seven-eyed belt*: according to I. A. Vüllers (*Lexicon Persico-Latinum Etymologicum* (Bonn, 1864)), this was part of the royal regalia of the Kayânid rulers, set with seven jewels in the colours of the seven planets.

16: 34 *his ruby form in turquoise robes*: red is the colour of joy and of health as well as that of Canopus and Mars/Bahrâm; turquoise (*pîrûza*) robes are blue robes of mourning, the colour of the sky (cf. §36: 438). The pun on *pîrûza*, 'turquoise'/*pîrûz*, 'victorious' anticipates Bahrâm's ultimate victory.

17: 4 *what another poet spake*: the poet alludes to Firdawsî's treatment of the story of Bahrâm's war on the Persians in the *Shâhnâma*; he will improve upon Firdawsî, as Firdawsî did upon his predecessors (cf. §17: 10–11).

18: 53 *and called him "Sinner"*: the epithet given to Yazdigird was *Bizihkâr*, 'the Sinner'.

18: 57 *hammer cold iron*: to do something useless.

19: 44–7 *Who else . . . goes down*: these lines serve to legitimize Bahrâm's claim to the throne: *Gushtâsp* made Zoroastrianism the official religion of Iran, *Ardashîr* founded the Sassanian dynasty, *Kayûmars* was the first Iranian monarch. See further the Glossary.

22: 3–7 *the Lion . . . Saturn's hand*: this horoscope predicts Bahrâm's successful rule and anticipates future events. Leo ascendant indicates a firm and prosperous rule; the conjunction of the sun with Mercury (which must be in Gemini, the house of the sun's apogee and Mercury's own house, though Wilson (ii. 95 n. 834) places them in Cancer) suggests nobility tempered by intellect; that of Venus and the moon in Taurus (the moon's house of exaltation) predicts a strong feminine influence, in particular in respect of love, since Venus is in her own house. Mars, in exaltation in Capricorn, suggests boldness, tempered by reflection (Saturn in Libra, its house of exaltation); Jupiter in his own house Sagittarius suggests nobility combined with enterprise. Leo, Aries, and Sagittarius are in trine, indicating mutual reinforcement of kingly qualities; Leo and Taurus are in quartile, suggesting conflict (which will be overcome by the combined powers of Venus and the moon in Taurus); Leo and Libra are in sextile, as are Jupiter and Saturn, connoting mutual reinforcement of their positive qualities in this friendly aspect.

23: 2 *the seven-stepped throne*: like the 'seven-eyed belt' (see note to §16: 29 above), the seven-stepped throne was presumably a royal symbol of the Kayânids, the seven steps representing the seven regions of the world.

24: 53 *Venus, ruler of the age*: each planet was said to rule over one 7,000-year cycle of time (cf. note to §2: 22 above); the association of Venus with Taurus connotes that part of the cycle ruled by Venus and the moon (cf. §22: 4–6 and note to §22: 3–7 above), the powers of love and guidance.

25: 3 *Jupiter's house is in the Bow*: Jupiter's (diurnal) house is in Sagittarius, and Jupiter is the king of the planets; the sense is that Bahrâm's kingly skill in hunting surpassed all measure.

25: 5 *the stallion danced beneath his lord*: a restive horse is an emblem of the appetites of the animal soul, which must be kept in check. On the image of the king in the centre of a circle, see Introduction, p. xxvi.

25: 8 *it wants a fire to roast the chine*: a possible allusion to an episode in the *Shâhnâma* in which Rustam, after an onager hunt, lights a fire to roast the meat; he then falls asleep, enabling his foes to steal his horse.

25: 13 *Fitna her name*: the poet plays on the various senses of *fitna*: its primary meaning of 'putting to the test', as gold is tested by fire; its Koranic sense as 'trial' or 'test' of faith and as punishment for unbelief; its connotations of physical attraction and sexual temptation, of incitement to morally reprehensible acts, of civil disturbance and sedition; its connection with magic (see further J.-C. Vadet, 'Quelques remarques sur la racine *ftn* dans le Coran et la plus ancienne littérature musulmane', *Revue des études islamiques*, 37 (1969), 81–101; and see Introduction, p. xxiii–xxiv). The letters of Fitna's name in its Arabic orthography, *f-t-n-t*, add up to 80 + 400 + 50 + 400 = 890 > 8 + 9 + 0 = 17; on the significance of this number, see Introduction, p. xxviii.

25: 15 *pâlûda*: a sweet made of starch, sugar or honey, and rose-water; the term also means 'strained, purified'.

25: 49 *death to disturbers*: cf. Koran 2: 194, 'Fight them [the unbe-lievers] so that there will be no disturbance [*fitnatun*], and religion shall be God's (alone).'

25: 64 *all Oman's price*: Oman was noted for its pearl fisheries; Fitna's rubies outdo its pearls in value.

25: 71 *The Moon to Dragon I've given*: the moon is in eclipse when passing through the 'Dragon's Tail', its descending nodes. Fitna's association with the moon, emphasized in this and the next section (cf. §26: 59–60, 90) establishes her role as spiritual guide and links her with the concept of the moon as mediator between the celestial and material worlds and as figuring the Universal Intellect (whose powers are analogous to those of speech, the moon's twenty-eight stations corresponding to the twenty-eight letters of the Arabic alphabet).

25: 75 *sixty steps . . . a fair place to sit*: in the sexagesimal system of calculation known as *hisâb al-munajjimîn*, 'the reckoning of the as-tronomers', a whole is composed of sixty parts. Bahrâm's age at the end of his reign is put at 60 years (§52: 11), creating a symmetry between these two episodes. The *place to sit* is in Persian *manzar*, 'belvedere', a place to observe, that is, for Bahrâm to observe the lesson about to be taught him.

25: 80 *The Sun does bear the Calf in Spring*: the sun enters the house of Taurus in mid-spring (21 Apr.–20 May); Taurus (ruled by Venus) is the moon's house of exaltation (cf. §26: 60).

26: 18 *to cleanse that mirror of its rust*: Dastgirdî glosses as 'to cleanse Fitna's mind of anxiety' (p. 115 n. 2), Wilson 'to put things in good order' (ii. 103 n. 926). The meaning seems rather to be to cleanse the mirror of Bahrâm's heart from the rust of ignorance. The heart was commonly likened to a mirror (mirrors were made of metal) which must be polished to make it susceptible to reflection; cf. Koran 83: 15, 'Their [the sinners'] hearts have been rusted by that which they practised,' and the Prophetic Tradition, 'Hearts may become rusty as does iron'; and see Franz Rosenthal, *Knowledge Triumphant: The Conception of Knowledge in Medieval Islam* (Leiden, 1970), 188–90.

26: 20 *his royal eagle reached the moon*: literally, the eagle emblem on his (black) parasol, emblem of sovereignty, reached the moon's apogee.

26: 25 *its carpet was the azure dome*: the tower was so high that it seemed the sky had cast a carpet before it.

26: 59 *This fortnight's moon . . . seven adornments*: *har haft*, 'all seven', are the seven cosmetic adornments of henna (to dye the hands and feet), indigo (to dye the eyebrows), rouge, white powder, collyrium, talc (to improve the lustre of the face), and galia (a mixture of perfumes). There is a correspondence between their colours and those of the Seven Domes: henna (red-brown, i.e. sandal), indigo (blue-green?), rouge (red), powder (white), collyrium (blue), talc (yellowish), and galia (black). The *fortnight's moon* is the full moon.

26: 61 *see what a jewel adorned that beast*: a further reference to the moon in Taurus: Fitna's moon-like face, surrounded by the ox, is compared to the 'night-shining pearl' (*gawhar-i shab-chirâgh*), a luminous gem by the light of which the 'cow that comes from the sea' is said to graze by night (cf. Dastgirdî, p. 117 n. 9), also a metaphor for the moon.

26: 81 *he made 'Disturbance' seated be*: a pun on *fitna nishândan*, 'to put down sedition'.

26: 90 *the Sky-Dragon*: the moon's descending node, which causes its eclipse (cf. note to §25: 71 above).

27: 1 *from Fish to Moon*: from the earth (said to be supported by an ox resting on a fish) to the heavens.

27: 22 *The Khân of Khâns marched out from Chîn*: historically, this refers to the Hayatila (Hephthalites or White Huns), of Turkish stock, topically perhaps to the Khwârazmians, also of Turkish stock (see Introduction, p. xiii). *Chîn* (Turkestan) is a general term for any enemy of Turkish extraction.

27: 50 *juggled with balls*: a reference to *huqqa-bâzî*, a game with cups and balls ('shell-game'); Bahrâm's 'ball' is his army.

27: 59 *Bahrâmian war*: 'Martian'; the Persian name for Mars is Bahrâm.

27: 69 *the sphere disclosed a bowl of blood*: the red sun is compared to the executioner's bowl or basin, which catches the blood shed by his sword.

27: 97–8 *Persian song . . . Arab bards*: *Persian song*, the epic and heroic poems sung by Persian minstrels, is contrasted with the polished panegyrics of the Arab poets.

28: 12 *from lions take their name*: many Turkish rulers took names which meant 'lion' (e.g. Arslân; see note to §5: 16 above). On the Iranian heroes and kings mentioned in lines 11–12, see the Glossary.

28: 20 *My hare's sleep*: referring to the belief that a hare sleeps with its eyes open and can thus see danger approaching.

28: 67 *be it the Fish*: even if it be the depths in which the fish that supports the earth resides (cf. note to §27: 1 above).

28: 84 *Davidian mail . . . Ark*: the Koranic David was famed as an armourer (Koran 21: 81, 34: 11), as were Indians for making fine swords. *Largesse* is in Persian *júd*; in the Koranic story of Noah the name of the mountain on which the Ark settled is Júdí (Koran 11: 45).

29: 5 *its boilings seven . . . elixirs*: the 'seven boilings', or 'fusions', refers to the alchemical procedure of producing the 'seven fusible metals' (gold, silver, copper, iron, tin, plumbago, and antimony) by the distillation of quicksilver and 'red sulphur' (see note to §35: 301 below). An alternative is to create an elixir (*kímiyá*) which will produce pure gold. The sense is that Bahrám's love for the princesses (his 'elixirs') relieved his agitation.

30: 16 *Wise roses in the furnace hid*: to protect themselves from the cold, the roses, in their wisdom (*hikmat*), hid in the furnace, where, in the crucible sealed with clay (*gil-i hikmat*, 'philosophers' clay', used by alchemists and goldsmiths), they were transformed into rose-water.

30: 18 *The winter chamber*: *tábkhána*, a chamber whose roof and walls were hollow and heated by warm air from the fire.

30: 21 *like Hindus at their prayer*: the black smoke of sandalwood and aloes surrounding the bright fire looked like black Hindu worshippers.

30: 29 *The Joy of Hindus*: the bright fire, compared to fair Turks and Greeks, brought joy to the black Hindus (the coals or smoke surrounding it).

30: 30–1 *The torch of Jonah . . . Abraham's | Rose garden*: these are signs of prophecy, drawn from the Koran and from legends about the prophets: from within the belly of the whale Jonah could see the depths of the sea as though illuminated by a torch; Moses was brought close to God by the fire of the Burning Bush near Sinai (cf. Koran 20: 10–16, 28: 30–2); Jesus prayed for God to send him a feast as a sign of his prophecy (cf. Koran 5: 113–15); the fiery furnace in which Abraham was cast became cool for him according to the Koran (21: 69–70); while in legend it became a rose garden.

30: 68 *Shída, brilliant as the sun*: pun on *shíd*, 'sun'.

30: 100 *Simnár's design*: the portraits of the seven princesses in Khavarnaq (see §15: 9–16).

30: 107 *Bahrâm's aspect*: as Bahrâm is the Persian name for Mars, this may mean the day governed by Mars (Tuesday). In Zoroastrian angelology, Bahrâm is the angel who presides over the twentieth day of the Persian solar month.

31: 5 *the seven planets' natures*: the association of the planets with the days of the week goes back to ancient Babylon; it passed into Islamic thought from Greek–Hellenistic sources, as did that of the planets with certain colours. Nizâmî's use of the seven-day week is anachronistic for the Sassanian period, as in the Sassanian calendar each day of the month was independent (with its own patron-angel) and there was no division into weeks.

32: 2 *Shammâsî temple . . . Abbasid black*: the fire-temple was served by white-robed priests; the eponymous Shammâs was said to have instituted fire-worship. Black was the emblematic colour of the Abbasid caliphs.

32: 27 *red and yellow*: surkhî va-zardî, colours that indicate good health.

32: 45 *Iram's green . . . black lot*: a pun on savâd, meaning 'the (dark) verdure around a city' (Iram), 'the black (ink) of the pen', 'learning': 'it made men write my story as if it were a fable.' On Iram, see the Glossary.

32: 49 *scraping Heaven with an axe*: attempting the impossible.

32: 73–4 *my pawn . . . that castle*: however I manœuvred, my pawn was always blocked by the queen ( *farzîn*, literally 'vizier', the Persian equivalent of our queen in chess).

32: 130a *snake's basket*: the basket in which the snake-charmer keeps his snake.

32: 136 *the ring-juggling sphere*: the 'rings' are the planetary spheres.

32: 188 *our turquoise fort*: the sky.

32: 193 *who taxes paid from Paradise*: the garden, which seemed to have been devised from hourîs' forms, was so much more beautiful than they that the hourîs were obliged to pay taxes to it.

32: 199 *like it free*: the cypress is called 'free' (âzâd) because it is ever-green, hence does not yellow in autumn, and bears no fruit; tall and straight, it does not interlace with other trees.

32: 209 *Khuzistan*: a region in south-western Iran famed for its production of sugar-cane.

32: 219 *sugar and candles are well joined*: literally, 'each sugar-lump [maiden] bore a candle'; sugar and candles are appurtenances of feasts, especially wedding feasts.

32: 224 *Greek troops before, Ethiops behind*: unveiled, she displayed a fair (Greek) face and black (Ethiop) curls.

32: 226 *others of earth, of pure light she*: while the other maids were human (created from earth), she seemed an angel (created from light).

32: 240 *Pleiads and Moon well-mated be*: the Pleiades, the third of the twenty-eight lunar mansions, are in the house of Taurus, suggesting that the moon is also in that house and that this 'moon' may be expected to exert a strong influence over her lover, with whom she is in accord.

32: 271–4 *Turktâz . . . Turkish raid*: a pun on the names Turktâz, 'Turkish raid', and Turktâzî, 'Turkish raider'. (Ritter and Rypka and the Moscow edition have *Turknâz*, 'Turkish wiles', for Turktâz.)

32: 323 *the sky became a puppeteer*: an allusion to the shadow-play (cf. note to §4: 16 above); the 'puppets' are both the planets, which influence men's lives, and the beauties, who similarly influence the protagonist.

32: 358 *a date . . . a needle*: metaphors for the sexual act.

32: 402 *candles came before*: the brightness of her face made the candles pale.

32: 413 *Nihavand*: a town near the mountain of the same name in western Iran.

32: 430 *pearl-hung ear . . . iron*: a pun on *na'lak*, a type of ear-ring, and *na'l*, 'horseshoe' (iron); casting a horseshoe into the fire after having written the name of the beloved on it was a magical spell to engender passion.

32: 458 *beyond | this Abadan there is no town*: an Arabic proverb meaning one has reached the furthest point possible: 'let be what will be.' Abadan ('Abbâdân) is a town formerly located on the coast of the Persian Gulf but now on an island on the left bank of the Shatt al-Arab.

32: 465 *the mat*: the leather mat was, like the bowl or basin (see note to §27: 69 above), associated with the executioner's trade; such mats were spread for the condemned to kneel upon. A leather mat was also spread to provide a smooth surface for dancing.

32: 514 *king-like, 'neath parasol of night*: a black parasol was part of the royal regalia of certain rulers.

32: 515 *fish-bone's less prized than fish's back*: the bone is white, the edible back is black.

32: 519 *no colour beyond black is known*: black was considered the most perfect of the seven colours; the saying is proverbial. Black is also the colour of Saturn, the furthest from earth of the seven planets (the 'seven thrones').

33: 25 *Qârûn*: the Koranic Qârûn (Biblical Korah), famed for his great wealth, was punished by God for boasting of his riches and oppressing his people (cf. Koran 28: 77–83).

33: 31 *Ayâz*: the favourite slave of the Ghaznavid ruler Mahmûd (r. 999–1030); type of the ideal beloved.

33: 95 *like Venus in sextile*: a sextile (60°) relationship between planets indicates friendship and love. Solomon, as king, is the equivalent of the sun.

33: 101 *the Tablet*: the Preserved or Well-Guarded Tablet, said to be inscribed with God's knowledge.

33: 116 *Rizvân*: the angel who is guardian of Paradise.

33: 133 *within God's shrine*: Wilson glosses as the Ka'ba in Mecca (ii. 145 n. 1418), but more probably the temple of Solomon in Jerusalem is meant.

33: 192 *was cooked up*: literally, 'came from that old woman's oven'; witches were said to be able to raise storms by means of their cauldrons. There is also an allusion to the Flood, which in popular tradition (based on Koran 11: 41, 'When Our decree was issued and the oven boiled forth') was said to have poured out of the oven of an old woman in Kufa (Iraq).

33: 229 *the Calf of Gold*: the calf worshipped by the Israelites during Moses' absence on Sinai (see e.g. Koran 20: 84–98).

33: 230 *yellow ochre*: *tîn-i asfar*, clay containing hydrated iron oxide, used medicinally as a stimulant; also, an alchemical term for gold.

34: 51 *who brings bad news to men*: a pun on Bishr's name, which means 'joy', 'good tidings' (Wilson reads Bashr, 'mankind'; but see Krotkoff, 'Colour and Number', 115–16 n. 43).

34: 82 *this talk of Plan and Pen*: literally, 'how long will you attribute this design to the Pen?' meaning the divine Pen of God's power which inscribed all that was to be on the Preserved Tablet (see note to §33: 101 above).

34: 91 *this high-branched tree*: Dastgirdî glosses, 'the high-branched tree of the mysteries of creation' (p. 204 n. 1). In the Koran, Adam was cast out of Paradise for eating from the 'tree of eternity' (20: 121); a good word is compared to 'a good tree whose roots are firm and whose branches reach the heavens' (14: 25).

34: 244 *the bride-price*: the *kâbîn* or *mahr* was the amount the groom agreed to pay the bride, part in advance, the remainder reserved to be paid in the event of divorce.

34: 249 *Better than yellow robes are green*: perhaps an allusion to the green colour sacred to Islam, contrasted with the yellow garments Jews were sometimes obliged to wear.

35: 2 *the navel of the week*: so called because Tuesday comes in the middle of the Muslim week, which begins on Saturday and ends on Friday.

35: 13 *she brought pure rubies to the mine*: she offered the rubies of precious speech to the mine, Bahrâm, dressed in ruby red.

35: 14 *Russia*: Rûs, i.e. Slavonia.

35: 31 *Venus had given her Mercury's milk*: she possessed the beauty of Venus, the wisdom and cleverness of Mercury.

35: 46 *the Brazen Fort*: Rû'în-Diz, the name of the fortress of Nizâmî's patron (cf. §53: 53), here alludes to the conquest of the eponymous 'Brazen Fort', protected by talismans, by the Kayânid prince Isfandiyâr in the *Shâhnâma*.

35: 57 *talismans*: these were generally images (sometimes, as here, sculptures or automata) engraved on stone and metal and intended for magical purposes (e.g. warning against the approach of enemies; protecting treasures). The properties of the materials of which they were composed, as well as the astrological aspects under which they were made and which rendered them efficacious, were of great importance, and there is a considerable body of literature on the subject, for example, the eleventh-century *Ghâyat al-Hakîm* ('The Philosopher's Goal'; German translation by H. Ritter and M. Plessner, *'Picatrix': Das Ziel des Weisen von pseudo-Maǧrītī* (London, 1962; repr: 1978); English summary, pp. lix–lxxv).

35: 80 *by door, not roof*: an allusion to the romance *Vîs and Râmîn* by Fakhr al-Dîn Gurgânî (*c*.1054), a story of adulterous love; in one episode the lover, Râmîn, clandestinely visits his beloved Vîs (married to the ageing King Mawbad) by entering her chamber by the roof.

35: 114 *with flasks of poison round*: the portrait, whose beauty makes it seem like sweet honey, is surrounded by the severed heads of the princess's suitors, which are compared to flasks of poison.

35: 133–4 *heart . . . mind*: literally, 'liver', the seat of the emotions, and 'heart', the seat of affection and love.

35: 140 *Shírín's castle, Farhâd's grave*: *Shírín's castle* (near the town of Qasr-i Shirin in the mountains of south-western Iranian Kurdistan), believed to have been the palace built by Shírín in her desire to be near Khusraw Parvíz (Nizâmí tells the story in *Khusraw and Shírín*; see Introduction, p. x), was in actuality a summer residence of the Sassanian emperors; in Islamic times it was in ruins. The rock tomb known as *Farhâd's grave* is just south of Qasr-i Shirin. On Farhâd, Khusraw, and Shírín, see also the Glossary.

35: 162 *a spiritual connection*: just as there are specific astrological relationships that render talismans efficacious (see note to §35: 57 above), there are others that will render them ineffective by loosing (reversing) their original connections. The prince, by studying the configuration of the stars, found an auspicious time for his endeavour.

35: 257 *a bead of blue*: a blue glass bead was said to be efficacious against the Evil Eye.

35: 268 *the symbols' secret sense*: the princess's gloss clearly conceals a deeper meaning; for a discussion of this crucial central tale, which provides the transition from black to white through red (cf. §35: 298), see Krotkoff, 'Colour and Number', 106–7.

35: 288 *Venus and Canopus*: the prince is compared to Canopus because of his red robes.

35: 301 *red sulphur*: gûgird-i surkh, also an alchemical pseudonym for gold; it and quicksilver are used together to obtain the seven fusible metals (see note to §29: 5 above). In esoteric thought red sulphur denotes the Universal Man, the product of the hermetic action of red.

35: 302 *the vital spirit*: the *vital* or 'animal' *spirit* (ravân), originating in the heart from the mixture of the pure vapour of the blood and inhaled air, moves through the arteries to the organs and supports the body's functions (see M. W. Dols, *Majnūn: The Madman in Medieval Islamic Society* (Oxford, 1992), 25).

36: 2 *bright sky-like robes*: literally, the king, world-illuming as the sun, and like it ruler of the world, donned turquoise (pírúza) robes, the colour of the sphere, in triumph ( pírúzí; cf. note to §16: 34 above). This contrasts with the blue (azraq) mourning robes donned by Mâhân at the end of the tale (see note to §36: 438 below).

36: 12 *Mâhân*: the name means 'moons' or 'like the moon' (mâh).

36: 13 *a thousand Turks his Hindu slaves*: beautiful Turks bowed before Mâhân's beauty like Indian slaves.

36: 59 *his whipping post*: the ruler's tripod, set up when punishment is to be administered.

36: 66 *like the wind*: literally, 'with whom, like the wind, do you share your breaths?'

36: 67 *Mâhân the clever*: literally, 'Mâhân-i Kûshyâr', i.e. a descendent of, or like, Kûshyâr. The Persian mathematician and astronomer Kûshyâr (Gûshyâr) ibn Labbân (971–1029) was the teacher of the philosopher Ibn Sînâ (Avicenna; d. 1037).

36: 78 *Hâyil*: the name means 'horrible, frightful' (Bausani translates 'Orrore').

36: 85 *tied on its camel a golden drum*: dawn bound on the camel-coloured (pale) sky the golden kettledrum of the sun.

36: 106 *Lâ hawl*: Lâ hawl wa-lâ quwwa illâ billâh, 'There is no power and no strength but in God', a prayer recited when one has escaped from danger.

36: 107 *ghouls*: demons who lead people astray and draw them to their deaths, often taking human form to deceive them.

36: 109 *Haylâ . . . Ghaylâ*: 'horrible', 'ghoulish'.

36: 130 *the guards of Hell*: zabâniyya (pl. zabâniyyât), the 'violent thrusters' (from Arabic zabana, 'to push') of Koran 96: 19; there is a pun in this line and the next with the Persian zabân, 'tongue', as the demons are said to spurt tongue-like flames from their mouths.

36: 131 *clattered horns and blades*: certain beggars would clatter sheep's horns and shoulder-blades together, demanding alms; the sense is 'threatening'.

36: 138 *a seven-headed dragon's hight*: the dragon is the world: the seven heads represent the seven planets or spheres, the four wings the four elements.

36: 234 *There's no power*: see note to §36: 106 above.

36: 279 *sandal-tree*: since sandalwood is a cure for headache and for melancholy (cf. note to §3: 46 above), it would be expected that by remaining in the tree Mâhân would be cured of his melancholic nature (see §36: 166) as well as of his troubles. The flowers of the sandal-tree are red.

36: 308–9 *Seventeen Prinesses . . . of the moon*: on the esoteric significance of the number seventeen, see Introduction, p. xxvii. The *seventeen aspects of the moon* (reading, with Ritter and Rypka, and Bausani, *khaslat*, 'quality') may refer to the seventeenth lunar station, al-iklîl, considered unlucky. Dastgirdî (p. 257 n. 2) and the Moscow edition read *khasl*, the seventeenth and final throw in the game of *nard*, which ends the game, meaning that these maidens were more beautiful than any.

36: 353  *sugar . . . rose-water*: in the marriage ceremony it is the custom for the bride to scatter sugar on the groom, and for him to sprinkle rose-water on the bride.

36: 363  *a foul afreet*: an *'ifrît* is one of the most horrible of the race of *jinn*, non-humans who harass humans, and who include demons and ghouls.

36: 366  *tûz bark*: 'the bark of a tree which is very tough and strong and is used to bind bows and horses' saddles' (Dastgirdî, p. 261 n. 15); in ancient Iran it was also used for copying books in order to preserve them.

36: 384  *the White Dîv*: a gigantic demon described as black-skinned and white-haired, killed by the hero Rustam.

36: 411  *this bathhouse . . . rubbish-heap*: bathhouses were adorned with pictures (often representing the ages of man), and provided a common metaphor for the world; the Prophet compared this world to a dung-heap covered with green growth, which appears fair but is in reality foul.

36: 418–19  *to Him Who aids . . . show me the way*: cf. Koran 25: 32, 'And thy Lord is sufficient Guide and Helper.'

36: 423  *in his own form*: his good intent became materialized in his own form in Khizr.

36: 438  *sky-like, he took the hue of Time*: Dastgirdî glosses, 'he donned blue (*azraq*), like the colour of time, which shows deception (*zarq*), and because of being in Time's colour escaped from its calamities' (p. 267 n. 1). Blue is the colour both of mourning and of Sufi robes, signifying renunciation of the world.

36: 441–3  *That flower blue . . . sun-worshipper*: the heliotrope; its yellow centre is the 'disk' received from the sun.

37: 30  *a pit*: i.e. that he would not find water, but that a calamity lay in wait for him.

37: 40  *brought water forth . . . mouth*: a pun on *âb*, 'water', 'lustre', 'honour': the jewels were so brilliant that they would make the viewer's eyes water, but, since their lustre could not provide water for the thirsting man, they brought tears of sorrow to his eyes; they also caused Bad to display his lack of honour.

37: 73  *the narcissus*: Good's eyes.

37: 92  *Her Babylonian charms*: Babylonians were famed as magicians and sorcerers.

37: 222 *Aaron . . . bells*: dawn is compared to Aaron (Hârûn), the brother of Moses, in Muslim tradition the 'watchman' over God's people. The guards of a royal palace wore belts hung with bells to prevent them from going to sleep at night.

37: 226 *Venus and Mercury*: he joined love and beauty (Venus) with wisdom (Mercury).

37: 243 *the dîv's ill*: epileptics were believed to be possessed by demons.

37: 320 *the traveller . . . Mubashshir*: used here ironically, the name *Mubashshir* means 'bringer of good news'. *The traveller (safarî)* suggests, also ironically, an itinerant Sufi or preacher.

38: 1 *this willow vault*: the sky, so called because of its greenish colour.

38: 3 *the fifth kingdom*: the fifth clime, Iran; Venus, the sphere's musician, who rules over Libra, the sign of the fifth clime, demonstrated her submission to Bahrâm's rule. The sun·is the first planet to see Venus and Mars together; hence the significance of dawn in the opening lines.

38: 27 *that gardens circled, like a shrine*: his garden was so beautiful it seemed like the Ka'ba at Mecca, the other gardens like pilgrims circumambulating the shrine in worship.

38: 50 *Sufi-like*: the Sufis were accustomed to dance in a circle to music in order to induce an ecstatic state.

38: 88 *Manhood humanity beguiled*: manly passion (*mardî*) overcame his judgement, a sign of humanity (*mardumî*).

38: 91 *a chamber high*: *ghurfa*, used in the Koran (25: 76, 39: 21) for the chambers (or 'lofty mansions') in Paradise, promised to believers. That the room is made of bricks suggests the tension between the spiritual and physical aspects of love resolved at the tale's end.

38: 114 *like boats*: the girls' rounded breasts floating upon the water seemed like small boats.

38: 117 *milky streams . . . Shîrîn's castle*: the castle of Shîrîn (see note to §35: 140 above) had a conduit, built by Farhâd, which brought milk from the mountain pastures to fill its pools. The *milky streams* are the maidens' fair bodies.

38: 121 *Resurrection's dawn*: a pun on *qâmat*, 'stature, form', and *Qiyâmat*, 'Resurrection', used metaphorically for a great disturbance.

38: 153 *Bakht*: the maiden's name means 'Fortune'.

38: 154 *veil . . . mode*: a pun on *parda*, which means both 'veil' and 'musical mode'.

38: 202 *The Judas-tree has flowered*: a sexual metaphor, as are those in the lines which follow.

38: 213 *yellow wallflower . . . white jasmine*: his white face had become yellow with suffering; a yellow complexion is associated with disappointment and lovesickness.

38: 232 *bailiff . . . guard*: the *muhtasib*, the inspector of public morals or public censor, and the *shihna* or police chief of a town.

38: 243 *moth . . . light*: moth and flame are traditional metaphors for lover and beloved.

38: 298 *the eyes of hundred beasts*: the *beasts*, embodied in the disruptive animals, represent the appetites of the animal soul.

38: 301 *my Hour*: the 'appointed hour' of his death.

39: 1 *Jupiter and Saturn . . . Fish for Ram*: trine is the distance of four zodiacal signs between planets (= 120°), an auspicious aspect; the time is the vernal equinox, the Iranian New Year, when the sun passes from Pisces (Fish) into Aries (Ram).

39: 3 *Salsabîl*: a stream in Paradise.

39: 17 *without the Resurrection*: an allusion to Koran 82: 2–3: 'When the heaven is cleft asunder and the stars are scattered, and the rivers are diverted, and the graves are laid open, then everyone will know that which he has brought forward, and that which he has left behind.'

39: 18 *the fenugreek . . . saffron*: the dew on the fenugreek is compared to tears, its yellow blossom to saffron, which imparts happiness.

39: 20 *like Scripture*: literally, 'the rose, like the scribe of revelation [*kâtib al-wahy*], inscribed with the Water of Life a writ to shed the poppies' blood', i.e. to make their red flowers blossom. *Kâtib al-wahy*, 'scribe of revelation', was an epithet of the caliph 'Uthmân (r. 644–56), who supervised the written recension of the Koran.

40: 3 *A burdened messenger . . . six sides*: literally, a messenger bearing a *chahâr-bandî* (see note to §7: 60 above). A six-sided pavilion is a royal one, erected by Bahrâm for the New Year's feast.

40: 17 *his collar*: an emblem of royalty.

40: 18 *a vizier*: on the story of Bahrâm, his evil vizier, his encounter with the shepherd, etc. (§§40–50), and its source in Nizâm al-Mulk's Siyâsatnâma, see Introduction, p. xxiv.

40: 47 *are lawful*: shedding their blood or confiscating their wealth is legally allowable.

41: 17 *the reins of Heaven*: i.e. of the king's horse.

41: 43 *the alms-collector*: the ʿāmil-i sadaqāt collects Muslims' taxes (*zakāt, sadaqa*) on their wealth. A fifth of all wealth goes to the Bayt al-Māl, the public treasury, to be spent for charitable purposes. Nizām al-Mulk uses the same term, anachronistic for pre-Islamic Iran, in the *Siyāsatnāma*.

41: 70 *My human exemplar*: nimūdār-i ādamiyyat. Nimūdār, 'exemplar', 'model', is also the astrological term for 'rectification' (animodar), a 'method of estimating the Ascendant when [its] precise time is not known' (E. P. Elwell-Sutton, *The Horoscope of Asadulla Mirza* (Leiden, 1977), 83). According to the philosopher Nasīr al-Dīn Tūsī, man the microcosm is the symbol (*nimūdār*) of the macrocosm and a composite of the influences of both worlds.

41: 77 *the king kills, the vizier forgives*: it is a topos that viziers intercede for those the king has condemned to death.

42: 2 *Dawn, with one stroke of its two swords*: 'Single-Stroke' was the epithet of Sām, the grandfather of Rustam, who killed a dragon with one stroke; the *two swords* are false and true dawn, the moon is compared to the dragon.

42: 22 *a guardsman fell*: literally, a zabānī, one of the guardians of Hell; cf. note to §36: 130 above.

43: 7 *Ghūr*: a Turkish tribal dynasty known for its savagery. The Ghurid ruler ʿAlāʾ al-Dīn Jahān-Sūz ('World-Burner') sacked the city of Ghazna in 1150–1 and conquered Lahore in 1186, putting an end to Ghaznavid rule; Rāst-Rawshan is called ʿālam-sūz (§40: 66), which is synonymous, perhaps in a topical allusion.

45: 17 *shell-like*: I, the owner of the stolen pearl, was consigned to the pit (prison) like the oyster-shell to the depths of the sea.

46: 5 *gave name to "nought"*: her mouth was so small that it could be considered as nothing.

47: 2 *custom-house*: rasadgāh, a place where customs and imposts were collected (and perhaps also land-tax; cf. §47: 12); the revenues were spent on public works. Dastgirdī glosses, 'a border post manned by troops' (p. 338 n. 9); possibly both functions were combined. (The term also means 'observatory'; cf. §3: 52 and note to §3: 51–2 above.)

48: 25 *I'd no pen*: that is, to write my complaint against him; the poet plays on the traditional opposition between pen and sword (cf. §40: 44, §48: 22–3).

48: 26 *Me, a clod*: meaning, do you think me a piece of dirt to fear being dissolved by the water of the king's justice?

50: 2 *in this brick-kiln . . . was like damp bricks*: was near falling apart from worry. Bricks (*khisht*) are made from clay and straw and dried in the sun; the *brick-kiln* is the world.

52: 11 *that cypress tall . . . violets*: the tall cypress is the king; *jasmine on his violets* means the appearance of white hair among his black.

52: 16–18 *one tomb, the other vice*: a pun on *gûr*, 'onager'/'grave', and *âhû*, 'gazelle'/'vice'.

52: 28 *Companion of the Cave*: Dastgirdî glosses *yâr-i ghâr* as 'the solitude sought by Bahrâm' (p. 351 n. 1), Wilson as 'the Divine Beloved' (ii. 200 n. 2005). The epithet is used of the Prophet's uncle Abû Bakr, his companion in the cave in which they hid on the flight from Mecca to Medina; by association it may be applied to the Prophet (who received the revelation from Gabriel in a cave at Hirâ near Mecca) and to God. (See further the Introduction, pp. xxxiii–xxxiv.) In the *Shâhnâma* Bahrâm dies a natural death; in some historical sources he disappears into a swamp or a deep pool; according to Abû Mansûr Thaʿâlibî's (d. 1038) history of the Persian kings, Bahrâm disappears into a pit while pursuing an onager.

52: 33 *the stone within the serpent's head*: the snake-stone (cf. note to §7: 54 above) is found in the snake's brain.

52: 39 *that elephant | had dreamed, and gone to Hindustan*: a proverbial expression: just as the elephant dreams of returning to its home in India, the king has returned to his (spiritual) home.

52: 40 *Time held in check the mighty king*: *pîl-band* means to be put in check by the elephant, in Persian chess the equivalent of our bishop.

52: 45 *many spiders, but no flies*: an allusion to the spider which concealed with its web the mouth of the cave in which the Prophet and Abû Bakr hid on their flight from Mecca to Medina (see note to §52: 28 above).

52: 47 *snake-like*: like snakes guarding a treasure (cf. §52: 27).

52: 60 *a mother of earth, and one of blood*: man, who is composed of the four elements, is both the product of earth (likewise so composed) and of the physical mother who gives birth to him and nurtures him.

52: 66 *birds' milk*: something impossible.

52: 79 *four jars in the dyer's shop*: the four humours, associated with four colours: sanguine (red blood), phlegmatic (white phlegm), bilious (yellow bile), splenetic (black bile).

52: 91 *these fancies' Teukros*: i.e. you control the forms of the heavens. On Teukros, see note to §10: 27 above.

52: 94 *One Line, Point of origin*: the Unicity of the Creator, from which all creation stems; represented by the *alif*, the first letter of the alphabet, first in the name of God (Allah) and of the primal man, Adam.

52: 99 *the veil of light*: see note to §3: 59 above.

52: 101 *grief's market-place*: literally, 'grief's crossroads' (*chahâr-sû*), the meeting-place of the four directions; market-stalls were set up at crossroads.

52: 102–3 *A room . . . four-banded bag*: the *room* is the world, its *chimneys* the four elements. The *two-doored house* is also the world, from one door of which one enters and from the other leaves; robbers were said to choose houses with two doors, for ease of escape. On the *four-banded bag*, see note to §7: 60 above.

52: 108 *nought but these two worlds*: Bausani interprets this and the following lines (109–11) as evidence for Nizâmî's belief in the possibility of multiple worlds; see 'Nizami di Gangia et la "pluralità dei mondi"', *Rivista degli studi orientale*, 46 (1971), 197–215. Both Dastgirdî (p. 357 n. 6) and Wilson (ii. 203–4 n. 2038) gloss 'these two worlds' as those of body and soul.

52: 109 *this cave*: Dastgirdî (p. 357 n. 6) and Wilson (ii. 204 n. 2039) gloss the cave as 'the world of the body, the material world'; but the 'cave of initiation' and the Platonic cave are also suggested (see Introduction, p. xxxiii).

52: 112 *These seven four-sided tablets*: literally, 'these seven tablets with four natures', i.e. the seven spheres of the heavens and the four elements of earth.

52: 121 *how long seek profit from this ice*: literally, 'how long make beer?' i.e. attempt the impossible; another figurative meaning of 'to make beer' is 'to boast'.

52: 136 *your pulpit, scaffold*: Dastgirdî glosses, 'Do not think that Heaven's nine steps [sc. spheres] are the steps of the pulpit,' and notes the frequent comparison of the sky to a scaffold (p. 259 n. 13); Wilson translates, 'high places'. The *pulpit* (*minbar*) is a construction with steps which the preacher mounts to deliver his sermon in the mosque, in which he pronounces the name of the current ruler; the *scaffold* (*dâr*) is also the cross, used for executions. Perhaps an allusion to the Sufi martyr Hallâj (d. 922), executed for heterodox beliefs, who is depicted in mystical literature as forsaking the pulpit for the cross.

52: 137 *You seek for life . . . one Messiah*: referring to the Muslim belief that Jesus was taken down alive from the cross and ascended directly into Heaven (see Koran 4: 158–61; alternatives are that another person was substituted for him, or that he died a natural death (cf. Koran 3: 55–6) ).

52: 146 *where Jesus' love, where donkey-bead*: an allusion to the donkey on which Jesus rode, which was thereby ennobled; the meaning is that the humble can be made high. Donkey-beads are blue beads worn by donkeys to protect against the Evil Eye. There is a pun on *mihr*, 'love'/*muhra*, 'bead'.

53: 4 *Bakhtîshû's judgement, Jesus' fame*: (Jibrîl ibn) Bakhtîshû' (d. 817; the name means 'saved by Jesus') was the Nestorian Christian physician of the Abbasid caliph Hârûn al-Rashîd; the poet puns on the elements of his name, *Bakht*, 'fortune' (Persian), and Ishû', 'Jesus'. Jesus was famed as a healer.

53: 17 *Maintainer . . . arrived*: the *maintainer of the world* is the *qâ'im*, who protects this age; the *one not yet arrived* is the Mahdî, who will appear at the end of days, but whose arrival is rendered unnecessary by the ruler's justice (cf. note to §5: 14 above).

53: 22 *persian manna*: *turanjabîn*, a medicinal compound of honey and thorns.

53: 37 *from nought*: literally, 'from two letters', *kâf* and *nûn*, which spell *kun*, the Divine Fiat.

53: 45 *to Mercury fresh ears of corn*: Virgo (Arabic *sunbula*, an ear of corn) is Mercury's nocturnal house and the sign of his exaltation; Mercury is the scribe of the heavens. The meaning is that the poet's 'virgin thoughts', embodied in the brides of his poem, are full of nourishment.

53: 46 *story-tellers love not each other*: a proverb; the meaning is that Mercury is not jealous of the poet's skill but admires it.

53: 48 *his brazen fort*: the patron's fortress Rû'în Diz (cf. §53: 53).

53: 51 *diamonds*: representing his severity towards his enemies.

53: 53 *The golden nail*: the nail which holds the earth in place.

53: 55 *The Mount of Mercy . . . Bû Qubays*: two mountains near Mecca.

53: 61 *who pardons sins, wears Cathay robes*: a pun on *khitâ* 'Cathay'/ *khatâ*, 'sin'.

53: 63–4 *five hundred and ninety-three . . . fourteenth Ramazân*: the date of the poem's completion: 14 Ramadan 593 = 31 July 1197.

# GLOSSARY

*Alexander* (Iskandar, Sikandar): the Greek ruler (d. 323 BCE) who conquered Persia; he was said to have been tutored by Aristotle (cf. §6: 36). On his legendary journey through the Realms of Darkness in search of the Water of Life (q.v.) he was accompanied by the mysterious prophet-sage Khizr (q.v.), who succeeded where Alexander failed.

*Alp Arslân*: the second Seljuk sultan (r. 1063–72).

*Amul*: a city in Mazandaran (northern Iran) located on the Caspian Sea, in Nizâmî's time a flourishing centre of industry and trade.

*'Anqâ*: see Sîmurgh.

*Anûshîrvân*: see Nûshîrvân.

*Âq Sonqor*: the father of Nizâmî's patron 'Alâ' al-Dîn Körp Arslân (see Introduction, p. xiii).

*Ârash*: the legendary archer who with one extraordinary shot from his marvellous bow defined the boundaries between Iran and Tûrân (the Turkish lands of Central Asia and Transoxiana).

*Ardashîr Bâbak* (Bâbakân): founder of the Sassanian dynasty (r. 226–41).

*Artang* (Arzhang): an extra-canonical work by Mânî (q.v.), illustrated with drawings and paintings including astrological images and depictions of the final Judgement; the type of beautiful painting.

*Baghdad*: the Iraqi city, capital of the Abbasid caliphate.

*Bahman*: son of the Kayânid prince Isfandiyâr (q.v.) and ancestor of Ardashîr (q.v.).

*Bilqîs*: the legendary Queen of Sheba, wife of Solomon (q.v.).

*Bîsitûn*: a mountain east of Kirmanshah in western Iran famed for its Parthian and Sassanian rock-carvings, often confused with those of nearby Taq-i Bustan. According to local legend, the carvings were made on the order of Khusraw Parvîz (q.v.), who, jealous of the love of the engineer Farhâd (q.v.) for Shîrîn (q.v.), commanded him to hew a tunnel through the mountain (the story is retold in Nizâmî's *Khusraw and Shîrîn*). Bîsitûn (or Bihistûn, from the Old Persian *bagastana*, 'place of the gods'), read in Persian as *bî-sutûn*, 'without columns', provides a source of puns throughout the *Haft Paykar*.

*Canopus* (Suhayl): a bright star in the constellation Argus which rises from the direction of Yemen.

*Cathay* (Khitâ, Khitây): Qarakhitay, a region of Chinese Turkestan.

*Chîn*: 'China', (Chinese) Turkestan. The 'Chinese' were known for their artistic skills and for their Buddhist temples adorned with idols and wall paintings. The term is also used of any Turkish invader from the east.

*Darius* (Dârâ): the Achaemenid Darius III (r. 335–330 BCE), in the eastern Persian historical tradition the last Kayânid ruler, defeated by Alexander (q.v.) and subsequently murdered by his own generals.

*Daylam*: a region in north-western Iran (now part of Gilan), whose natives (Daylamites) were known for their dark curling hair.

*dirham*: a silver coin; generally, 'money'.

*dihqân*: a member of the ancient Iranian landed aristocracy.

*dîv*: a demon, one of the non-human race of *jinn*, who torments people and leads them astray.

*Faghfûr*: in the Muslim sources, a title of the emperor of China.

*Farhâd*: the famed engineer, builder and sculptor, who loved the beautiful Shîrîn (q.v.), and threw himself from the mountain of Bîsitûn (q.v.) when he received the false report of her death.

*Farîdûn*: an early Iranian king who, with the help of the hero Kâva, defeated Zahhâk (q.v.) and restored legitimate rule to Iran; famed for his sagacity.

*farr*: the aura signifying divine favour to a ruler.

*Firdawsî*: the author of the *Shâhnâma*; see Introduction, pp. xxii–xxiv.

*Gabriel* (Jibrâ'îl): the angel, divine messenger and source of inspiration, who revealed the Koran to the Prophet Muhammad and was the Prophet's guide on his Ascent.

*Gîv*: a hero in Firdawsî's *Shâhnâma*, son-in-law of Rustam (q.v.).

*gûr*: the Persian for 'onager'/'grave'; see Introduction, pp. xvi, xx–xxii.

*Gushtâsp*: the Kayânid (q.v.) ruler who made Zoroastrianism the official religion of Iran.

*halvâ*: a sweet made from oil, flour or other cereal, and honey, sweetened with saffron (a stimulant said to induce joy).

*Hindu*: used generally of all Indians (inhabitants of Hind), characterized for their blackness and believed to worship fire; known proverbially as watchmen and house-servants, also as thieves.

*hourî*: a female denizen of Paradise; used figuratively for a beautiful woman.

*Îraj*: son of *Farîdûn* (q.v.), on whom the latter bestowed Iran when dividing rule of the world among his three sons.

*Iram*: a legendary city filled with palaces and gardens, 'many-columned Iram' was said to have been built in Aden by the Arabian king Shaddâd, of the tribe of 'Âd, in imitation of Paradise. According to the Koran (89: 7–15) it was destroyed by God as punishment for

Shaddâd's excessive pride. Many legends have been elaborated about this city buried in the sand and filled with fabulous treasures.

*Isfahan*: a city in Western central Iran, in Islamic times an important political and cultural centre.

*Isfandiyâr*: a Kayânid (q.v.) prince, son of Gushtâsp (q.v.), who performed a series of seven famous exploits; he was killed by Rustam (q.v.).

*Jamshîd* ( Jam): an early Iranian king who, in the *Shâhnâma*, was deposed by his nobles when he became over-proud, and replaced by the usurper Zahhâk (q.v.). Famed for his love of pleasure, he brought many of the elements of culture to Iran, including the discovery of wine.

*Jesus*: known in the Islamic tradition primarily for his life-giving powers and his studiousness.

*Joseph* (Yûsuf ): the biblical prophet, in Islam a figure of beauty, piety, and prophecy. In the Koranic story (Koran 12), elaborated in legends of the prophets, Joseph was thrown into a pit by his jealous brothers, who told his father Jacob that he had been eaten by wolves; 'Joseph in the pit' is a figure for one (usually innocent) who has fallen into trouble. Joseph was rescued and sold into Egypt as a slave, where his beauty made his master's wife (Zulaykhâ (q.v.) ) fall in love with him, but with divine aid he resisted temptation; he often appears as a type of the ideal or spiritual beloved, irresistible but unattainable.

*Kaʿba*: the sacred shrine at Mecca to which Muslims make pilgrimage.

*Kâvûs*: see Kaykâvûs.

*Kawsar*: a pool in Paradise.

*Kayânids*: the second pre-Islamic Iranian dynasty, founded by Kayqubâd (q.v.), whose last ruler was Darius (q.v.).

*Kaykâvûs*: a Kayânid (q.v.) ruler known for his weak nature and his many mishaps, among them his attempt to ascend to Heaven on a throne borne by eagles; when he fell from the sky into the forests of Mazandaran and was captured, he was rescued by Rustam (q.v.).

*Kaykhusraw*: the eighth Kayânid (q.v.) ruler, son of Siyâvash (q.v.) and grandson of Kaykâvûs (q.v.) and a renowned warrior.

*Kayqubâd*: founder of the Kayânid (q.v.) dynasty.

*Kayûmars*: the first Iranian king, who established the institution of monarchy.

*Khallukh*: a region in Turkestan.

*Khân*: a title used by Turkish chieftains and rulers.

*Khâqân*: the title of the kings of Turkestan (Chîn).

*Khizr*: a mysterious, saintly figure, guide to those in distress, who found the Water of Life (q.v.) denied to Alexander (q.v.).

*Khurasan*: north-eastern Iran, bounded on the north by the Oxus river.

*Khusraw II Parvîz*: Sassanian ruler (r. 590–627), known for his love for Shîrîn (q.v.); his adviser was the minstrel Bârbad (cf. §6: 38).

*Khuttal*: a region in Badakhshan (north-eastern Afghanistan) known for the beauty of its inhabitants.

*Khwarazm*: a region in Central Asia north of the Oxus; in Nizâmî's time the empire of Khwarazm stretched westward to the region of the Khazars (north of the Caspian Sea).

*Kisrâ*: the title of the kings of Persia, an Arabization of Khusraw (=Chosroes).

*Magi, Magian* (Mâjûs): the Zoroastrian priesthood (=Magus).

*Malikshâh*: The third Seljuk sultan (r. 1032–92), whose vizier was Nizâm al-Mulk (q.v.).

*Mânî*: the founder of the Manichean religion (d. 274, 276, or 277), famed for his book the Artang (q.v.) with its exquisite paintings.

*nard*: the Persian form of backgammon.

*Nizâm al-Mulk*: the vizier of Malikshâh (q.v.) and author of the *Siyâsatnâma*, murdered in 1092 by an Ismaili assassin.

*Nûshîrvân* (Anûshîrvân): A Sassanian king known for his justice and wisdom; his vizier was the sage Buzarjmihr (cf. §6: 37).

*Parvîz*: see Khusraw II Parvîz.

*perî*: 'fairy', one of the non-human races; used figuratively of a beautiful woman.

*Qaysar*: 'Caesar', title of the emperors of Rûm (q.v.) (Byzantium).

*qibla*: the Muslim direction of prayer, facing Mecca.

*Rayy*: A city in Iran near present-day Tehran. Once a major cultural and political centre, it was sacked by the Mongols in 1221 and completely devastated.

*Rû'în-Diz*: the fortress belonging to Nizâmî's patron.

*Rûm*: Byzantium (Rûmî = 'Greek', 'Byzantine'). The Greeks were known for their fair complexions, their fine fabrics, and their engineering and artistic skills.

*Rustam*: one of the hero-kings of Sistan and champion of the Kayânids (q.v.), whose deeds are recounted in the *Shâhnâma*, and to whose famous horse Rakhsh Nizâmî alludes (§5: 15).

*sâqî*: a cupbearer.

*Shâhnâma*: see Firdawsî.

*Sharî'a*: Islamic law, embodied in the Koran and in the example of the Prophet (whose words and actions are collected in the Prophetic Traditions, Hadîth); the moral and spiritual guide to human conduct.

*Sheba*: see Bilqîs.

*Shîrîn*: the Armenian princess loved by Khusraw Parvîz (q.v.) and by the architect Farhâd (q.v.), heroine of Nizâmî's romance *Khusraw and Shîrîn*. On her castle with its pools of milk, see the notes to §35: 140, §38: 117.

*Shushtar*: Susa, a city in south-western Iran famous for its silks.

*Sikandar*: see Alexander.

*Sîmurgh*: A fabulous bird said to live far from human sight and to be possessed of great wisdom; sometimes conflated with the ʿAnqâ, a bird resembling the Phoenix. In the *Shâhnâma* the Sîmurgh is the foster-father and teacher of Zâl, father or Rustam (q.v.); in mystical literature it became a symbol of the divine essence and of the spiritual guide.

*Siqlab*: Slavonia, in southern Russia.

*Siyâmak*: son of Kayumars (q.v.); in the *Shâhnâma*, he is killed by the Black Demon.

*Siyâvash*: a Kayânid (q.v.) prince, son of Kaykâvûs (q.v.), who in the *Shâhnâma* was wrongfully accused of adultery with his stepmother; forced to flee Iran, he was subsequently incited to rebel against his father, and met a cruel death.

*Solomon* (Sulaymân): the Koranic prophet and king, known for his great wisdom, to whom God gave mastery over the demons; archetype of the ideal ruler, combining temporal and sacral kingship.

*Stream of Life*: see Water of Life.

*Suhayl*: see Canopus.

*Taraz*: a region in Turkestan known for the beauty of its inhabitants.

*Water of Life*: the miraculous stream or fountain sought in the Realms of Darkness by Alexander (q.v.), found by Khizr (q.v.).

*Zahhâk* (Bîvârasb): the usurper placed on the throne following the deposition and murder of Jamshîd (q.v.), who inaugurated a thousand-year reign of tyranny. A demonic figure, he is said to have had serpents growing from his shoulders which he fed on human brains. He was ultimately vanquished by Farîdûn (q.v.).

*Zand*: a commentary on the Zoroastrian scripture, the Avesta.

*Zangî*: 'Black', 'Negro'; the historical Zanj were black slaves who revolted against the Abbasid caliphate in the ninth century.

*Zulaykhâ*: the wife of the Egyptian lord who fell in love with Joseph (q.v.) ('Potiphar's wife').

# THE WORLD'S CLASSICS

*A Select List*

**HANS ANDERSEN: Fairy Tales**
*Translated by L. W. Kingsland*
*Introduction by Naomi Lewis*
*Illustrated by Vilhelm Pedersen and Lorenz Frølich*

**JANE AUSTEN: Emma**
*Edited by James Kinsley and David Lodge*

Mansfield Park
*Edited by James Kinsley and John Lucas*

**J. M. BARRIE: Peter Pan in Kensington Gardens & Peter and Wendy**
*Edited by Peter Hollindale*

**WILLIAM BECKFORD: Vathek**
*Edited by Roger Lonsdale*

**CHARLOTTE BRONTË: Jane Eyre**
*Edited by Margaret Smith*

**THOMAS CARLYLE: The French Revolution**
*Edited by K. J. Fielding and David Sorensen*

**LEWIS CARROLL: Alice's Adventures in Wonderland**
*and* Through the Looking Glass
*Edited by Roger Lancelyn Green*
*Illustrated by John Tenniel*

**MIGUEL DE CERVANTES: Don Quixote**
*Translated by Charles Jarvis*
*Edited by E. C. Riley*

**GEOFFREY CHAUCER: The Canterbury Tales**
*Translated by David Wright*

**ANTON CHEKHOV: The Russian Master and Other Stories**
*Translated by Ronald Hingley*

**JOSEPH CONRAD: Victory**
*Edited by John Batchelor*
*Introduction by Tony Tanner*

**DANTE ALIGHIERI: The Divine Comedy**
*Translated by C. H. Sisson*
*Edited by David Higgins*